HEROIC SONG AND HEROIC LEGEND

HEROIC SONG

and

HEROIC LEGEND

JAN DE VRIES

Translated by
B. J. TIMMER

LONDON
OXFORD UNIVERSITY PRESS
NEW YORK TORONTO
1963

Oxford University Press, Amen House, London E.C.4

GLASGOW NEW YORK TORONTO MELBOURNE WELLINGTON
BOMBAY CALCUTTA MADRAS KARACHI LAHORE DACCA
CAPE TOWN SALISBURY NAIROBI IBADAN ACCRA
KUALA LUMPUR HONG KONG

Originally published in Holland by
Uitgeverij Het Spectrum N.V.,
Utrecht and Antwerp,

1959

*Printed in Great Britain
by Butler & Tanner Ltd., Frome and London*

PREFACE

EVERYONE knows a few epic poems, even if for most people this knowledge is only fragmentary. There are not many children who have read the whole of the *Iliad* or the *Odyssey* at school, and not much is normally known about the *Chanson de Roland* or the *Nibelungenlied*, except that they are very old poems and therefore difficult to digest.

In order to appreciate these creations of earlier days one should learn to see them against the background of their time. This book is intended to give a general introduction to the reading of an heroic epic, of whichever nation or kind it may be. If it should stimulate the reader to make a closer acquaintance with this poetry, I would consider myself amply rewarded. For it has not so much been my intention to impart knowledge, as to provide a background for the reading of such poetry.

The notes have purposely been kept within limits. If I had wanted to give a complete survey of all that has appeared about this literature, the list of books would have become very extensive. The professional scholar will find many gaps, but I wanted to include only what has led me to a better understanding or incited me to contradiction. I have therefore given only a selection from my own reading, and this selection was determined by the nature of my observations.

J. De V.

CONTENTS

I

THE HOMERIC EPIC

Homer's *Iliad* and *Odyssey* surpass any of the other epic poems in the world. He is the first poet of Greece and directly or indirectly the paragon of most epic poetry and certainly of the main epics of Europe. The fascinating contents, the beautiful form, the grand style and the richness of images of his language lend these poems the great charm which, after so many centuries, is still felt by anyone who reads them. They may serve as an example in another respect. All the problems which arise in connexion with the French *Song of Roland* or the German epic of the Nibelungs are to be found in the *Iliad* and the *Odyssey*. It is here that they were posed for the first time and here for the first time their solution was attempted.

The *Iliad* deals with an episode in the struggle for Troy. In the tenth and last year of the siege the Greeks suffer the greatest set-backs. The cause is Achilles' wrath: Agamemnon, the leader of the Greek army, has ordered the female slave Briseis, allotted to Achilles as part of the booty, to be led away from the latter's tent and, angered at this, Achilles decides not to take further part in the struggle. The consequences of this are soon felt. The Trojans under Hector now appear to have the upper hand: they push back the Greeks in spite of their brave resistance. They even penetrate to the fleet of ships riding at anchor, and the Greeks have difficulty in preventing the Trojans from setting them on fire. Agamemnon is forced to yield to Achilles, but the latter is too embittered to forgive and forget the insult he has suffered. He is only willing to send his friend Patroclus with his Myrmidons into the field against the Trojans. He even gives his friend his own armour, but warns him to avoid a fight with Hector. But when Hector, in the heat of battle, notices the coat of mail and the shield of Achilles, he wants to measure his strength against the bravest hero of the Greeks with the result that Patroclus falls. This produces a change in Achilles. What he did not want to do when the Greek leaders implored him, in the interest of the general cause, no longer to abstain from the fight, he is now prepared to do in order to take personal revenge. After he has been given a new suit of armour, made by the god Hephaestus himself to replace the one captured by Hector, he throws himself into the battle and does not stop until he has killed Hector. The way in which he avenges the loss of his closest friend Patroclus on the dead Hector is terrible, almost inhuman. He drags his body, tied to the chariot, three times through the sand round the walls of Troy. The epic ends with the funeral of Patroclus and with Achilles' victory over himself: he allows himself to be persuaded by the prayers of Hector's father Priam to give Hector's body back to the Trojans, so that he can be given an honourable funeral.

This story is enlivened by numerous episodes in which other Greek heroes play their parts. Paramount among them is Diomedes, who ranks scarcely below Achilles in courage and readiness to fight. Menelaus too is much in the foreground: no wonder, as the fight had started in order to avenge an insult to him. The Trojan prince Paris had abducted Helen, wife of Menelaus, and taken her to Troy. So Helen, praised as the most beautiful woman of the day, is the main issue in the ten-year struggle for Troy. In several places in the poem the gods interfere: they hold consultations on Mount Olympus about the development of the fight; they take sides in it and quarrel about the fate of the heroes; they even descend to earth to take part in the fight. All these side issues make the *Iliad* rich in variety. At times it even appears that the course of the main action is slowed down or interrupted by these episodes, and yet one feels again and again that a master holds the threads of the whole variegated fabric firmly in his hands.

What is the origin of this masterpiece? How are we to judge the work of a poet of whom we know nothing more than that antiquity called him Homer? Can this poem, in which scholars have more than once seen an apparent lack of unity, be considered the personal creation of a single poet at all?

As far back as the seventeenth century a negative answer was given to this question. In 1664 the Abbot François Hédelin d'Aubignac wrote a book on the subject which was not, however, published till 1717, nearly forty years after his death.[1] In it, he argued that the *Iliad* was the concatenation of a number of smaller lays which were the work of various poets. Homer was only the final editor who joined together into a whole the poems that had existed long before him, and whose art really consisted in successfully making such a beautiful, close unity that for many centuries the epic had been taken for the original creation of the 'divine' Homer. This discovery, which ought to have caused a great stir for its novelty and daring, remained almost unnoticed: the time was not yet ripe for it. In 1735 the English scholar Blackwell voiced the generally accepted opinion,[2] honouring Homer as the genuine natural poet who, without any compulsion of rules and prescriptions, created this masterpiece.

D'Aubignac's view, however, was not condemned to remain buried among unsuccessful hypotheses. It was waiting for a more favourable era, which came at the end of the eighteenth century, in 1795, when the German scholar F. A. Wolf, without giving his great predecessor the honour due to him, again broached the problem of the unity of the *Iliad*.[3] Even if classical tradition named Homer as the poet of the *Iliad*, he could not have been ignorant of a series of lays composed long before him. Before the tenth century B.C., when Homer was assumed to have lived, there had been many predecessors who had dealt with the same material in short episodic lays which together formed the story of the fall of Troy. In the course of centuries these songs were recited by bards and continually changed by them until, in the middle of the sixth century, the Athenian tyrant Pisistratus had them joined together in their present form and written down. This view appeared to be very attractive at the end of the eighteenth century. The German scholar Karl Lachmann gave it a definitive form; after he had shown that the *Nibelungenlied* was made up out of short lays he applied his art of analysis to the *Iliad* as well, and arrived at the conclusion that the epic was composed of sixteen lays.[4]

---

[1] *Conjectures académiques ou Dissertation sur l'Iliade.*
[2] *Enquiry into the life and writings of Homer.*
[3] *Prolegomena ad Homerum.*   [4] *Betrachtungen über Homers Ilias,* 1837–41.

This *Lieder* theory prevailed almost unchallenged for a long time. Even that great authority on Greek literature U. von Wilamowitz-Moellendorff applied his ingenuity to the analysis of the *Iliad*.[1] But when he wrote his book he had to defend himself against the view that the poem was not a more or less mechanical conglomeration of originally independent songs, but the creation of one single artist.[2] For doubt had arisen as to the correctness of the *Lieder* theory chiefly because, in the attempt at analysis, every investigator arrived at results entirely different from his predecessor's. The splitting up into independent lays was therefore far from evident.

What, then, were the criteria for such an anatomy of the *Iliad*? First of all, there were the internal contradictions which were supposed to exist in the poem. Thus on the one hand it is said that Agamemnon is King of Argos, but on the other that Diomedes rules in Argos. This, then, could point to two parallel traditions which later came to be placed side by side in the *Iliad*. If Homer had been sole author, surely this discrepancy could not have escaped him. It may be asked, however, whether the poet would have minded about this. If Diomedes ruled in Argos and if Agamemnon, as sovereign of the whole Peloponnese, naturally extended his authority over that district also, is there then a real discrepancy when Argos is placed under the rule of both heroes?[3]

Again, to give an example from the *Odyssey*: in Book xxii, Eurycleia tells Odysseus to take off his rags, although earlier he had already fought against the suitors clad in his armour. If there is a discrepancy here, then it is one which cannot be laid to the poet's charge as an oversight, for he gains the highest effect precisely through this scene. Should we not bear in mind the wise words which Goethe spoke to Eckermann in such a case?[4] 'The imagination has its own laws, over which the intellect can and should have no hold.'

In the *Iliad*, Patroclus visits Nestor to obtain information from him, by order of Achilles.[5] Nestor is here seen again as a garrulous old man, for he proceeds to reminisce at length about his youth.

---

[1] *Die Ilias und Homer*, 1916.
[2] C. Rothe, *Die Ilias als Dichtung*, 1910.
[3] A. Bougot, *Étude sur l'Iliade d'Homère*, Paris 1888, p. 29.
[4] *Gespräche mit Eckermann*, 5. VII. 1827.
[5] *Iliad* xi. 655 ff.

Quite uncalled for, it may be objected, and certainly unworthy of a poet like Homer. Yet, when properly considered, how well thought out! For Nestor is stirring up the wounded Machaon and how could he do this better than by diverting his thoughts to the stories (the *mythoi*) of the past?[1]

An attempt has been made in another way to carry through a division not based on the idea of originally independent songs. People thought it possible to show that the *Iliad* had grown by the later insertion of additional material from an older and shorter epic made by Homer. This 'interpolation' theory, which has also done much damage in the field of the Germanic epic, found an easy prey in the *Iliad*. For it seemed possible to point out older and later parts on purely material grounds.

To do this, it is necessary to take a closer look at the history which is found in the epic. For it does deal with real history. It was Schliemann, convinced from his youth that the siege of Troy had really taken place, who discovered the town by his excavations in the hill of Hissarlik on the Hellespont. Here he found the traces of various strata of habitation one above another and thought that he had found the dwelling-place of Priam in the settlement of Troy II, dated between 2500 and 2000 B.C. Later investigations have not borne out this assumption. A later level of occupation was evidently taken as the remnants of the famous town, and when remains of Mycenaean culture were discovered, they were considered to be an indication that the Troy of the *Iliad* must have stood here. When it appeared, however, that this Mycenaean town had not been destroyed by force of arms but by an earthquake, this view had also to be abandoned, and the general view now is that the Troy VIIa stratum is the town in question. The archaeological finds show that this town must have been destroyed in about 1200 B.C. If one bears in mind that Greek tradition itself placed the fall of Troy in 1184, one may indeed be astonished that archaeological discoveries and historical tradition agree so completely.

Homer himself lived in the second half of the eighth century B.C. and so there are about four centuries between the *Iliad* and the fall of Troy. The Mycenaean civilization, which flourished at the time

[1] Cf. E. Drerup, *Das Homerproblem in der Gegenwart*, Würzburg 1921.

of the Trojan War, had long since collapsed through the so-called
Dorian invasion about 1000 B.C. After that, Greek civilization proper
had gradually been built up. Now it can be assumed that Homer,
with his own time in mind, would be bound to show in many places
that he is an eighth-century man, but, equally, he may have heard
much about the civilization of Mycenae from ancient sources.

So it strikes us at once that Homer calls the Greeks Achaeans;
the Dorians do not exist for him, the Ionians are hardly mentioned.[1]
This alone points to Mycenaean conditions. Agamemnon and
Nestor are represented as powerful kings who ruled in Argos and
Pylos. The highly praised riches of Orchomenos had long since
disappeared in Homer's day. Iron is mentioned as a rarity and so
we are still entirely in the Bronze Age. The shield covering the
whole body and the chariot are typically Mycenaean. Nestor's
goblet,[2] which is described as an old heirloom, has come to light
in an early Mycenaean find. Meriones' helmet, with its decoration
of boar's teeth, belongs to the same early period.[3]

This is part only of the evidence which shows that in many respects
the *Iliad* reflects the civilization of the Mycenaean period. But it
also holds good even for the *Odyssey*, which many investigators
consider to be so much later that it cannot possibly have been written
by the poet of the *Iliad*. In the palace of Alcinous there was a frieze
of *kyanos*[4] (lapis lazuli), but decorations made of this material have
been found in ornaments in Tiryns—and they go as far back as
Cretan times.

On the other hand there are also features that are clearly later.
Cremation is the typical way of rendering the last honour to the
dead, but Mycenaean civilization only knew burial. The chariot,
which is of oriental origin, belongs to the twelfth century. Riding
on horseback was introduced later. Nevertheless, it is said of Odysseus
and Diomedes that they are sitting on horseback, even if this does
occur in a Book that for many other reasons is considered to be a
later addition.[5] But there are even more recent, post-Homeric
elements. The fight of hoplites, which occurs in some places,[6] is

---

[1] *Iliad* xiii. 685, and *Odyssey* vi. 162.   [2] *Iliad* xi. 632.
[3] *Iliad* x. 261.   [4] *Odyssey* vii. 87.   [5] *Iliad* x. 531 and 541.
[6] *Iliad* xiii. 130 ff., 339 ff., and xvii. 168–217.

only conceivable after the middle of the seventh century. Still more remarkable is the story of the Trojan women proceeding in supplication to the life-size image of the seated Athene and spreading a beautifully woven mantle on her lap.[1] Here we have a fixed point in time, the year 630, Bethe proclaims.[2] Such a procession can have taken place only after this date, because then the Panathenaea were instituted and so, in its present form, the *Iliad* must be placed after this date. This cannot be gainsaid, but naturally there remains the possibility that a later artist, an Athenian rhapsode, added these lines. It need not be surprising to find that every century in which this most popular epic of the Greeks was recited has left its traces in it.

However this may be, the appreciation of the difference in civilization between the thirteenth and the eighth centuries B.C. is more important. Is it possible, on the basis of these differences, to find out which parts of the epic go back to the Mycenaean period and which can have arisen in Homer's day only? If so, one might distinguish in the poem as handed down an older layer which must have suffered various additions in the eighth century, and which would have been expanded into the poem in its present form. But the result of this investigation, made with great expectations, is disappointing. The earlier and later layers are inextricably interwoven. The important evidence of the Mycenaean boar's-teeth helmet of Meriones occurs in the Doloneia, a Book which is almost universally considered to belong to the latest parts of the epic.

The language of the Homeric poems, too, is of greatly varying origin. Besides words which are so old that one can only guess at their meaning, there are others which belong to the normal Attic dialect. As long ago as the beginning of the eighteenth century the English scholar Richard Bentley (1662 to 1742) made the brilliant discovery that a line only has its proper metrical form if, before an initial vowel, the semi-vowel *wau* or *digamma* is added, i.e. a *w*-sound which was lost in the later development of the language. This was taken to be a perfect means of separating early and late, for if lines which had originally contained this *w*-sound were metrically flawless without it, they must have been composed at a later time than

---

[1] *Iliad* vi. 302.   [2] E. Bethe, *Homer* i, p. 314.

others that could not do without the *wau*. An edition[1] was even made in which the *wau* was restored, and the lines in which this was metrically not possible were printed in small type at the foot of the page as interpolations. But on closer examination this method appeared to be too arbitrary, for in the language of poetry *wau*-forms were evidently still used at a time when this sound had long since disappeared from normal usage. Similarly, there are great differences in the dialect that is used. The Ionic dialect may be taken to be the normal one, but in it occur older, so-called Aeolic, forms and it has been said that an Aeolic veil lies over the language. In other words, these forms were not so much Aeolic, but rather remnants of an older form of the language which also underlies the Ionic dialect.[2] But there is more: there are also Arcadian–Cypriot elements of language which are supposed to have belonged to the very earliest tradition. Hence the Swedish scholar Nilsson suggests[3] that these latter elements of language point to a state in which the Aeolic and Arcadian languages were spoken in each other's neighbourhood, which was the case on the east coast of Greece before the Dorian invasion. When the Aeolians later crossed into Asia Minor, they passed the epic poetry on to the Ionians, who then transposed it into their own dialect but retained many Aeolic forms which, owing to the metre, could hardly be replaced. The result, at all events, was an artificial language which made it possible for the singers in the oral tradition to choose forms in accordance with their immediate need. This also explains why they were able to make an optional use of the *wau*.[4] In this connexion, pseudo-archaic words are particularly interesting. They prove that the later Attic dialect was interspersed with archaic words on the basis of an age-old tradition in accordance with or under compulsion of the metre.[5] Thus we obtain this picture: an eighth-century poet expanded older lays whose language was Aeolic with pieces composed in his own Ionic dialect: he himself used the artificial language current then and mixed his Ionic dialect with genuine or even spurious forms from the other

[1] The edition by Van Leeuwen and Mendes da Costa, 1887.
[2] Cf. Drerup, op. cit., pp. 111 ff.
[3] *Homer and Mycenae*, London 1933, p. 177.
[4] Cf. Albin Lesky, *Geschichte der griechischen Literatur*, Berne 1957, pp. 61–62.
[5] Cf. Ch. Autran, *Homère et les origines sacerdotales de l'épopée grecque*, i, p. 34.

dialects. Thus, two things result from investigation of the language. There was an uninterrupted tradition of epic songs suitably couched in an artificial language with archaic colouring, but underlying this tradition there was a poetical activity reaching back into the Mycenaean period—the time when the siege of Troy took place.

A few words must be said about the metre: the hexameter. The modern reader has grown so accustomed to this measure that he no longer realizes with what difficulty the Greek language has been pressed into this mould. The hexameter can never have grown out of the nature of the Greek language itself. There is no place in this measure for a series of normally accentuated Greek words. Hence there is every reason to consider this non-Greek measure as an inheritance from a non-Greek past; or, to put it differently, it is pre-Hellenic. Where does it come from? Pausanias tells us[1] that it was invented by the mythical Olen, who is supposed to have been a priest of Apollo in Delphi and on Delos. This is a valuable indication of its origin in sacral poetry; the hexameter was originally the vehicle of the oracles and the hymns. If Apollo was indeed a god originating in Asia Minor, it is reasonable to assume that his priests took the metre of his oracles with them to Greece. So it is interesting to see that the epic poets chose precisely this measure. Does it point to a relation between the epic art of poetry and that of hymns? This is a question to which we shall return later.[2]

Before we draw any conclusions from what has been said so far, we will briefly discuss the *Odyssey*. This poem, with its often charming description of travel adventures, with its homely settings at the court of Alcinous or in the palace of Odysseus, contrasts so much in tone with the martial *Iliad* that already in ancient days a sharp line of division was drawn between them. If the *Iliad* was the work of Homer, the chorizontes thought the *Odyssey* was at least a century later. And again the hunt was on for later forms of language, or later elements of civilization, in order to prove this. In the end the result was equally negative.

A different argument was based on what was called the poor composition of the *Odyssey*. Surely an artist like Homer could not be guilty of that? What does this deficiency really consist of? The

---

[1] Book x. 5, 7–8.   [2] Cf. Autran, op. cit., p. 125.

first four Books, the Telemachy, so called because Telemachus, the son of Odysseus, is the main character in them, were supposed to be a later addition to the original older song of Odysseus. Is this a certainty? If one noticed such a disposition of material in a modern novel one would be inclined to give the author high credit for it. Is not Telemachus' search for traces of his father a splendid beginning which focuses our attention in ever-growing tension on Odysseus, the hero proper? Formally, at least, these first Books are closely linked with the subsequent poem, for in the first Book Athene sees to it that Hermes is sent to Calypso in order to effect the rescue of Odysseus, and this actually takes place in the fifth Book. The first four Books are not so very much detached from the rest of the poem. Let us further remember how 'modern', but at the same time how well-considered, is a device that the poet uses, in that the story of Odysseus, after the events described in the *Iliad*, is not told from the very beginning. It is in the middle of the poem, when the hero has arrived at the court of the Phaeacians, that a singer recounts his past adventures and the hero, deeply moved, adds to these his own reminiscences. One can only agree with Lesky when he says: 'The *Odyssey* displays a strength of composition and a mastery of the art of narrative such as are only inherent in a very great work of art. In this respect it is unmistakably a unity, even if one cannot deny that in later times various other parts have been added to it.' [1]

Is it, then, the work of Homer after all? Present scholarship does indeed incline towards this view. There is no line of division between the heroic tale of the *Iliad* and the seemingly so much more 'romantic' adventures of Odysseus the seafarer.[2] If differences in style can be pointed out, they are to be explained not from a difference in age but from the different character of the material.[3] Even Nilsson has to admit that the figure of Odysseus still belongs to the Mycenaean era, even if the story of his wanderings and his return home is probably a tale made about him in later times and adorned with all sorts of sea adventures.[4] But we should bear in mind how old these seafaring stories were among the seafaring Greek people: the

[1] See Lesky, op. cit., p. 55.
[2] Cf. W. Schadewaldt, *Von Homers Welt und Werk*, p. 122.
[3] Cf. E. Bethe, *Homer* i, p. 32.   [4] Cf. *Homer and Mycenae*, p. 258.

legend of the Argonauts is also full of them. And indeed, in the days of old pre-Hellenic Crete there had already been extensive navigation to the coasts of Asia Minor and Egypt. And did not the Sporades and the Cyclades tempt people to the venture of navigation?

Thus, far from being a point of departure, Homer is the crowning end of a very long development. The stories of Achilles and Odysseus had been celebrated in song and transmitted as such for centuries, before they became crystallized into the perfect form that Homer eventually gave them. How rich was the development which the heroic legends already attained at an early age will at once become apparent from the fact that Homer himself refers to numerous other legends. The *Iliad* contains memories of the story of Meleager and the Caledonian boar, as well as the legend of the Seven against Thebes, those of Heracles, Perseus and Orestes, and the myths of Minos, Deucalion, Bellerophon, and Niobe. Homer also knew the legends of the Lycian heroes Glaucus, Pandarus, and Sarpedon. Together, this forms an impressive body of legends which were treated poetically, and which give us an inkling of the extent and rich variety of the epic tradition, at the end of which the *Iliad* and the *Odyssey* appear as its ripest fruits.

One is therefore justified in assuming that the legend of the fall of Troy had been treated long before Homer composed his poems. There was indeed much more to be told than merely the events of the fifty days in which the action of the *Iliad* takes place. Twelve days have to be deducted for the time that elapses between the beginning of the poem and the preparation for the fight, and another twelve for the burning of Patroclus' corpse and again as much for that of Hector's body. The action proper therefore takes place in only a fortnight. But the struggle lasted for ten years. It had its cause and its preparation. It ended with the capture and destruction of Troy, which is not told by Homer, and was followed by the stories of the return of the various Greek heroes. All this was known to Homer, for he alludes to it. The background of his story is the whole cycle of poems from the *Cypria* to the *Nostoi*. From later sources we know, at least by name, the poems that belong to it, sometimes even the names of the poets. The introduction, the

Cypria by Stasinus of Cyprus, ran from the judgement of Paris to the death of Palamedes. Then follow the contents of the *Iliad*. The events up to the death of Achilles were dealt with in the *Aethiopis*; what happened after that up to the capture of the town was described by Lesches of Mytilene in the 'Little Iliad'. Arctinus sang of the destruction of Ilion in the *Iliou persis*. Agias of Troezen dealt with the return of the heroes, with the exception of that of Odysseus, which was told by Homer. The end is formed by the *Telegonia*, ascribed to Eugamnon of Cyrene, in which is told how Odysseus accidentally meets with his death through his own son, Telegonus. All this forms one whole, and from it Homer made his choice. As far as we know these poets were contemporary with Homer or lived after him. It is easy to understand how the magnificent example of the *Iliad* and the *Odyssey* incited other poets to make poems of the other parts of the Trojan drama. But this does not alter the fact that long before Homer there must have been a tradition of epic poetry reaching far back into the past and combining independent elements such as the stories of the return of the various heroes.

Thus, using only fifty days out of so large a canvas comprising many years, the *Iliad* shows the poet's surprisingly firm grasp. Who was this Homer, so often depicted as the blind singer? What was the purpose of his work? What were the thoughts that inspired him?

About 680 B.C. Callinus mentions Homer, but, remarkably enough, as the poet of an entirely different epic, the *Thebaid*. He is the singer of Chios and tradition calls him blind. This brings to mind the singer Demodocus at the court of Alcinous, of whom the *Odyssey* tells that the Muse loved him and had deprived him of the light of his eyes but had given him sweet song instead.[1] Perhaps it was a gentle complaint of Homer himself who found consolation for his blindness in the poetic images that arose in his soul. That he was not born blind is proved by the lively similes with which he adorns and illustrates his epic story. These metaphors bear witness to a mind receptive to the beauties of nature and life. Whether it is the horse that, boldly snorting, trots to the races, or the lion lying in

---

[1] Cf. *Odyssey* viii, 64.

wait for the herd, one is always struck by the freshness of the image and the visual power of the description.

These similes are the work of the poet himself, who writes, however, in a language fixed by long tradition. He has sometimes been blamed for excessive use of stereotyped expressions; but we shall discuss their function later on, when we deal with the art of recitation of the epic singers. Modern poetry, with its extreme demand for originality, has little sympathy with an art which puts itself humbly in the service of a time-honoured tradition. And yet, how moving the genuine poet can be in his fresh, graphic description, even when bound by a traditional usage of language. Hector's farewell to Andromache, with its deeply moving description of the son Astyanax whom Hector embraced, is rightly famous; he is frightened by the brass cuirass and the nodding horse-tail crest on the helmet.[1] In this passage full of human tenderness no less than twenty-eight stereotyped phrases have been found,[2] but they are in exactly the right place, so that each word seems as if it were new born and contributes to the building up of an entirely original scene.

No wonder that Homer lived on in Greek tradition as the only genuine epic poet. He was a divine artist. His language is to be praised, but no less the composition of the poem as a whole. 'Sing to me, Goddess, of the pernicious wrath of Peleus' son Achilles, who caused a thousand griefs to the Achaeans and sent many powerful souls into Hades.' Thus the poet begins his epic. So he does not want to deal with the Trojan War, but only with the short span of less than two months over which Achilles' wrath cast its shadow. When we consider the range of the Trojan cycle which he knew from the *Cypria* to the *Nostoi*, as appears from allusions, we cannot but admire the firm grasp with which he chose and controlled his material. This epic poet—and we shall see that this holds for all epic poets—scorns the idea of dealing with a piece of history, a rhymed chronicle, but takes from it the drama of a particular hero, Achilles or Odysseus, and depicts this against the background of events. It is possible that before Homer there was an older song

---

[1] Cf. *Iliad* vi, 370–502.
[2] Cf. G. R. Levy, *The Sword from the Rock*, London 1953, p. 185.

about Achilles' wrath,[1] but he has built out of it an epic of twenty-four books in which the war around Troy is also given such importance that for many books we leave Achilles sulking in his tent, while outside the heroic deeds of Trojans and Achaeans demand our full attention. But it would really not be inconceivable that he himself had the idea of making Achilles the main character of an action chosen by him. What would this *menis* of Achilles mean to us without its greatest victim, Patroclus? And Patroclus, we may assume, is a creation of Homer himself. Even Hector, the Trojan hero with a Greek name, seems to have been his own creation.

Critics here used to think that they were able to indicate the origin of this idea. The *Aethiopis*, one of the cyclic epics, deals with the end of the struggle for Troy, in which Achilles, as his mother Thetis had predicted to him, dies young through a treacherous attack by Paris. This poem resembles the *Iliad* in many respects. The hero Memnon has come from Ethiopia to help the Trojans; like Achilles, he wears armour forged by the god Hephaestus. In the fight he kills several Greek heroes, among them Nestor's son Antilochus, who had been too young at the beginning of the war to take part in the expedition. Later, when Antilochus comes of age, he joins the Greek army, to Nestor's great anger, as he had wanted to keep the boy far from the battle. Achilles, to whom Antilochus turns for help, soothes Nestor and takes a particular liking to the boy. When Antilochus has fallen, Thetis tells Achilles what has happened and he at once throws himself into the fight to avenge the boy's death. Meanwhile Zeus weighs on his scales the fate of Memnon against that of Achilles. Ajax, who is just at that moment fighting against Memnon, is pushed aside by Achilles and in a fierce fight the Ethiopian hero is killed.

Thus the plan of the *Iliad* shows a great resemblance to that of the *Aethiopis*. Put Patroclus in Antilochus' place and Hector in that of Memnon and one has the structure of the Homeric epic. But even in certain details there is a resemblance. Both poems contain an episode in which Nestor goes in danger of his life because Paris kills one of the horses of his chariot. In the *Iliad* it is Diomedes who saves him, in the *Aethiopis* it is Nestor's own son Antilochus. Undoubtedly,

[1] Thus Bethe, *Homer* i, p. 311.

the latter representation makes for a closer unity, for it shows an underlying and more consistently sustained idea. Again, one can point to the scenes in which Zeus weighs the fate of the heroes. In both poems Thetis warns her son that victory in the approaching battle will mean that his own death is at hand.[1]

These resemblances are so striking that a connexion between the two poems must be assumed. It is understandable that at first it was thought that the 'divine' *Iliad* must have been the model for the lost poem of the Moorish hero Memnon.[2] But since Heinrich Pestalozzi reconstructed the lost *Aethiopis* and considered it the model for the *Iliad,* the case has been precisely the reverse. Schadewaldt has proved in detail that Pestalozzi's view must be correct[3] and he has also shown in a penetrating study how Homer built up his masterpiece by shifting persons and motifs. One of the advantages gained by this was that the struggle for Troy, the end of which is told in the *Memnonis,* is still in full swing in the *Iliad.* Thus Homer has the opportunity of giving a lively description of the fight near the fortified camp of the Greek ships. But what is especially admirable is the way in which Homer has interwoven the action of the poem and the figure of Achilles. In the *Aethiopis* Antilochus dies in an attempt to save his father and Achilles avenges him, because he has taken a great liking to the brave boy. But in the *Iliad* Achilles avenges his own bosom-friend Patroclus who, moreover, falls in the fight against Hector through his own audacity. Patroclus' death is the final result of a long chain of events which all spring from the person of Achilles. How moving it is to see Patroclus in Achilles' armour, for it will be the cause of his death, which Achilles will feel so grievously. If the *Memnonis* is later, its poet would have very much watered down the subject of the *Iliad;* if it is earlier, it turns out that Homer has created moving drama out of a *fait divers* of the struggle for Troy.

Schadewaldt's view has on the whole been accepted in spite of occasional opposition.[4] With legitimate pride Homer opens his

---

[1] See Lesky, op. cit., p. 30.   [2] Bethe, *Homer* ii, p. 243.

[3] In his book *Von Homers Welt und Werk*, Stuttgart 1951.

[4] J. Th. Kakridis, *Homeric Researches* (Skrifter utg. av kgl. Human. Vetenskapssamfundet i Lund, XLV, 1949), pp. 83 ff., had already argued for the probability of this relationship.

poem with the promise to sing of the wrath of Achilles, for it is this wrath which inspires the whole *Iliad*. It should be remembered that it is not only the psychological explanation of the dramatic development, but it positively determines the ethical character of the *Iliad*. Why does Achilles sulk? Because a girl has been taken away from him by the army leader, Agamemnon. What is the result of this wrath? That the whole Greek army is endangered, many Greek heroes fall and, among these, his own friend Patroclus. Is there any kind of balance between the cause and the ultimate results? Was Achilles right in avenging a personal insult at the cost of so many victims? This far exceeds the measure of what is allowed, it is what the Greeks call *hubris*, the over-confidence which defies the wrath of the gods.

There can be no doubt: Homer intended his poem to illustrate this *hubris* which leads man to his downfall. For it is not only Achilles who goes too far. Patroclus too, in his victory, ignores the limits imposed on him, by wanting to measure his strength against Hector in spite of Achilles' warning. And Hector himself becomes the victim of his *hubris*; three times he is warned by Polydamas, but in spite of this he goes to meet his downfall. And Agamemnon? And Diomedes? Again and again the poet illustrates in his heroes the tragic results of *hubris*.

But *hubris* is avenged by the gods. The world of the gods—who would still dare to mention it in connexion with Homer's poems? Has it not been said that Homer is really the creator of Greek mythology, that he has given later generations the plastic image of the gods? Who does not recall in this connexion those scenes of anger, adultery, and cruelty; those ridiculous situations in which the gods appear? It seems so often that in serene indifference this world of feasting, bickering gods, revelling in sensuality, is drawn as a humorous background to human suffering drenched in blood and tears. And yet, in spite of this *chronique scandaleuse*, at which an Aristophanes or a Lucian could laugh so irreverently, the Greeks believed in these same gods. And Homer likewise believed in them. He was convinced that the gods punish the sins of mankind, that retribution is in their hands. Again and again Homeric poetry proclaims the existence of a supreme power which heeds the moral doings of men and rewards or punishes accordingly.[1] Homer made this whole apparatus of gods subservient to the ethical construction of his poem; it serves to show that, in accordance with the laws of a moral world-order, action is influenced and governed by the gods. Zeus deceives Agamemnon with a dream in order that he shall be made humble. Apollo sends the pious Aeneas to his death so that Hector shall remain alive. Not for a moment do we lose sight of the fact that men act and fight in their blindness, but that, watchful and enthroned on Mount Olympus, the gods let the thread of fate go through their hands.

In his *Poetics*[2] Aristotle makes the true remark that Homer did not confuse the hearer by superabundance and variety of subject-matter, but by poetic concentration, placed a single leading motif in the centre of the action, broadening this out and splitting it up by inserted episodes. This in itself is perfectly true, but it is not the whole truth. Homer is not merely a technically gifted poet; he is also an artist who wants to give expression to a great vision in his work. His high moral sense caused him to see in the epic material handed down to him more than a series of interesting events and adventures. He saw moral powers at work in them, perhaps the same that he saw at work in his own day. He saw especially that the Trojan legend was a drama full of deep emotion, and that the fall of the noblest heroes was caused by their own fault.

He did more than this. That series of fights presented a spectacle of courage and contempt of death; those ancient heroes were examples of the highest military virtues. But were they also models to be followed? Perhaps for the Mycenaean period, which reminds us so vividly of the period of the Vikings, but certainly not for the century in which Homer himself lived. That century had different standards of human dignity and demanded a different moral attitude of man. This new spirit he allows to shine through his work. The *Odyssey* is full of it. We need only think of the country of the Phaeacians and the sweet figure of Nausicaa; the swineherd Eumaeus and the maidservant Euryclea are drawn with tenderness, even if they are mere slaves; Penelope's faithfulness adds lustre to the whole

[1] Thus R. Herkenrath S.J., *Der ethische Aufbau der Ilias und Odyssee*, Paderborn 1928, p. 329.   [2] Ch. 23.

poem. The *Iliad* too has episodes full of warm human feeling. We have already mentioned the scene of Hector's farewell. But even more moving is Priam's prayer to Achilles; here the father who has lost his son and the fellow-soldier who has lost his friend meet, and behold—Achilles' wrath melts away in tears. He rises to a state of compassion that can console and forgive the enemy.

Thus Homer did not really continue or bring to a culminating point the old epic tradition based on heroic ideals. On the contrary, he may be called the artist who broke and conquered this tradition. Schadewaldt remarks[1] that by telling the story of the heroes in a new manner, and also by placing the actions of the heroes as handed down in an ambiguous light, entangling them in guilt and revealing a new inner life in them, Homer raised the heroic element in a certain respect, namely by developing in it the human character. For the hero is complete and unbroken as an image of glorified human nature. Achilles, however, is 'all too human', broken as he is by the *hubris* in which he allows himself to be entangled. For this *hubris*, once the characteristic of the triumphant hero, brings about his downfall. The Achilles of the Priam scene is closer to us, appeals more to our feeling, than the ever-triumphant fighter against the Trojans. Is it because of the shattered state of modern life that we can accept Achilles so much more easily? If so, Homer has given him the character in which we recognize ourselves, and precisely by doing so he has taken Achilles down from the lofty heroic plane to the common human level.

It would not be difficult to show the same in the *Odyssey*. It is even more human than the *Iliad*, and is therefore rightly considered as the work of Homer's old age when a milder outlook on life saw the granite of the old heroic legend crumbling more and more. And in this Homer shows himself to be a man of his own time. For how much the world had changed! Navigation and colonization had brought the Greeks in touch with the Near East; not the royal court, but the *polis* formed the centre of their thoughts and endeavours. The struggle for Troy was overshadowed by the new wars which were now carried out on a grander scale and for more important purposes. This way of life, too, had become problematic; men felt

[1] See op. cit., p. 197.

their destiny in the vehement pulsation of life in which no heroic ideals lifted up the spirit, but only too human passions clashed. How else could a poet make a living reality of that legend of prehistoric times, the ten-year siege of a town in a remote corner of Asia Minor, and the people of Smyrna and Ephesus, other than by depicting in it the tragedy of man entangled in guilt, common to all?

The admirable structure of both poems, with their numerous episodes in which the thread of the story is never lost, with the frequent references to earlier or later parts, and particularly their size, which presupposes long labour and a well-thought-out plan, has raised the question whether they can be considered as the creation of a poet working in an oral tradition. Should we not in fact think of an artist with the stylus in his hand—recording, connecting, and checking his thoughts and ideas? At the time when it was still thought that the epic was the fruit of an oral tradition alive among the people, this question hardly arose. When it did, it was at once rejected, because the art of writing did not yet exist in Homer's day.[1] But our attitude towards this question is, at present, entirely different. The deciphering of the documents found in Pylos was a surprise which forced us to reconsider many established opinions. It is true that the so-called linear-B script which is to be dated between 1400 and 1200 B.C. was used for administrative purposes only, as far as we know at present. But what seems still improbable before 1200, the time of the fall of Troy, may well have been possible for the age of 800, the time when the Homeric poems came into being. With A. Lesky[2] I am inclined to say that, especially after the masterly analysis of the *Iliad* by Schadewaldt, everything now seems to point to the fact that Homer put his poems in writing. Of all the poems that belonged to the huge cycle they were by far the longest. It was precisely the use of writing which enabled Homer to compose, out of the overwhelming mass of material that was orally handed down and ever increasing, a properly constructed epic

---

[1] Cf. S. J. Suys-Reitsma, *Het Homerisch epos als orale schepping van een dichter-hetairie*, Amsterdam 1955, p. 35.

[2] Cf. 'Mündlichkeit und Schriftlichkeit im homerischen Epos', in *Festschrift für D. Kralik*, Horn 1954, pp. 1–9.

which, governed by one thought, recreated the rich contents so as to form a whole that was well thought out from beginning to end. Here one cannot but think of a preconceived plan which he worked out with other poems in mind. One would almost be inclined to think that it was precisely this written epic, which could only arise then, which also signified the end of the creative oral tradition.

A new light falls on the problem of the heroic epic, viewed from the *Iliad* and the *Odyssey*. We know that already at the time of Mycenae poets sang of the adventures of their heroes. We can understand how from century to century the memory of their deeds was preserved, even how they grew in fame and importance in the veneration of later generations. And then we suddenly find that the entire heroic age has become a mere empty shadow, because modern man no longer sees in it the depiction of his own needs and desires. But heroic legend has an indestructible core; it can suddenly undergo an entirely unexpected metamorphosis. In spite of all its heroic splendour, it has also enough humanity to move later generations. It is rich enough to adapt itself—even to be filled with a new spirit. It can present heroes who retain their validity within a purely human sphere.

But at the same time we feel that the epic cannot go further than Homer in this respect: one more step forward, and man takes the place of the hero; then the heroic world is deprived of its glory. Then also the time came when tragedy took over the role of the epic, and the development from Aeschylus to Euripides shows how the human element increasingly gained the upper hand over the original heroic element.

Thus the Homeric epic teaches us that for many centuries heroic poems could be handed down, and that through this tradition there developed, from generation to generation, a system of forms and possibilities of artistic expression of tyrannical coercion. Owing to this inexhaustible stock of fixed formulae and procedures, the art of the epic was able to preserve a certain level even if its practitioners were mediocre and not very creative. This tradition, rich in memories and possibilities, awaited the great mind that suddenly caused everything sublime and at the same time deeply human that lay hidden in it, to shine forth in full splendour. Homer is inconceivable without his many anonymous predecessors, but they would be of limited importance to us if it were not that out of their activity, lying hidden in the silence of centuries, a great work of art was finally born.

Scarcely anywhere is the problem of the relation between tradition and personal creation so burning a question as in the field of the heroic epic. Can we use Homer as a beacon when presently we try to unravel the origin of the *Song of Roland* or the *Nibelungenlied*? At any rate we should remember that a development which can be demonstrated so clearly in the Greek epic need not lose any of its probability if we can demonstrate it in French or German epic poetry in a similar way.

2

THE OLD FRENCH EPIC

FOR the appreciation of French epic poems it would, at first sight, seem to be an advantage that we can more or less clearly detect their historical foundations. Whereas, properly speaking, we know the history of the fall of Troy from the *Iliad* only—for the archaeological finds merely confirm that about 1200 B.C. a war was fought for this town—a poem like the *Song of Roland* deals with a fight about which medieval documents give us some information. It will soon appear, however, that this apparent advantage may also turn into a disadvantage, because the relationship between the historical fact and the song made about it may be extremely dubious.

As the historical background of the *Song of Roland* is well known to us from old sources, we shall first discuss this poem as the typical representative of Old French epic poetry. After that, we shall glance briefly at the cycle of Guillaume d'Orange, in order to find out how far our conclusions are confirmed or contradicted by it.

The *Chanson de Roland* describes the defeat sustained by the rearguard of Charlemagne's army in the Roncevaux pass on 15 August 778, when the emperor, after his campaign in Spain, returned to France over the Pyrenees. In his *Life of Charlemagne* Einhard gives the following account.[1] After their arrival in the Pyrenees, the rearguard was suddenly attacked by the Basques (who had lain in ambush on the densely wooded mountain tops) and killed to the last man. When night fell the Basques escaped with a rich booty. Among those killed were Eggihard, the emperor's bailiff, Anselmus, the *comes palatii*, and Hrodlandus, the Margrave of Brittany. Revenge was not possible, as the enemy had dispersed in the inaccessible mountains.

In general, the *Song of Roland* tells of the same event. It is, how-

---

[1] 'Vita Caroli' in *Monumenta Germaniae historica Scriptores* iii, p. 447.

ever, not the Basques who make the attack but the Saracens, who to a later generation were France's typical enemies in Spain. Moreover, the margrave whom Einhard mentioned at the end has now been raised to the position of main character, and from him the poem has received its name. For the rest, however, there is such striking agreement that a direct connexion between the historical fact and the song made about it cannot be denied.

How are we to explain this? The simplest solution seems to be to assume that shortly after the defeat (which, one may rightly suppose, was much more serious than Einhard made it out to be) a song was made about it which in the course of the centuries developed into the *Song of Roland*. Gaston Paris therefore gave that definition of the Old French epic which later was to give so much offence: the Germanic spirit in a Romance dress. Only it was uncertain which form one had to assume for those oldest poems. Medieval sources more than once speak of *cantilenae* sung by country people; they deal with the heroes of the old days, and are also called *carmina rustica*. These were probably lyrical poems, and as they appear to have originated in, or shortly after, the time of Charlemagne, they must have been composed in the Frankish language. This was the conclusion which Gaston Paris, the authority on the history of Old French literature, arrived at.[1]

But why should lyrical poems form the basis of an epic tradition? Is it not much more likely that the famous persons and striking events were sung in narrative poetry from the beginning? The Italian scholar Pio Rajna pointed out that the French and German epic agreed in a large number of motifs and he concluded that, for the Frankish period, Germanic epic poetry of a similar nature can be assumed on both sides of the Rhine.[2] This view, for which comparison with the German epic (later pushed a little too much into the background) found some support, based itself on a famous statement made by Einhard in his biography of Charlemagne: 'The emperor ordered ancient songs about the deeds and wars of the

---

[1] *Histoire poétique de Charlemagne*, Paris 1865, ²1905, pp. 43–44.
[2] *Le origine dell'epopea francese*, Florence 1884, and also G. Gröber, 'Romanische Literaturgeschichte', in *Grundriß der romanischen Philologie* ii. 1, Strasbourg 1902, 447 ff.

old kings to be noted down, so that their memory should be preserved.'[1] Should one not think of epic poems rather than lyrical songs in this connexion? Poeta Saxo, who rendered Einhard's chronicle into poetry in about 890, says: 'Even now it is well enough known: folk-songs celebrate his father and his ancestors and sing of Pippin, Charles, Louis, Theoderic, Carloman and Chlotarius.'[2] 'Folk-songs' and 'sing': does this mean we still have to imagine a kind of ballad, such as are known from the later Middle Ages, or are they perhaps recited epic poems after all? When we remember that Virgil opens his *Aeneid* with the words *Arma virumque cano* and that Homer opens the *Iliad* with 'Sing of the wrath of Achilles', there would not seem any objection to taking the Poeta Saxo's *canunt* as a recitation of an epic. We shall see later on that it was not sung without musical accompaniment.

It will be clear that there is ample reason for uncertainty in the matter. Not only did the question whether these *carmina* were lyrical poems rather than short epic poems remain unsolved; there was likewise doubt about the original language in which this poetry was composed, whether it was Frankish or the corrupted Latin of the early Middle Ages. As it was also not quite clear how these old songs could have survived the tenth century, so heavily afflicted with war and anarchy, and developed eventually into the extant epics, the vague notion of the 'legend' was seized upon as a way out. This preserved materials and characters until a poet built up a *chanson* out of it, at the end of the eleventh or the beginning of the twelfth century.[3]

When no more agreement seemed to exist on the question of which form should be assumed for the transmission of historical facts and the songs made about them, the question was abandoned, for it had become so vague and uncertain that it could no longer

---

[1] *'Vita Caroli'*, ch. 29: Item barbara et antiquissima carmina quibus veterum regum actus et bella canebantur, scripsit memoriaeque mandavit.

[2] Lines 117–20: Est quoque jam notum; vulgaria carmina magnis
        Laudibus ejus avos et proavos celebrant,
        Pippinos, Carolos, Hludovicos et Theodricos
        Et Carlomannos Hlothariosque canunt.

[3] So Voretzsch, 'Das Merowingerepos und die fränkische Heldensage', in *Philologische Studien, Festgabe für E. Sievers*, Halle 1896, and P. Meyer, *Recherches sur l'épopée française*, Paris 1867.

offer any help in explaining the origin of the *chansons de geste*. There were obviously several possibilities. Each song could have its own prehistory. The emphasis should be laid on the known song. Its antecedents, annals, legends, chronicles, remained obscure through lack of explicit sources. What, then, was really the work of the poet of the *Song of Roland* as handed down? The Austrian scholar Becker answers: without Roland's grave at Blaye and without the situation of Roncevaux on the pilgrims' route from San Jago de Compostella, Roland's fame would never have arisen. If an auspicious fate had not led the talented poet to Roncevaux, Blaye, and Bordeaux at the time when memories of the rearguard fight were being collected and revived into a graphic picture for the edification of the pilgrims, and if on seeing the mountain tops and the abysses and on listening to the story of his informants he had not seen the fallen Franks rise up out of their graves and heard the sound of Roland's horn plaintively die away, we would not now possess a *Song of Roland*.[1]

This is the theme on which Bédier was presently to build up a whole symphony.[2] The creator of the work of art threatened to become a tool of an anonymous tradition, the last redactor of a subject-matter treated and worked over by innumerable *remanieurs* ever since the time of the Carolingians. What became of his greatness, his originality, his own powers? Strange questions, when we consider that Homer is in no way degraded by the tradition on which he builds and which he masters at the same time. It is certain that the poet of the *Song of Roland* must have been a great artist and that he drew freely on the spirit and the ideals of his own time. If one wants to get to know him, of what use are all these speculations about an older tradition? He becomes greater as he builds up out of less. At one stroke Bédier sweeps away the *carmina* and the legends, and makes the poet start his work on virgin soil. What would he have known about the defeat in the Pyrenees? What we too know about it: a few sentences in Einhard and some other historians and, particularly, legends collected or made by abbots eager for knowledge. With undeniable vividness Bédier describes the activity on such a pilgrims' route: along it stand churches and chapels, monasteries and

---

[1] Ph. Aug. Becker, *Grundriß der altfranzösischen Literatur* i, Heidelberg 1907, pp. 35–36.　　　　[2] *Les Légendes épiques*, 4 vols., Paris 1908–13.

B

hospices to edify and harbour the pilgrims. They are shown the relics preserved with veneration: Roland's horn at Bordeaux, his grave at Blaye, the cross erected by Charlemagne at Port de Cize, the bodies of Olivier and Ogier at Belin, let alone the numerous false certificates with which the clergy practised pious fraud. All these are for the edification of the pilgrim, and they produce some scanty alms. But with all these, on the whole, not very canonical relics, goes a legend, a story, a song. Then the *jongleur* appears on the scene, who also seeks to profit from these crowds of pilgrims by shortening their journey with a song and a jest. In the monasteries he will have been shown the manuscripts which preserve the memory of the tragedy that had occurred here. He reads in them the names of Roland, Olivier, and Bishop Turpin, and especially of the traitor Ganelon; he sees before him the majestic landscape where all this took place; he stands on the famous hill with the name of *angarda Rollan*; he looks upon almost the same shrubs and bushes that had grown among the bodies of Christians and pagans then; and in his imagination there arises the vision of the fatal fight. It assumes content and life: the *Chanson de Roland* matures in his mind.[1]

Poeta vindicatus could bed place as a title above Bédier's fascinating argument. And note in particular that Bédier speaks of a French *jongleur*, not of a Frankish *scop*. Not, then, Germanic thought in Romance dress; thought and subject-matter and form are all equally the property of a French poet of about 1100. That is the undeniable merit of Bédier's theory: if we still admire the *Song of Roland* it is not because of the venerable, centuries-old tradition of the subject-matter, but because of the noble art of the poet who has given its ultimate form to the story of Roncevaux. What was impossible in the appreciation of the *Iliad* or the *Odyssey*, the neglect of Homer as the creator of these immortal songs, threatened to happen in the case of the *Song of Roland*: the magnifying-glass of criticism was focused on the tradition instead of on the song itself; the poet was in danger of melting into the background as one of the many who were supposed to have dealt with this subject-matter.

This view was particularly suited to the recent conception of the art of poetry. The eighteenth century, with its indefatigible treat-

[1] Cf. vol. iii, pp. 115 ff.

ment of classical subject-matter in drama and epic, had had to yield to the nineteenth century, with its admiration for the individual character of the artist. Even if the notion of genius in the period of Romanticism had been reduced to more modest proportions, it still remained the pride of the artist not to work from old models but to create out of the fulness of life and, above all, out of the inexhaustible riches of his soul. For the Dutch poets of the Movement of the 1880's the essence of all genuine art was still 'the most individual expression of the most individual emotion'.

The question arises, however, whether these views of the art of poetry were not transferred to medieval conditions too rashly. A respectful attachment to tradition of any kind is characteristic of the medieval period everywhere. Did a poet, such as Bédier imagined the poet of the *Song of Roland* to have been, really fit in at that time: a man who dealt with legendary subject-matter without examples, and who with lively imagination recreated the scanty data of an obscure past into a mighty work of art? Was Homer less great because he had been a link in a centuries-old tradition? It was inevitable that the one-sidedness of Bédier's view should come to be increasingly felt.

It is really rather remarkable that he himself did not realize how improbable his explanation was. How could one imagine that, three centuries after the tragedy of Roncevaux, a *jongleur* hit upon the idea of treating this subject? It was suggested to him by the clergy who, to the greater glory of their churches and monasteries, wished to have their relics consecrated in a beautiful legend. But what kind of relics were they? Roland's horn, Olivier's grave. In what way had these very worldly objects come to be thought worthy of being placed in a church, and being shown there to the faithful for their pious adoration? Such apocryphal saints must surely have been forced upon the Church by a very powerful tradition. Roland's horn must therefore have been hallowed by an entirely different tradition from that of the Church. And what else would have given these relics their importance but precisely those stories that were current about Roland and Olivier of old? In order, as it were, to command the recognition of the Church, these stories must certainly have been entirely different from the dull sentences of an Einhard or a dry chronicle, which Bédier so much liked to put forward as sources, but which, at least as far as the latter is concerned, are rather the reflection of a tradition which existed outside the walls of church or monastery.[1] And so the *cantilenae* which Bédier had wished to expel re-emerged as an indispensable link in the historical development of the *chansons de geste*.[2]

But Bédier could not of course be refuted by general considerations; it had to be proved that there had indeed been older versions of this material. Now the *Song of Roland* itself refers to an older source, a *geste Francor*,[3] but it has to be admitted that, as is usual with such source references, the evidence mostly serves to confirm extremely unimportant things. At any rate there must have been a *gesta Francorum*; the question is merely what it was like. Was it in prose or in poetry, written in Latin or in the vernacular? Perhaps one might say that this does not really matter. The main thing is that it can be assumed that the poet of the *Song of Roland* knew an older source (whatever its nature) which dealt with the episode of Roncevaux, not in the sense of Einhard's information but adorned with a number of romantic and heroic—possibly also hagiographical— additions.[4] Apart from this, we know a chronicle, the *Historia Caroli Magni*, which is ascribed to Bishop Turpin who died in 800, but which must actually have been a document of the twelfth century. It is thought that this chronicle drew its material from *chansons de geste* and that, moreover, a Latin poem in hexameters can be detected in the text.[5] This poem has been characterized as a kind of saint's life, a *Passio Beati Rotolandi Martiris*, but there are no indications of this and it can only be defended, it seems to me, once one accepts Bédier's theory. What can be said is that it seems very improbable that such a poem should have been composed in Latin after the *Song of Roland*. If the pseudo-Turpin is later than the *Chanson de Roland*, the underlying Latin poem may have been considerably older. In Germany, too, legendary matter was treated in Latin: a typical example is the Latin *Waltharius*. And even this poem in hexa-

[1] Cf. F. Lot, in *Romania* liv (1926), pp. 357–80.

[2] Cf. R. Fawtier, *La Chanson de Roland*, 1933.

[3] *Chanson de Roland*, ll. 1433 and 3262.

[4] Cf. M. Delbouille, *Sur la genèse de la Chanson de Roland*, Brussels 1954, p. 99.

[5] Cf. A. Burger, *Romania* lxx (1948–9), pp. 449–51.

meters does not at all rule out the possibility that songs in the vernacular existed before, by the side of, and after this epic with its classical colouring. If one considers further that influence of the *Waltharius* on the *Song of Roland* may actually be assumed,[1] one can conclude that such an influence must have worked from the Latin poem by Ekkehard on a similar Latin *Song of Roland*. Together with the evidence of the above-mentioned *geste Francor*, this consideration allows us to assume that the poet of the *Song of Roland* did have predecessors and that he was able to base himself on these.

How far can this tradition be traced back? It is a well-known phenomenon that the names of famous heroes of poetry are often chosen when a new-born child has to be baptized. The two best-known figures of the *Song of Roland*, the heroes Roland and Olivier, were frequently chosen as baptismal names from about 1040—even for children of the same family, as if people wanted to fix a similar bond of loyalty between two brothers. Naturally, this fashion in names could only arise when these had become famous: the parents did not consult old chronicles, but took the names from life. At the time, then, there was already a poem in which the two heroes played their part as known to us. Now, the name Olivier arose from *Olivarius*, itself derived from *oliva*, the name of the olive-tree. This form is typically Northern French, for in the South the tree is called *olivum*. The name Olivarius, too, is mainly found in the area of the Lower Loire. These are, it seems to me, surprising data, which make it extremely probable (to put it at its mildest) that there was a powerful and certainly poetic Roland tradition in the Anjou area.[2]

But it was not limited to that area. New discoveries can bring surprising results. A Spanish text, *Nota Emilianense*, written in Visigothic script from the period 1065 to 1075, contains, at the year 778, a description of the battle of Roncevaux. Here too the Saracens have already replaced the Basques. Among the paladins mentioned are Rodlane and Olibero, again the two inseparable friends. Besides these there appear Ghigelmo Alcorbitanas or Guillaume d'Orange with his cousin Bertrand, Ogier with the short sword, all of them

---

[1] Cf. M. Wilmotte, *L'Épopée française*, p. 84.
[2] Cf. R. Lajeune, *Recherches sur le thème: Les chansons de geste et l'histoire*, Liège 1948, pp. 200–04, and M. Delbouille, op. cit., pp. 106 and 161 ff.

famous heroes of the Carolingian epic who do not play any part in our *Chanson de Roland*. The Spanish *Nota* therefore knows a whole series of French heroic songs. The forms of the names are clearly Romanized; that of Roland shows a South French form. It is further remarkable that no mention is made of Ganelon, from which it may perhaps be deduced that at the time a song was known in which the part of the traitor did not yet appear. This Spanish text cannot possibly have drawn on Carolingian annals, as is at once clear from the fact that of all the heroes mentioned only Roland is known as an historical figure in the battle of Roncevaux. But it should also be noted that the poetic tradition underlying the *Nota* is different from that of the *Song of Roland*. Different Roland songs therefore existed in the first half of the eleventh century in the South and in the North of France. So there was a widespread tradition, and the *Song of Roland* is the last and the most successful representative of it.[1]

Thus the poet of the *Song of Roland* comes to be placed against a varied and colourful background. He has been rescued from his isolation. If we ask the question: how did the poet know the story of the tragic event, it is difficult to give a definite answer to it. There are so many possibilities. Is it right to say that the legend arose, at the latest, in the beginning of the eleventh century as a poetic creation which was then fed from an inspiration at once historical and ecclesiastical? But then the question must be answered: what precisely was the inducement at that time to give a poetic treatment to the defeat at Roncevaux? If one goes back to the beginning of the eleventh century, because the appearance of the names Roland and Olivier prevents us from thinking of a later period, one should also bear in mind that this does not mean that an even earlier poetic treatment of the material can be excluded. Granted that at that time the popularity of the story evidently reached its climax, and that this may perhaps be ascribed to a particularly happy form of the story, we should still like to point out that, in the Margraviate of Brittany, this very legend may already have been given poetic treatment a good many years earlier. How else would the *comes* Hrodlandus, whom Einhard mentions as the last of the noblemen killed, have become so much the centre of the story? For this can be best explained if his tragic death

[1] D. Alonso, *Revista de Filologia Española* xxxvii (1956), pp. 1–94.

at Roncevaux made such a deep impression on his own people that he continued to live in the memory of the people as an heroic figure. The presupposed poem of about the year 1000 proves by the effect it had—an effect strengthened by the Christian names Roland and Olivier extending northwards to Jumièges, eastwards to Molesme, and southwards to Brioude and Lerins—that by then it had attained a form which could lay claim to more than purely local interest.

That the *Chanson de Roland* as handed down to us was not, as Bédier assumed, an original creation of a poet without any predecessors, is further proved by both its language and its poetic form. The same formulae for the glittering of armour in the sun, the tumult of battle, the challenges to fight are also found in the song of *Gormont and Isembart* which arose in Normandy, and in the oldest song about Guillaume d'Orange which comes from the South of France. At that time, therefore, there was already a general epic activity which extended to all parts of France and presupposes a continuous interaction between songs of this kind.

These three poems show the same poetic form, which was replaced in the course of the twelfth century by the rhyming couplets, used exclusively after that. At first such epic poems were written in a rather loose form: series of verses ending in the same assonance and of unequal length. In the *Song of Roland* each of these sections, called *laisses*, ends with the word *Aoi*, which has been explained, perhaps rightly, as the vowels of the motto *Pax vobis*. It is assumed that the last verse of a *laisse* ends on a long drawn-out tone, a kind of pause. If this is true, then, together with the use of the motto *Pax vobis*, this could point to the influence of, or origin from, Church music. This would not be so surprising for the *Song of Roland* which, as we shall see later, shows unmistakable clerical influence in other respects too. But the *Chanson de Gormont* points to quite a different connexion. Here the *laisses* are rounded off by a four-line stanza which was probably chanted. This particularly suggested to Salverda de Grave that the song was originally composed in stanzas, and he thinks this a clue to the thesis so often put forward, that the epic song arose from the lyric.[1] This is undoubtedly too bold a state-

---

[1] Cf. *Mededeelingen der Akademie van Wetenschappen te Amsterdam* liii A, No. 11, pp. 273–301.

ment. Yet it seems probable to me that there may be a pointer here to the recitation of the oldest epic songs. For there are undeniable points of agreement with the late-medieval ballad, a similar recited two- or four-line stanza rounded off by a chanted refrain. Is it possible that the oldest *chanson de geste* had a similar form? And does this not also explain why medieval sources tell us that the country people were familiar with heroic subject-matter, and that they always spoke of 'singing' (*cantare*)? A definitive answer cannot be given to such questions, yet they make us suspect that the heroic song had a long prehistory which may have been considerably more complicated than tradition suggests at first sight.

If, therefore, we are inclined to consider the *Song of Roland* as the end of a very long and literary development, and not at all as a masterpiece that suddenly sprang up out of nothing, this does not mean that we wish to degrade the poet to a *remanieur* of an older text. We did not do so in the case of Homer. It is actually owing to Bédier that we hail the creator of this song as a genuine artist. It is clear that this poet was anything but a man who merely repeated old songs— rather one who had his own view of them and filled them with the spirit of his own time. Not a *jongleur* who made propaganda for monastic relics at the instruction of an abbot, but a deeply religious man who saw in the tragedy of Roncevaux a warning for the age in which he himself lived.

Let us first of all reject all attempts at dissecting this poem with the scalpel of criticism. In the first place there is the famous Baligant episode. When the drama of Roncevaux is finished and Charlemagne has lamented the fallen heroes on the battlefield, that is, when the *Song of Roland* proper has come to its tragic end, there follows an epilogue. A new and even more dangerous opponent appears: Baligant of Babylon, which in the language of the medieval poems means Cairo. For over a thousand lines there is talk of his attack and defeat. The critics think that this whole episode could well be dispensed with. Roland plays no part in it, and it separates the hero's death and the revenge on the traitor Ganelon. But the question is not whether our modern taste would like to do without this section, but rather whether the poet did not put it there intentionally. The mere fact—and the whole tradition of the *Song of Roland* confirms this—that the original text already contained this episode, serves as a warning that we should not decide to reject it too quickly. What was the poet's intention? In the final part of the poem, after the *preux de France* have fallen in the fight against the treacherous Saracens, the emperor himself comes to the fore. The material of the poem is no longer an old legend about a still older defeat, but broadens into a picture of the fight between the Christians and the infidels. For centuries this fight had been smouldering, and occasionally it had flared up briefly into battles near the Spanish borderland. At the end of the eleventh century, at the time when the *Song of Roland* was composed, it entered a new and more decisive stage, a general European stage. The crusades with their breathtaking drama were to occupy the whole of the twelfth century. The champion of Christendom in arms is Charlemagne—radiant symbol of the fight for Christ. In the last fight against Baligant, Charlemagne receives a blow on his helmet, so that he totters.

> Mais Deus ne volt qu'il seit mort ne vencut:
> Seint Gabriel est repairét a lui.
> Si li demandet: 'Reis magnes, que fais-tu?' [1]

And the emperor raises himself and with one blow splits the head of the heathen 'tresqu'en la barbe blanche'. Roland had fallen for the good cause, but Charlemagne triumphs and sets an example to the flower of French knighthood who, with the slogan 'Dieu le veut', will presently go and wrest the Holy City of Christianity from the heathen.

When Charlemagne dismounts on the battlefield of Roncevaux, he decides not to disarm that night. He has buckled on his white cuirass, donned his golden helmet adorned with jewels, girded on his sword Joyeuse, and thus he stands before our eyes as the warlike protector of the Christian faith. But the poet gives this figure a deep, symbolical meaning with the words:

> Asez savum de la lance parler
> Dunt nostre Sire fut en la cruiz nasfrét.

To say 'the poet', is not perhaps justified, for the Holy Lance was

[1] Lines 3609–11.

not found till 1098 by the crusaders at the siege of Antioch,[1] and it is improbable that the *Song of Roland* originated after this date. It has, therefore, been suggested that these lines allude not to this lance but to a different one, an older relic.[2] However this may be, whether the poet himself wrote these lines or whether a later *jongleur* was inspired to add them entirely on his own, this passage fits in perfectly with the spirit of the poem. Armed with this lance, Charlemagne has been raised from his temporal state of Frankish Emperor to that of the fighter for the Christian faith, chosen by God. For that reason, it can be said that the poet was a truly pious man, able to remodel an old heroic legend into an ardent testimony of faith in the eternal mission of Christianity.

If the poet thus rises above his subject-matter, he nevertheless stands firmly in the middle of a long and fruitful tradition which shows other flashes of a new conception, giving to the chronicle-report on the battle in the Pyrenees an element of deep humanity that shows the true poetic spirit. I have already mentioned the two friends with the well-known characteristic: 'Rollanz est proz et Olivier est sage.' This contrast between the impetuous Roland and the staid Olivier comes out again and again, not least in the famous scene in which Olivier advises blowing the horn, because the situation has grown so desperate that the emperor's help has to be invoked. But Roland refuses, because it would injure his honour: 'male chançun n'en deit estre cantu' (l. 1466). Who would not be reminded of the *hubris* of Achilles who sends his faithful friend Patroclus to his death? It is probably not an accidental similarity, and has been thought to be a direct imitation of the situation in the *Iliad*, which must have reached the French poet through many intermediaries.[3] But if we consider these intermediaries: Virgil, Statius, Dictys, Dares, Waltharius; then that older poem still comes to mind which, to a high degree of probability, may now be assumed to have been written in Latin hexameters.[4] Undoubtedly it was the work of a cleric, a monk like that Ekkehard who describes, at times with un-

---

[1] Cf. K. Heisig, in *Zeitschrift für romanische Philologie* lv (1935), p. 70.

[2] Cf. A. Junker, in *Germanisch-Romanische Monatsschrift* xxxvii (1956), p. 103.

[3] Cf. E. R. Curtius, *Europäische Literatur und lateinisches Mittelalter*, pp. 174 ff. (English ed.: *European Literature and the Latin Middle Ages* pp. 165 f.).

[4] It is also best to explain the typical name Olivarius in this way.

deniable relish, the unequal struggle of Walter against Gunther and Hagen in the narrow mountain pass (a narrow pass here too!) of the Vosges. And this Waltharius is supposed to have come from Aquitaine, so very close indeed to the other pass, that of Roncevaux. The threads of this epic tradition are strangely intermingled. It seems to me that there must have been some exchange between these verse-writing clerics. On the other hand, it must not be forgotten that, just as in the case of the German epic, an impulse from the classical epic was needed to give rise to poems of the type of the *chansons de geste* among the peoples of Western Europe. With this I do not wish to fall back upon Bédier's thesis, that before the *Song of Roland* there had been nothing but annals, legends in monasteries, and a Latin monk's epic. I still consider it probable—and the development of the German, or, let us say, of the East Frankish epic fully confirms it—that short songs with epic content were current in the vernacular. They would have remained short songs, as was the case in Scandinavia, where people never went beyond the Eddic type of lay, or else they would have disappeared, if, at an auspicious moment, Virgil's example had not stimulated the creation of a full-length epic poem.

As for this Latin *Song of Roland*, which has now become most likely, and which we took to be the predecessor of the Old French poem, it may be assumed to have been almost certainly shorter and more concise in content: without the episodes which in the poem as handed down testify to the pious and at the same time Christian militant spirit of the French poet—hence without the Baligant episode and the 'crusading' spirit. But the *faits divers* of Roncevaux, which Einhard relates soberly and with obvious restraint, had grown and had been raised to a higher plane. The two friends Roland and Olivier, suggested to the poet by classical examples, belong to those happy inspirations which infuse the breath of immortality into a work of literary creation.

Earlier on we mentioned that some *chansons de geste* which are usually considered as the oldest examples of this unusually well-developed genre have a metrical form that was later abandoned: the eight-syllable *laisse* with an unequal number of lines bound together by assonance. To this genre, apart from the *Song of Roland*, belong the *Chançun de Willelme* and the song of *Gormont and Isembart*. Unfortunately, the latter is a mere fragment of 661 lines lacking both beginning and end, but what we have of it is sufficient to give an impression of what may, without exaggeration, be called a little masterpiece. The song deals with the battle of Saucourt in 881, when an army of Vikings ravaging Normandy was defeated by Louis III. A really successful victory over the Vikings was a fact of exceptional importance in those dark days; the long-suffering people recovered their breath and hoped for better days. A German poet wrote a song in praise of this victory, a French *jongleur* made an epic tale of it. What strikes us at once is the unity of the Frankish kingdom, then still very real, despite early signs of the opposition which drew that line of separation between the western and the eastern part which was to gain such a decisive and often fatal significance in the history of Europe.

The French song[1] shifts the accent from the historical fact to the personal human tragedy, which is a general characteristic of epic poetry. We noted this in the *Iliad* and will find it again in German epic poetry. In this song, too, a Ganelon figure appears, the Frankish nobleman Isembart, exiled by the king, who had sought refuge with the Viking Gormont. He had gained power and authority in England at the time. Taken up by him, Isembart had abjured his faith and urged his new lord to invade France so that he could revenge himself on the king. The fragment starts in the middle of Gormont's fight against the Frankish army, which, as is usual in epic poetry of all nations, is described as a series of duels. The Viking performs miracles of valour and fells one Frankish knight after another, until ultimately he is vanquished by the king himself. Then Isembart continues the fight. The monotony threatened by this is enlivened by an episode in which he finds himself opposite his father, which almost gives rise to the fight between father and son so popular elsewhere. The poem ends with the fatal wounding of Isembart, and his bitter remorse at his apostasy from his faith and his lord.

The poem is dated about 1080. At this same time, the chronicle of Saint-Requier mentions the Viking attack in which the church

---

[1] Edited by Bayot, Paris 1921; see my article on this in *Romania* lxxx (1959), pp. 34–62.

there was plundered and destroyed. In his chronicle of events the writer does not enter into details, as they were still 'on everyone's lips'. At once Bédier sees in this chronicle's contribution towards the history of this epic tradition, proof that the epic ultimately goes back to a clerical tradition. Naturally it must again be the monks of Saint-Requier who noted down this story in their chronicle and who urged a *jongleur*, to the greater glory of their monastery, to make a poem of it in the vernacular.

This poem, however, shows, as we remarked above, so many peculiarities of style in common with the *Song of Roland* and the *Chançun de Willelme*, that at any rate the *jongleur* must have been supported in the art of epic poetry by a long previous tradition. He had predecessors: why not predecessors who had also sung about this Viking invasion? Is the distance between the battle itself and the poem made about it—hardly two centuries—so great that we cannot assume a continuous tradition? It need not always even have been in poetic form, and the monks of Saint-Requier may also have had their share in it. It is remarkable that in this poem too there is mention of a relic: it is said that one of those taking part in the battle had presented to the monastery a dish of pure gold which he had taken away from Gormont. Is it not likely that the abbot should have tried to exploit the story of Saucourt for the benefit of his monastery? But is it not equally likely that this Viking invasion, which caused so much damage to the area and ended in a glorious victory for the Frankish king, was preserved in the memory of the people? One need not assume a dependence of lay epics on the tradition of monasteries, but rather a continuous interchange between both, which contributed towards preserving and embellishing this feat of arms. The relic preserved with piety by the monks will at times have been shown to the believers, and that in itself is a conclusive explanation of the fact, so often doubted, that a tradition which provided both the explanation and the illustration could be handed down to each following generation.

The third song which is written in the old-fashioned form of *laisses* is called the *Chançun de Willelme*,[1] and it was only discovered

---

[1] The text is printed by G. Baist as *l'Archanz* (La Chançun de Willelme), Freiburg i. Br. 1909.

in 1903. This poem of over 3,550 lines is considered to be a trivial, manufactured work without any art of composition. It deals with a fight against the Saracens at Archant near Bourges. The fight takes place in William's absence and the French are defeated. William's cousin loses his troops and is forced to invoke William's help; William comes to his rescue with the men he has been able to scrape together in all haste, but likewise suffers a heavy defeat. In the meantime his wife Guibourc has gathered together fresh troops, and again a great slaughter takes place. William kills the leader of the Saracens but finds Vivian dying on the battlefield. As he cannot overcome the enemy, he turns for help to King Louis, who is only prepared to give his aid after William has called him all sorts of names for his cowardice and ingratitude. William is ultimately rescued by the popular figure of the huge Rainoart, who crushes with his club everything that stands in his way.

What is remarkable about this poem is that it presupposes an already fully developed legend. All the familiar figures from the legend of Guillaume d'Orange appear in it: the cousin Vivian, whose tragic death forms the subject of a separate chanson, the faithful and energetic Guibourc, the humorous figure of Rainoart, and finally the weak and unreliable king, quite a different figure from Charlemagne. Surveying the contents in broad outline, we are struck by the similarity with the *Song of Roland*. In both cases there is the unequal fight of a handful of people in the king's absence; both tell of the lamentable death of a young hero, in the one case Vivian, in the other Roland; in both it is the king's army that turns the scale, but it arrives too late because it is prevented from interfering in time: in the *Song of Roland* by the treachery of Ganelon, in the other song by the king's false attitude. The struggle against the Saracens evidently provided the poets of the eleventh century with ample material.

But whereas the *Song of Roland* towers like a high peak above the epic poetry of the Carolingian era, the tradition of Guillaume d'Orange forms a range of which not one peak reaches as high as the *Song of Roland*. Round the figure of William a whole cycle of poems has grown, depicting his life from his youthful adventures to the monkhood which closes his heroic life. The main figures of his circle, however, have also been dealt with in separate poems. I shall first give a brief survey of the main poems of this cycle.

First of all there is the *Enfances Guillaume*. It tells of the adventures of William's youth; concentrating, naturally, on fights with the Moors. He comes to the court of Charlemagne who gives him his own sword Joyeuse, a mythical dwarf's weapon which is already supposed to have been worn by Clovis. In William's time Charlemagne is already an old man. It is really his son, Louis the Pious, who is the central background figure in William's cycle. But how different the situations have become! This cycle remembers the imprint of the evil reign of the later Capetians: the king is weak in power—for he cannot hold his own against his great vassals—and weak in character, for he distributes his favours according to his moods, and is anything but kindly disposed towards his most faithful servant. This comes out in the next poem of the cycle, *Le Couronnement de Louis*: Charlemagne, who feels his end approaching, calls a diet of the realm at Aachen in order to transfer the crown to his son. He delivers an oration in which he admonishes his son Louis to fulfil the duties of a king. The latter hesitates before the tremendous task which weighs upon a Frankish emperor. In the end William intervenes, seizes the crown, and himself places it on the head of the child, promising to defend the young monarch against the presumptions of all his high barons. This in fact turns out to be necessary, for whenever William is absent (one of his adventures takes him to Italy where he fights with the giant Corsolt, who strikes off the tip of his nose, thus being the cause of the hero's nickname, *Guillaume au court nez*), the vassals rebel, and the danger is not warded off until William has rushed to the king's aid. Is the king afraid of this all-powerful baron who towers high above all the other noblemen, and is he too painfully reminded of the success of this man's ancestor, the major-domo, who pushed the king aside? At any rate the poem hints clearly at the end that William will not receive much gratitude for his faithfulness.

This is shown in *Le Charroi de Nîmes*. In distributing his fiefs, Louis has 'forgotten' his faithful counsellor, who vehemently reproaches him for his ingratitude, refuses everything that the king offers him in his fear, in particular some hereditary lands that legally belong to another baron's family. In the end, in bitter mockery, he asks for the land of the Saracens as fief, which he himself will have to conquer first. Then follows the siege of Nîmes, where William uses a stratagem which reminds us of the peat-barge of Breda but which ultimately is only a variant of the Trojan horse. In *La Prise d'Orange* he seizes the town which is to be his place of residence and the home of the Saracen princess Orable, who after being baptized is called Guibourc and becomes a faithful and extremely energetic wife to him.

Besides William, his cousin Vivian plays an important part: there is a poem, *Enfances*, about him, too, and there is also *Aliscans*, which tells of his death. The contents of these songs also provide the material for the above-mentioned *Chançun de Willelme*. At the end of the cycle comes *Le Moniage Guillaume*. After the death of Guibourc, the hero withdraws to the monastery of Aniane. But even beneath the monk's habit the knight will show. This comes out in some comic episodes, such as the fight with the robbers who demand from him one piece of his armour after the other, which William humbly hands over to them because the abbot had ordered him to do so. But when the villains even demand his shirt, he flies into a rage and kills them with the jaw-bone of a donkey. This is undoubtedly a typical monks' legend that is also found elsewhere: the *Chronicle of Novalese* tells it of Waltharius.

Naturally such an extensive cycle of legends did not spring up suddenly. There are old poems in it, but many more later ones. We see how successive generations of *jongleurs* have treated this fine material. We can even observe how these legends gradually came down from the sphere of the knightly court to that of the fair. A comic figure like Rainoart would have irritated the old barons, though he raised a broad smile on the faces of farmers and labourers. But, as always, these are all accretions round an old and genuine heroic core.

The hero is an historical figure: Guillaume de Toulouse, who had become a count in 790, and is known as the faithful counsellor of Louis the Pious. In 793 he fought against the Saracens on the bank of the Orbieu, in 801 or 803 he took part in the conquest of Catalonia, and in 806 he entered a monastery at Gellone. He died on 28 May

812. While his life made him a figure that fully deserved a place in heroic epic poetry, his pious end gave rise to hagiographical legends. The founder of the monastery at Gellone was later worshipped as a saint. He is the prototype of the hero of Carolingian legend, in which the intermingling of knightly stories and monastic legends arose from the life of the man himself.

It would be far from true to say that all the adventures that are told of Guillaume d'Orange can originally be ascribed to him. Hence again the ingenious hunt for other prototypes who were supposed later to have merged into him. No wonder, therefore, that Bédier, in his book about this cycle,[1] can make fun of the *seize Guillaumes* who together have to share the honour of having been the prototype of this hero.

These questions may be left aside. What is interesting, however, is to assess the nature of this tradition. How far can we trace it back? The monks of Gellone naturally composed a legend for their saint and traces of it will no doubt have remained in the *Moniage Guillaume*. They did not even scruple to draw up false documents, like that of 804 in which the names of Vuilhelmus and his wife Vuitburg appear. But even such a false piece of evidence is important: it proves the early interest in the warrior-saint.

In 827 Ermoldus Nigellus made a poem in praise of Louis the Pious, *In Honorem Hludovici*, which contains a passage that seems to be the direct example for an episode in *Le Couronnement de Louis*, the oration about the duties of a king, which Charlemagne delivers to his son.

Towards the year 1030 we find the next trace of the epic tradition: in the so-called *Hague Fragment*. This is a Latin story which mentions the siege of a town, and personages familiar from the William cycle.[2] In several places it is clear from the language that the prose is a paraphrase of a poem in hexameters, for which the diction of Virgil and Ovid had plainly served as an example. This Latin William epic can therefore be compared with the German *Waltharius* which will be discussed in the following chapter. A poem in Latin was obviously the work of a cleric, and so it affords another

[1] *Les Légendes épiques* i, 'Le Cycle de Guillaume d'Orange', ²1914, pp. 195–223.
[2] The text is given by G. Paris, *Histoire poétique de Charlemagne*, pp. 465–8.

proof that the learned cleric was in fact also concerned with these stories of chivalry. But this does not mean that he must have been the first. How would he have chosen such materials if they had not been ready to hand? And where else would he have found them but in the old legends that were told and recited at the courts of the lords of the castles?

In the case of Guillaume d'Orange the monastic tradition, naturally, is strongly represented. To it belong the *Vita Benedicti Abbatis Annianensis* of about 823, and especially the *Vita Guillelmi*, which, however, dates from about 1122—that is after various poems, such as the *Prise d'Orange*, were already in existence.

There was, therefore, every reason for Bédier to take this very cycle as his starting point in support of his thesis that the *chansons de geste* had arisen along the pilgrims' routes and in connexion with them. It is certain that the canonization of Guillaume de Toulouse strongly promoted the development of the extensive cycle of legends around his figure, but it does not sufficiently explain the nature of the knightly tales told or invented. There is more in these poems— fierce fights with Moors, the conquest of towns, stratagems, the winning of a Saracen bride—which will have appealed to a lay audience. We have mentioned the Spanish document, the *Nota Emilianense* of about 1070, in which Guillaume d'Orange and his cousin Bertrand also take part in the battle of Roncevaux. This would have been unthinkable if at the time the cycle of William had not already gained such fame that he was considered indispensable in the fight of the *Song of Roland*.

That is why the cycle of William is so extremely important. Nowhere else can we indicate so clearly how monastic legends and secular songs share the honour of having brought an heroic figure like that of William to its full development.[1] At the same time it will be clear that, to us who stand at the end of this long and closely interwoven series of traditions, it is extremely difficult to disentangle the threads of such a tangled web.

I shall therefore end these reflections by quoting the conclusion arrived at by the Spanish scholar Martin de Riquer.[2] After point-

---

[1] Cf. C. Voretzsch, *Einführung in das Studium der altfranzösischen Literatur*, Halle 1913, pp. 226 ff.   [2] In his book *Los Cantares de Gesta Franceses*, Madrid 1952, p. 207.

ing to the series of the oldest testimonies: Ermoldus Nigellus, *Hague Fragment*, and *Chançun de Willelme*, he continues: 'There was a transmission of historical facts in the cultured Latin of learned poets, and there must have been a similar one in the much simpler Latin of the hagiographical texts of the monasteries. Further, nothing stands in the way of the logical supposition that preserved in the castles there was the oral as well as the written memory of the heroic deeds of those warriors whom the knights, rightly or wrongly, considered as their ancestors. It is not without reason that the word *geste* in Old French often means no more than "pedigree". Nor does anything prevent the assumption that, after the wars and the glorious feats of arms, poems arose which celebrated the heroes and their important deeds; that has perhaps always been the case and perhaps it still happens even in our day.'

Thus we see the investigations of most recent times revert to the line of thought of Gaston Paris and Pio Rajna, not without having learned a good deal from the intermediate investigations, especially those of Bédier. The words of August Becker are still worthy of consideration.[1] 'What I object to is the assurance with which, on the basis of suspect sources and without observing the necessary caution, people have presupposed original poems and then plunged head over heels into the abyss of pure speculation. To me, the great danger is that the preserved texts do not count any more; the interest is only in their lost hypothetical predecessors.'

Anyone dealing with a *chanson de geste* should take this warning to heart, for it contains a good deal of truth. Anyone, however, who wishes to investigate the genre of the heroic song is forced again and again to get away from texts handed down, because he becomes convinced that they are only the *rari nantes in gurgite vasto*, the wreckage more or less accidentally washed up on the shore of medieval heroic poetry. Our eyes are not—at least, not exclusively—focused on the sound work of art that has ultimately been preserved for posterity as the fruit of so many vain and lost attempts; we wish to try to penetrate into that dark past in which the heroic song germinated and, gradually gaining in strength, unfolded into immortal songs like the *Iliad* and the *Song of Roland*.

[1] Cf. *Der südfranzösische Sagenkreis*, p. 43.

3

THE GERMANIC HEROIC SONGS

WHAT is so sadly lacking in Old French literature, that is, poetry from the time of Charlemagne himself, is amply provided by Germanic literature. About the year 800, a profusion of heroic epic poetry was known among the Germanic peoples. In South Germany there is not only the fragment of the *Lay of Hildebrand*, but also the epic of *Waltharius* written in beautiful Latin; from England we have, besides the so-called *Finnsburg Fragment*, the epic of *Beowulf*; from Scandinavia some heroic songs dealing with the Sigurd and the Nibelung legends. Here, then, we actually possess what the chronicle writers talk about when they say that, among the country people, *cantilenae* dealing with one or other of the heroic legends were sung. But the development has already progressed: we have not only the short song but even the complete epic, either in Latin, like the *Waltharius*, or in the vernacular, like *Beowulf*. We get the impression that we have virtually the complete material from which we can reconstruct the historical development of the Germanic epic.

Let us revert for a moment to what we said about the Homeric epic. The German scholar Karl Lachmann explained the *Nibelungenlied* as a string of twelve short songs, each of which dealt with a complete episode of the great drama. In order to form an idea of these old and short songs one has only to consider the nature of such poems as the *Lay of Hildebrand*, the *Finnsburg Fragment*, or the Eddic lays. Here we are not, as in the case of the Old French epic, completely in the dark, with hypotheses springing up like mushrooms. Here we can build on solid facts. Any theory of the origin of the epic can firmly be put to the test. If we try to consider Lachmann's view more closely, we find that it raises difficulties. For he supposed that each of his suggested short songs dealt with only an episode of the contents of the *Nibelungenlied*—such as the journey to Brünhild,

Kriemhild's marriage, Siegfried's death. Obviously we have to start from the idea that the audience already knew the legend as a whole, so that they could place each episode within the whole. For how could their interest be aroused if they heard such an episode recited without knowing in what context it belonged? This is precisely what Lachmann assumes: behind these short songs the whole complex to which they belong looms up in the minds of the audience, just as behind the *Iliad*—to place the question in an even broader context—the whole cycle about the journey to Troy must be assumed to be present in the audience's minds. So in the case of the German epic: a complete legend of the Nibelungs, yet not a Nibelung epic. But what was there, then? One may have in mind the oral tradition, i.e. the 'legend', telling of Siegfried's death and the fall of the Nibelungs. But what was the form of this legend? Was it a prose tale such as we later know of in the fairy-tales? That is possible, but we know even less of the existence of such a legend than of that of heroic poetry in one form or another, of which at any rate the *cantilenae* mentioned in the chronicles give an indication.

We should like to have an idea of the pre-literary stage of the epic, and this early stage would have to be less flimsy and vague than that ubiquitous but nowhere tangible oral legend. In our consideration of the problem we should like to fix the place of those songs repeatedly mentioned in German and French sources; and how else could this be done but by accepting such short epic songs within the picture of such a development? But this is where the difficulty crops up. It is true that the Old Norse *Edda* has some poems which belong together: the lay of Regin, telling of Sigurd's stay with the smith, the lay of Fafnir, telling of the fight with the dragon, that of Sigrdrifa, telling of the hero's visit to the Valkyrie. They form a whole; they are a continuous story. But there are many other heroic lays which form one complete whole, such as, for example, those of Helgi. They do not, therefore, constitute a part of a much larger context; nor do lays such as those about Hildebrand or the fight around Finnsburg. So the short epic song as we know it does not deal with a part of a legend, but with a legend as a whole.

This deprives Lachmann's theory of its real basis. The Swiss scholar Andreas Heusler therefore suggested a different solution to the problem, although naturally, like his great predecessor, he started from short lays, for both the sources as preserved and the demand of a logical train of thought force us to do so.[1] The question regarding the nature of these *cantilenae* demanded a different answer from that given by Lachmann. Heusler had in mind poems that did not lift an episode out of a larger unit, but poems whose contents formed a coherent whole. A complete lay therefore, but recited in a concise and sober style.

His explanation was supported by the fact that the material of the *Nibelungenlied* clearly falls apart into two sections that were separated from the beginning. The first part deals with the story of Siegfried, the second part deals with the fall of the Burgundians. Originally these two legends had nothing to do with each other, for Siegfried was a Frankish hero who was in no way connected with the history of the Burgundians. The contents of the epic would certainly have been too extensive to be treated in a short song, but each of the separate parts would not have been too extensive for such a treatment. The proof is given by the two songs of Atli which occur in the *Edda*. They deal with a story that is a variant of the fall of the Burgundian kings of the German tradition.

Heusler arrives at the following conclusion: in the fifth century there were two short heroic lays, a Frankish song of Brünhild and a song of the fall of the Burgundians, which through some intermediary stages ultimately led to two Austrian poems dealing with the first and the second marriage of Kriemhild, and from whose amalgamation in the years 1200 to 1205 the *Nibelungenlied* as handed down to us will have arisen. The Eddic lays of Sigurd and Atli must have been an echo of those oldest fifth-century songs.[2]

Heusler had an entirely different idea from Lachmann, who imagined a joining together of short episodic songs into a continuous whole; whereas Heusler's hypothesis could be described as one of expansion: the contents always remained the same, but they were told with ever-increasing wealth of circumstance. There is, first of

---

[1] Cf. his *Lied und Epos in germanischer Sagendichtung*, Dortmund 1905, and *Nibelungensage und Nibelungenlied*, Dortmund 1921.

[2] See *Nibelungensage und Nibelungenlied*, p. 79.

all, a great difference in style between an Eddic lay and a German epic. The former is short, and hence muddled at times; the poet seizes upon the main incidents and leaves the intermediary stages in darkness: the hearer must imagine these for himself and so he must have a knowledge of the legend to begin with. The style of the epic, however, is broad, often very circumstantial; the poet leaves nothing out and tells unimportant details with great minuteness. The Eddic poet is in a hurry and seems to be afraid of boring his audience; the poet of the epic likes to go on as long as possible, and he knows that he is most fascinating when he describes all the details in well chosen words. Hence the great minuteness in narrating a wedding feast or a messenger's journey, which the Eddic poet would hardly consider worth mentioning. Hence, too, the preference for dialogues even when they are virtually superfluous. When the heroes speak in an Eddic song, they say something essential which influences the course of the action; when they talk in the *Nibelungenlied* they often merely utter the phrases of conventional politeness. We should therefore picture the epic as the rich development of material originally told in a concise form, and this was achieved because a richer and more confident art was able to tell the story in easy-going detail, perhaps even sounding complacent.

I have already mentioned that Heusler's conception was based on the facts of the Old Norse *Edda* tradition: it was not mere imagination. The lays which he chose as the basis of his hypothesis are there on the parchment. They are limited in size and rarely exceed a total of a hundred four-line stanzas. We even possess an example of the treatment of the same material in two different songs. The one has 43 stanzas, and the other 105. Both deal with the death of Gunther and Hagen and their sister Gudrun's subsequent revenge on Atli, the King of the Huns. The same matter could therefore be told in poems of different length. The second lay of Atli is fully twice as long but not really twice as circumstantial as the first. The first contains an episode in which Hagen's heart must be cut out of his body, at Atli's command. It is told vividly and graphically. First a slave is used, but when his heart is laid before Gunnar he sees from its trembling that it cannot be the heart of a hero: only when Hagen's heart is laid before him does Gunnar say:

> Here I have the heart of Högnit the valiant,
> Unlike to the heart of Hjalli the craven.
> Little it trembles as it lies on the platter,
> Still less did it tremble when it lay in his breast.[1]

This is a striking scene, built up in two parallel yet entirely contrasted parts. Now what happens to this scene in the second lay of Atli, which is twice as long? Here the cook is seized, but he wails so pitiably when they bind him and the knife is drawn that Hagen cannot bear it and lets him go; when they cut his own breast with the knife he laughs. The episode has not become longer, nor is it told more circumstantially; it is diluted and finds pleasure in a half-humorous, half-compassionate description of the cook, who is to be slaughtered himself this time.

The Eddic lays are dangerous material for the reconstruction of the epic development among the Germanic peoples. Although we do have a few that can be supposed to reach back into the eighth century, most of them are considerably later, and this applies especially to the lays of Sigurd. One has the impression that many lays are not at all concerned with the telling of this legend, but rather with a psychological approach to the feelings of the women who play such a tragic part in the life of the hero. The poet asks himself: how could Brünhild, who really loves Sigurd, send the hero to his death? What did Gudrun feel when her husband was stabbed beside her? At times this gives rise to long monologues in which the woman lays bare her heart. There is something else: the style of these songs is no longer as hard as the old ore of heroic song. It is softer and more sensitive. We are closer to the medieval knightly ballad. Most of the Sigurd lays belong to the twelfth century themselves and are therefore contemporary with the German *Nibelungenlied*.

It would be better to explain a German epic from German predecessors. But then we can only point to the *Lay of Hildebrand*. With this hero though, we enter a different field of heroic legend. He belongs not to the story of the Nibelungs but to the cycle of the

---

[1] All quotations from the *Edda* are from the translation by H. A. Belows, *The Poetic Edda* (1923).

Ostrogothic hero King Theoderic the Great [Theoderic of Verona]. These legends arose in the North of Italy among the Ostrogoths; they were next adopted by the Longobards who, after the fall of the Ostrogothic empire, likewise settled in Lombardy, which is called after them; they then reached Bavaria, and from there conquered the whole of the Germanic area as far as Iceland. The Austrian poems about Ortnit and Wolfdietrich belong to this tradition, just as much as the Norse prose story of Dietrich of Bern [Theoderic of Verona] which itself is built up of Low German poems. When we remember that this Theoderic of Verona is still prowling around as Derk with the Bear in the superstitions of the Dutch Eastern provinces, we realize the great popularity of this king: a fame which equals, even surpasses, that of Charlemagne. People are sometimes capricious in their preferences: the Frankish Charlemagne became the heroic emperor of the French, but the Gothic Theoderic that of the Germans.

How quickly a legend spread to the farthest corners of the Germanic region in these early Middle Ages is shown by a stanza cut into a Swedish runestone. The Rök inscription can be dated about 800. The stone was erected in honour of a man who fell in battle. His father gives the assurance that, although he is ninety years of age, he will beget another son who will avenge this murder: a family tragedy in a Swedish village. In the middle of this oath of revenge the following stanza has been cut:

> Theoderic the brave
> King of the Vikings
> Formerly ruled
> On the shore of the Reidmeer;
> Now sits on the Gothic
> Horse in armour
> The first of the heroes,
> The shield on the strap.

—a clear proof of how eagerly one tribe adopted the heroic legend of another. In the eighth century the stories of Siegfried, of Gunther and Hagen, of Theoderic the Great, are known in the farthest corners of Norway and Sweden.

Let us now first examine more closely the content of the *Lay of Hildebrand*. Old Hildebrand, retainer of King Theoderic, mounts guard before the approaching fight against Odoaker, who has young Hadubrand with him, the son of Hildebrand who, thirty years before, had gone into exile with his king. When Hildebrand left his wife, his son was only a new-born child. Now they stand on opposite sides as enemies in the outposts of both armies. The old man asks his young opponent to name his origin. From his answer it becomes clear that he is Hadubrand, but when the father makes himself known to him his son will not believe him, for he thinks he knows for certain that Hildebrand died long ago. 'By God almighty, know that you cannot seek battle with a closer relation,' the father says, and takes a ring from his arm and offers the young man this precious gift of his king as a token of his affection. But Hadubrand answers: 'One shall receive a gift with the spear, point against point; you are very cunning, old Hun, and seek to strike me with your spear. Seafarers told me that Hildebrand is dead. I see from your armour that you have a good lord and do not wander in this world as an exile.' Then Hildebrand calls out: 'Woe, a bitter fate is overtaking me. I wandered for sixty summers and winters away from my country. Now my own child is to hew me with the sword, or else I shall kill him. But you can easily capture a suit of armour from so old a man, if you have the strength and have any right to it.' But the young man insults his old opponent further, and Hildebrand, incensed, offers to fight him; then they will see who shall lose his armour to the other. The fight now begins: they hack on the white shields until these are whittled away with their weapons. . . . Here the fragment, which was accidentally preserved in a Kassel manuscript of about 800, breaks off. Not only is the end missing, but also the scribe has evidently omitted portions in the middle, or at any rate copied an already incomplete model. The outcome of the fight cannot be doubted: the father turns out to be the warrior with the greater strength and experience. He kills his own son. The fight of father against son is one of the famous themes of heroic legend. It is told of the Persian hero Rustum as well as of the Irish Cúchulainn. Its proper form is this: the father begets a son with a woman whom he leaves before the birth of the child, but he gives her a token of recognition, so that the son shall later seek him out and find him through this token. When the son is grown up he undertakes this expedition. But it is the son who causes the tragic end through his overconfidence: he meets his father, and, in spite of his suspicion that the man may be his father, out of pride he will not be the first to make himself known. The result is a fight in which the son is killed. On the body the father finds the token by which he recognizes his son. This fight, which dismays us because of its extreme tragedy, probably cannot be explained, as has been supposed, from the lives of warriors of old, who chose their own lord and so served outside their own country. Rather one ought to assume that its basis is an old, perhaps already an Indo-European myth.[1]

For us, however, the main point is whether this poem can serve to explain the development of epic poetry as Heusler imagined it. It does not really matter what we expect of the poem, for its content forms a complete whole in itself, which, although it has its place in the cycle of Dietrich of Bern, cannot be taken as an episodic song for that reason. No history precedes it, nor has it a sequel that presupposes this. The only requirement indispensable to a full understanding of the song is that for its background one should be familiar with the history of Theoderic's fight against Odoaker. Nor is the content such that it could expand, with padding, into a fully fledged epic; the story is too thin for that. It is therefore not the type of song that Heusler needs to prove his theory. But that is not really of very great importance. The main point is that by means of this unique fragment one can form an idea of the kind of lays that were current at the time of Charlemagne.

We can be certain that it is not at all a primitive poetic art. The poet builds on a long-established tradition: i.e. the repetition of the same thought in different words; the use of fixed-verse formulae such as: 'Hildebrand spoke, Heribrant's son'; the fixed epithets; the development of the action through dialogue—these are all features pointing to a traditional poetic style. The metrical form is that of Germanic poetry in general: a line with four lifts bound together by alliteration (*heuwun harmlicco huitte scilti*), while the number of syllables in the dip varies. There is every reason to assume that this system of alliteration goes back a long way. From a statement by

[1] See my essay 'Das Motiv des Vater-Sohn-Kampfes im Hildebrandslied', in *Germanisch-Romanische Monatsschrift* xxxiv (1953), pp. 257-74.

Tacitus, it follows that it was already known in Roman times. This may convince us that heroic poetry reaches very far back: that entire dark period, stretching from the Migration until written sources begin to appear, is also the period in which heroic song was alive. Is there any reason to think that things were different among the Franks who settled in Gaul? And if at the time of Charlemagne such songs were recited, is it then really necessary or even probable that the *Song of Roland* arose out of nothing, and would it not be better to assume that it forms the end of a long epic tradition in which both Germanic and Romance songs can find a place?

Now, it is remarkable that in this same period there was already epic poetry of an entirely different nature: we have the Latin *Waltharius* and the Anglo-Saxon *Beowulf*, poems of respectively 1,456 and 3,182 lines. If we bear in mind that the short epic lay (which, for that matter, in Scandinavia remained the exclusive form of heroic epic poetry) seems to have been older and more primitive in size and structure, we may well ask how it was possible that the large epic could also appear as early as the ninth and tenth centuries.

The poet of the *Waltharius* was the young monk Ekkehard of St. Gall,[1] who, as he says himself, made this poem at the command of his teacher as a specimen of Latin poetic style. This fixes the date of the poem between 920 and 930. It is obvious that a young cleric who has to prove himself a competent master of poetic Latin should first of all look at Virgil. But from the *Aeneid* he not only gathered a harvest of flowers of speech, but learned from it even more the clear disposition of material, and a vivid contrasting of people and situations.

Walter of Aquitaine, with the Frankish Hagen and the Burgundian princess Hiltgunt, had arrived as hostage at the court of Attila. Here the princes were given an excellent education, and, when of age, were appointed as leaders of the Hunnish troops. When Hagen fled, after King Gunther terminated the treaty with the Huns, Wal-

---

[1] I shall not discuss here the question whether we should not rather put Geraldus in his place, for which see H. Grégoire in *La Nouvelle Clio* iv (1952), pp. 319–20; W. Stach, in *Zeitschrift für deutsches Altertum* (1940), pp. 57 ff.; Langosch, in *Zeitschrift für deutsche Philologie* lxv (1940), pp. 121 ff.; Stackmann, in *Euphorion* xlv (1950), pp. 231 ff.; and K. Hauck, in *Germanisch-Romanische Monatsschrift* xxxv (1954), pp. 1–27.

ter, too, was seized by the desire for freedom and his native land. When he returns from a campaign in which he subjects a rebellious nation, he makes a plan to escape with Hiltgunt, with whom he has fallen in love. When Attila and his men are in a drunken sleep after an abundant feast, he escapes with Hiltgunt, taking with him a rich treasure from Attila's treasure chamber. In spite of Attila's wrath, none of his noblemen dares to pursue them. After a forty days' journey, the fugitives come to the Rhine. Gunther hears about them from the ferryman who ferries them across, especially about the treasure of gold which they have with them. His greed tempts him to obtain this, but Hagen, who has realized who the two fugitives are, urgently advises against it. Nevertheless, with twelve men, the king pursues Walter, who in the meantime has already reached the Vosges. Hagen must follow the king because of his oath of allegiance. Walter takes refuge in a mountain pass where only one opponent at a time can attack him, and in eleven successive duels that are vividly told he defeats eleven Frankish knights. Gunther and Hagen again pursue Walter, and do not shrink from attacking together. When, in this tremendous heroic fight, Gunther has lost a leg, Hagen his left eye, and Walter his right hand, they are reconciled and make lugubrious jokes about their wounds, which Hiltgunt dresses in the meantime. Each returns to his home and, after his father's death, Walter and Hiltgunt live happily together in Aquitaine for sixty years.

There is no reason to doubt the genuineness of this legend.[1] It seems likely to me, therefore, that Ekkehard rewrote a German heroic song in Latin hexameters, especially as fragments of an English *Waldere* poem, dating from about 900 and therefore even older, have come down, and also because the traces of this legend in later sources certainly do not all need to go back to the Latin monastic poem—which

---

[1] Although F. Genzmer in *Germanisch-Romanische Monatsschrift* xxxv (1954), pp. 161–78, defended the view that the poet knew no Old Germanic heroic song at all but had freely invented the whole story. The poem is full of features that are impossible in Germanic poetry. According to Genzmer the Old English poem *Waldere* is a version of this Latin poem used as reading matter in schools. While granting that the *Waltharius* is not a genuine Germanic epic, we should still consider that the monk Ekkehard or somebody else will as monk have had little contact with real heroic life.

probably did not become known outside the circle of the clergy. We have the impression that this poem also throws light on other legends. For the main reason for Gunther's decision to pursue Walter is his desire to obtain the gold treasure which the fugitives have with them. But thirst for gold is also one of the main motifs of the Nibelung legend. This appears very clearly in the Old Norse lays of Atli, but the hoard of the Nibelungs also plays a fatal part in the German legend, for it is actually for the sake of its possession that Kriemhild treacherously lures her brothers to Etzel's court, where Gunther meets his death. Thus Ekkehard did not work on virgin soil which he could plant with flowers gathered only from the *Aeneid*. There was a flourishing and widespread legend on which he could build. Naturally, this did not prevent him from treating the legend in accordance with his own feeling and perception. He was a monk, and although it is abundantly clear that the lives and fights of brave heroes were not at all repulsive to him, one can expect to find religious ideals reflected in this school-task.

Walter, the main figure, is a hero after his own heart. He is brave, of course, but he is also a pious knight. Involuntarily we are reminded of that other champion, Roland, who, through his over-confidence, was to die an early death. Walter is certainly drawn after the model of *pius Aeneas*. In several places Ekkehard stresses his faith in God. One might be inclined to think that these are only the obligatory genuflexions of the Christian monk. At any rate, Walter is especially noted for his virtues of courage and loyalty, the same virtues are always praised in Germanic epic poetry. Bound to Hagen by friendship, he cannot for a moment suspect that Hagen could enter into a fight with him, and especially in such a treacherous way as to attack him together with Gunther. But in Hagen loyalty reveals itself in a different way. It leads him into the same tragic conflict to which margrave Rüedeger succumbs in the *Nibelungenlied*: in the choice between loyalty to his comrade in arms or to his lord, it is the latter who wins and, with a bleeding heart, he has to turn against his friend.

But the fact that Ekkehard saw his heroes with the eyes of a monk appears from the somewhat acid humour with which he draws them. The true epic poet believes in his heroes, especially in the ideal which they represent. If necessary, fight for the sake of fighting; the hero's noblest qualities can only be developed through it. But Ekkehard's soul is really outside the circle of the old heroic legend. When, after the battle, the wounded heroes are sitting together, they joke about their wounds. We know this about Scandinavian heroes too, even if we sense a bravado which no longer seems genuine. What can one make of the mocking words which Hagen speaks to Walter?

> From now on, friend, will you hunt deer
> To make mittens out of their hides.
> Fill the right hand mitten with soft wool
> To deceive others with a semblance of a hand.
> But what will he say, when he sees that
> Contrary to custom you will fix the sword to the left,
> The wrong hand, and even worse, that
> When passion comes upon you
> You embrace your wife with the left hand
> In an embrace that is uncommon and even wrong?

Such humour is more in the style of monastic jokes than in that of genuine heroic legend. For that reason *Waltharius* is of little importance to the problem of the origin and development of heroic poetry, however important the epic may be as a literary phenomenon and as genuine testimony to the existence of old heroic poetry in the vernacular. This epic, which was made within the walls of the monastery and remained there, can hardly have had any significant influence outside them.

But how about *Beowulf*? There is no stranger poem in the whole of Germanic heroic poetry. In it Beowulf, the 'Bee-wolf', is the hero of two adventures—told in the first and the third part of the epic. At the court of the Danish King Hrothgar, the monster Grendel creates great havoc: every night he appears in the king's hall and drags one of the sleeping men away. The Geatish hero Beowulf hears about this and offers his services. He sleeps in the hall with his men, and in the middle of the night the monster appears and seizes one of the men with his claw. But Beowulf, undaunted, tears his arm off. The next morning he follows the bloody track which leads him to the shore of a lake. Without further thought he jumps into the water, dives to the bottom and there finds a den where he is attacked by Grendel's mother. His own sword is not able to pierce the monster's body. Then he wrestles with her, but is nearly overcome. He sees the ogre's sword and this enables him to cut through her throat. Then he finds Grendel himself dead on his bed; he decapitates him in order to take away the head as a trophy, but the sword melts in the monster's blood. He then makes his way unharmed to the surface. Hrothgar's men lose heart at the sight of the blood that colours the lake and go away in dismay, as they are convinced that Beowulf has lost his life in the depths. But Beowulf's own men show more confidence in their lord, and with them the hero returns in triumph to the hall of King Hrothgar. He is royally feasted and, laden with presents, departs for the land of the Geats.

The second part of the epic relates that Beowulf, on his return to his native land, offers the presents he has received to his king, and thus has the opportunity of giving a colourful report of his adventure. This means a repetition of what the poet has just been saying. We can only admire him for being able to introduce so much variation and mention so many new details that the hearer or reader continues to follow attentively Beowulf's report of his own heroic deeds. When the third part of the epic begins, many years have gone by. The king of the Geats is dead; all sorts of feuds with the Swedes have caused unrest; finally Beowulf is proclaimed king. Now, at the end of a blissful reign, a part of the coast is harassed by a dragon who ravages ever larger areas in his boldness. Beowulf resolves to fight him. With a number of followers he goes to the dragon's mound, but he considers it his royal duty to fight the dragon single-handed. Although he manages to conquer the dragon, he succumbs to the flames that issue from the monster's mouth. His retainer Wiglaf, who had come to his aid, scolds the other followers who had fled in cowardice for their lack of loyalty to their lord. Beowulf is now dying. The poem ends with the grand interment of Beowulf's mortal remains in an enormous mound; the burning of Patroclus may be placed beside this as a cultural and historical as well as poetic parallel.

Stories of fights with demonic beings and dragons easily give the impression of being fairy-tales, or, if one prefers the term, mythological tales. Yet it would be wrong to consider them as not fitting into a genuine heroic legend. There is certainly no reason to deny *Beowulf* the character of Germanic epic poetry. First of all, it contains numerous allusions to heroic legends known elsewhere, such as those of Sigmund, Ermanaric, Finn, and Offa. The poet fully realizes that he is moving in the sphere of the heroic. It is remarkable that the poet so often alludes to undeniably historical facts in which the tribe of the Geats occupies a central place. What he says of the fights with the Swedes is, even to us, one of the principal sources of our knowledge of the history of Sweden in the early Middle Ages. We may, then, draw the following conclusions: on the one hand, that in seventh-century England a richly developed heroic legend was current, which was by no means limited to the national past but also contained Frankish, Gothic, and Frisian material; on the other hand, that besides the inserted stories of historical events in Sweden, the main characters too, Beowulf of the land of the Geats, and Hrothgar of Denmark, point to an undeniable Scandinavian origin of these traditions. As the fight between the Geats and the Swedes took place after the emigration of the Angles and Saxons from their old homes in Slesvig, they cannot have brought these traditions along from their old native land. Hence, after the migration there was continual contact between the tribes living along the coast of the North Sea, and this contact concerned not only the exchange of merchandise, but also of legends and poems. How else could a story like that of the fight for Finnsburg, belonging to a Frisian–Danish tradition, be known to us from English sources only, namely, from a short fragment and from an episode connected with it in *Beowulf*? Friesland lost all memory of this legend, but England faithfully preserved it.

The main characters of *Beowulf* are historical. This is proved most strikingly in the case of the king of the Geats, Hygelac, for his name is found in Frankish historical sources: in 521 a king Chochilaicus invaded the territory of the present Zuider Zee with his fleet and sailed up the Rhine to the neighbourhood of Cleve; but Theodebert, the son of the Frankish king, pursued him after a battle, and defeated and killed him on the coast of Holland.[1] The Danish king, too, is known from other historical writings. But what about Beowulf? It

[1] Cf. Gregory of Tours, *Historiarum libri decem* iii, ch. 3.

C

is still uncertain whether he really was a historical figure. So little is known about him that he has been taken to be a mythical personality. But everything about him remains hidden under a veil of uncertainty. We cannot here enter into the many theories that have been propounded about him. Our purpose is solely to state that a not unimportant, partly historical, partly epic tradition at this early age came from Scandinavia to England, where it found a fertile soil in which to take root.

Can we say, therefore, that *Beowulf* is an English version of an original Geatish or Danish poem? This is again one of those many questions that remain without a clear answer. It is certain that the epic as we know it was the work of a Northumbrian poet. It is impossible that in Scandinavia in the sixth or seventh century, where to the end of the heathen period only short songs were composed, an epic of the size of *Beowulf* could have been written. The manuscript in which the poem has come down reveals the character of careful monastic labour; one can only imagine it in the library of an abbey or perhaps of a nobleman's stronghold. It is not at all an *aide-mémoire* of some *jongleur*; it is meant for educated readers.[1] The audience may indeed have consisted of clergy. A valuable testimony to this is contained in the letter written by Alcuin to the abbot of Lindisfarne in which he urged him that in a monastery only sacred writings should be read—the sermons of the Church Fathers and not the songs of the pagans—for '*Quid Hinieldus cum Christo?*' What has Ingeld to do with Christ?[2] Therefore, heroic songs were actually read in monasteries. Then why not also *Beowulf*?

A second point may have some bearing on this. Such an early and extensive epic is hardly imaginable without the example of Latin literature. Whether one is thinking of Virgil and Statius, or of Christian poets like Juvencus, pre-Latin epic seems an indispensable requisite for *Beowulf*. These authors were sedulously read in British monasteries. Bede and Alcuin prove it. Here and there the poet of *Beowulf* even deals with Biblical subjects, as if he wished to cast a Christian veil across the undoubtedly heathen theme. In all probability, therefore, the poet was an educated man—which does not

---

[1] Cf. W. P. Ker, *The Dark Ages* (1923), p. 251.
[2] Cf. *Monumenta Germaniae Historica Epistolae Carol.* ii, 124.

mean that he was not at the same time a great artist. His style has a noble dignity such as one can hardly associate with a *jongleur* who composed for the masses.

On the other hand, one wonders at the strange, weak structure. What truly epic poet would have hit on the idea of making a hero tell a story afresh from the beginning that he has just told circumstantially, by making him report on his adventures to the king. The fight with Grendel and that with the dragon do not form a logical whole; they are two independent deeds of Beowulf's, the former from his youth, the latter from his old age. The fight with Grendel especially stands on its own in Germanic heroic poetry, in which dragon-fights occur frequently enough. For that reason scholars have even suggested Irish examples,[1] especially in connexion with an Irish fairy-tale about a monster that puts his arm through the smoke-hole of a hut in order to steal children, and whose arm is then hacked off by the hero. It is not difficult to indicate the way by which Irish material could have come to the English epic. At about 700 there was a good deal of communication between Irish and English monasteries, especially from Iona. Is it possible to imagine an English Ekkehard who had heard tales in his monastery that had come over from Denmark and the land of the Geats, and who could also have heard Irish tales, and thus could himself have had the idea of making an epic? But there are objections to this. Scandinavia was still entirely heathen at this time. If historical and epic stories did come from there, it would seem improbable that they would find their way to a monastery. But how difficult it is to pronounce any opinion in regard to this dark period of history! Would it be entirely out of the question that in an English monastery where men toyed with the idea of converting the northern peoples, all potentially useful information about this distant and strange nation was being diligently collected for the missionaries who would one day undertake this dangerous task?

When we think of *Beowulf*, the example of Ekkehard is always before our eyes. Here too we have a poet who does not belie his Christian disposition, but who has a true taste for the feats of arms of famous heroes at the same time. The fight with the dragon, it

[1] Cf. J. Carney, *Studies in Irish Literature and History*, Dublin 1955, pp. 77–128.

need not be doubted, was the adventure of a Germanic hero no less than of a Greek hero. The last part of *Beowulf* may well therefore be founded on an old tradition. Is it likely, then, that the poet should, of his own accord, have added the Irish Grendel motif by way of introduction? But tradition is ever full of surprises: the adventure with Grendel is to be found in the Old Norse saga of Grettir. It is surely extremely unlikely that the author of this saga could ever have had a look at the *Beowulf* manuscript buried in a monastic library. Similarly, the assumption that he should have used as source the Irish fairy-tale of the monster with the hacked-off arm must be rejected, for the saga agrees with *Beowulf* in the name of the dagger with which Beowulf fights the dragon. There is therefore only one possibility: both Beowulf and the Icelandic saga go back to a Danish or Swedish poem which dealt with the fight with Grendel. Another indication, therefore, that, in the centuries immediately following the Migration, epic poems were already in existence and aroused such an interest that they could be brought over to England and to Iceland.

After all, one thing should not be forgotten. It may be true that *Beowulf* contains material that was gathered together from all directions, and that it owes its wide range to Latin examples, yet it also remains true that it has its roots in an old epic tradition of the Germanic tribes of England.[1] This is shown not only by the additional episodes which deal with genuine Germanic heroic material. It appears even more from the poetic style of the work itself. A monk trained in the classics does not find this in his Latin examples, even less does he invent it. The metrical structure of the line corresponds entirely with that of the German and Norse poems. The language, too, with its numerous fixed formulae and its typical style of variation, reminds us at once of the almost contemporary *Lay of Hildebrand*. If then, as an epic, the poem is a new creation, it also points back to the much older short heroic lay that is to be found among all Germanic tribes and which we have already shown reaches back to the Migration period. But nothing seems to prevent us from seeking its origin even farther back. Tacitus tells us that Arminius, the hero of Germania, was still celebrated in song a

[1] Cf. H. M. Chadwick, *The Heroic Age* (1912), pp. 73 ff.

hundred years after his death. This can no longer have been a simple song of praise. In the course of a century such a character will have grown into a true heroic figure, and hence there is every reason to assume that Germanic heroic epic poetry was already in existence at the time of the Romans. It does not seem superfluous to point out that against such a broad background of Germanic heroic poetry, Old French epic poetry need not have stood in such isolation as some scholars have suggested.

It is impossible within the narrow scope of this book to discuss all the products of Germanic epic poetry. Much will therefore have to be left out. But the *Nibelungenlied*, the crown and glory of the Germanic epic, deserves a final brief discussion. When, at the end of the eighteenth century, it was edited from a recently discovered manuscript by the Swiss Myller, Frederic the Great wrote to him, on 22 February 1784, that this miserable trash was not worth a shot of powder. One need not take a general's comparison of a literary work with gunshot too seriously, but the remarkable fact remains that a venerable relic of old national poetry met with so little response when it appeared in the age of classicism. And we can even understand Goethe saying: 'I have feasted at the Homeric as well as the Nibelungen table, but nothing is more in accordance with my character than the breadth and depth of ever-living nature, the works of the Greek poets and sculptors.' The age of Romanticism took a different view. In the years round about 1812 when Jakob Grimm discovered the manuscript of the *Lay of Hildebrand*, one surprise followed another. In 1815 *Beowulf* became known; in 1820 *Kudrun*; in 1830 the Old Saxon *Heliand*. A whole world opened up— a world which had lain buried in monastic libraries from the Middle Ages onwards.

At the beginning of this chapter we glanced at the prehistory of the *Nibelungenlied*. It reaches far back into the past. A whole chain of poems, which came into being and were lost again in the course of the centuries, link the Austrian epic from the beginning of the thirteenth century with its underlying facts, which belong to the time of Attila. It is outside our scope to unravel the mysterious development of this tradition; we shall here try only to determine the nature of the *Nibelungenlied* itself. It corresponds to *Beowulf* in that it consists of two parts which originally did not belong together. It surpasses *Beowulf* in that these parts are closely linked together. For, although the legend of Siegfried is entirely independent, and although the Frankish hero had nothing to do with the fall of the Burgundian kings, the epic describes how the death of Siegfried brought the Burgundian catastrophe in its train. This has no connexion at all with real history. It is purely poetic creation that sees or makes connexions where they do not exist in reality.

There are even sharper contrasts between the two parts of the German epic. The second part contains an at times breathtaking account of a genuine heroic story. The fight that breaks out at the banquet given by Etzel to his Burgundian brothers-in-law on their arrival, then the siege of the heroes in the hall that is set alight over their heads, the duels, the figures of Hagen and Rüedeger—all this to a large extent still has the ring of the old heroic legend. But the first part is entirely different. Banquets and journeys by messengers are described in easy-going prolixity, details of dress and armour hardly hold our attention for stanzas on end, especially as the poet seems to be concerned only with displaying royal pomp and splendour. At times the action does not seem to progress. The way in which Siegfried woos the beautiful daughter of the king, Kriemhild, betrays a noble nature such as one naturally encounters at the court of the Staufen, but which does not in the least accord with the crude milieu of fifth-century Worms. Let us be honest: when we come to the second part, we feel something like relief. Our flagging interest is revived again, for now the action gathers speed, tense scenes follow one another, and the events are full of breathtaking tragedy. The story of Siegfried, which ends so dramatically, is told as a charming idyll. We are astonished that the poet pushes the colourful scenes that were actually there—the story of Siegfried's youth with its dragon-fight and the winning of the hoard, the freeing of the maiden, the fight with the dwarf Alberich—entirely into the background, in order to describe with exhausting diffuseness tournaments and hunting scenes instead.

This is no longer a genuine heroic legend. It reminds us rather of the courtly romance which came to Germany from the France of Chrétien de Troyes in the twelfth century. There we find the picture of the cultured and knightly aristocracy with all the *courtoisie* and luxury of France under Philippe-Auguste, with their psychological interest in *amour courtois*, the service which the knight renders to his chosen one, the courtly tournament, and the richness of dress and banquet. There can be no doubt that the poet of the *Nibelungenlied* was familiar with the *roman courtois*; he wanted to imitate its elegant refinement at the Viennese court. One is, indeed, almost inclined to assume that in this case, too, a foreign example showed the Germanic heroic song the way to an extensive and colourful epic, even if it is not Virgil here, but Chrétien de Troyes. The *Nibelungenlied* is like a good hunk of boar's meat smothered in a delicious sauce from the French kitchen.

Two kinds of material, two styles, two ages, clash violently in the *Nibelungenlied*. Was it the poet's lack of ability, or was it perhaps a well-considered plan? Was the granite of the Burgundian heroic legend too much for him, and did he want to transform the undoubtedly more romantic and fairy-tale material of Siegfried's life into a knightly romance of the day with all the refinements of a then modern art? For the *Nibelungenlied* actually has no inner unity. It is astonishing that the same poet who could recount the fall of the Burgundians with all the starkness of an old heroic legend, should be so weak and soft at the beginning of his epic.

It would be too easy to consider this peculiarity in a work of art like the *Nibelungenlied* merely as a failing of the poet. Perhaps he meant it to be like that, and even if we regret that he arranged his work in this way, it is still our duty to try to understand his intentions. The almost brazen contrast between the heroism of the fifth century and the courtly life of the thirteenth cannot have escaped the poet. If he did not avoid this, or at least did not soften it, then he must have wished it thus. It is possible that he composed his poem in such a way that the charm of the beginning gradually darkens to the harshness of the tragic ending, and that he wanted to represent the death of the radiant Siegfried as such a gross injustice that Kriemhild's inhuman revenge is the only acceptable redemption for it. What a contrast it is: Gunther and Hagen at their happy knightly court at Worms and their bitter fight in the burning hall of Etzel. It is, of course, not known how much he took over from his predecessors, but the scene in which Gunther and Hagen keep guard after their arrival is magnificently drawn, and I, for one, would like to take this as the work of the last poet. The two heroes are seated on the bench in front of the hall where the Burgundians are sleeping. The moon is shining in a cloudy sky. Light and dark alternate. Kriemhild emerges from Etzel's palace with some of her faithful attendants, to find out whether she can take the Burgundians by surprise in their sleep. But she finds them watchful, and they see her too. Hagen has Siegfried's sword on his lap. He draws it half-way out of its sheath. The moonlight glitters on the white blade. Kriemhild sees it, and turns back into the stronghold.

That is all. What the woman must have felt, what hot thoughts of revenge must have welled up in her heart at the sight of that sword in the hands of the man who had killed Siegfried, the poet makes no attempt to describe. The situation speaks for itself. It is not the worst artists who sometimes conceal what is most important. For by doing precisely this, they create a picture which rises spontaneously and with an immediate sharp clarity in the reader's mind.

Two worlds, then, are seen beside, if not opposite, each other. One of Worms and Etzel's stronghold in the sphere of the Migration period; the second of about the year 1200. But there is more: there is Brünhild's Isenstein, situated far in the North, a mythical realm that seems to belong to the remotest past. Three worlds, therefore, which are continually overlapping, and, by doing so, shed all the more light on one another. Or perhaps more correctly, three worlds that are entirely cut off from one another and are placed beside one another without any connexion, but with characters continually moving to and fro between these completely incongruous spaces. Do they not feel that they do not belong there? Do their souls not suffer harm when suddenly they pass from one space into the other?

Siegfried, the hero of the dragon-fight and the liberation of the maiden, undoubtedly belongs to the highly archaic sphere of mythical, prehistoric times. How can he presently appear as a perfect and courtly knight at the medieval court of Worms without belying part of himself? The king of that same Worms, however, goes to Isenstein in search of adventure, and there loses his way in the world of the amazon Brünhild. He who adapts himself in such a way must belie his nature. And indeed both perish from this antithesis. Siegfried does not fit in in the Worms of Gunther, where he falls victim to women's intrigues; Gunther has brought back from the mythical Isenstein a wife who is not suited to him and who will be his ruin.

The characters move between two worlds of reality and semblance. What is Siegfried the strong hero doing at the highly civilized court of Worms? How dare the weak Gunther set his heart on the strong Brünhild? The two marriages celebrated with so much outward splendour are suitable in a certain sense, for Siegfried and Kriemhild are well matched in manly strength and female beauty as in every heroic legend. Gunther and Brünhild are a typical royal pair, both borne up by the grandeur of royal majesty. Yet both marriages are based on an inner falseness, because the partners have come together from such different worlds. Siegfried's role as Gunther's retainer is false: the hero belies his own nature when he puts his services at the disposal of the weak Gunther. This falseness ruins him, and it is precisely this false servitude which Brünhild will emphasize so as to raise herself above Kriemhild. The king, who has only a semblance of power, wants to show himself in the role of hero, and is so bold as to desire to marry a woman like Brünhild. How miserably he plays that role! Weakness always has deceit as an ally. Like a true maiden from fairy-tales, Brünhild has made the winning of herself dependent upon tasks which will reveal to her the courage and the strength of her future husband. Gunther is not equal to these, and he has to ask Siegfried to perform the trials of strength in his place. And Siegfried undertakes this unworthy deceitful role; invisible through his *Tarnkappe*, he takes Gunther's place.

Here, then, lie the actual roots of the tragedy of the Nibelungs. The quarrel of the women threatens to lead to the discovery of this deceit. So Gunther must at all costs see to it that the truth will never come out. Yet he cannot prevent himself from losing the nimbus of heroic strength in the eyes of Brünhild. The daily association with this weakling has revealed to her that he is not the husband she had dreamed of. One word from Siegfried is sufficient to dispel the semblance of heroism that he had gained by his deceit in Isenstein.

At any moment Siegfried, the man of the real world, can destroy Gunther's world of semblance. That everlasting menace is unbearable: Siegfried will have to be removed. With diabolical cunning a hunting party is planned, at which Hagen gets the opportunity to kill Siegfried.

With the hero's death the world of mythical prehistoric times has come to an end. It is only natural therefore that Brünhild, who belonged to the same sphere, should also disappear completely from the scene: it is as if she has returned to Isenstein. But now the struggle is between Kriemhild and her brothers. Ostensibly the issue is the revenge that will have to be taken for Siegfried, but, in reality, the struggle for power whose symbol is the Nibelung hoard lies behind it. This hoard, for which the people of this courtly world of semblance fight and which will ruin them pitiably, is also mythical. The *motif* of the hoard is very old: it appears much more openly in the *Edda* songs. But whereas in the North the treasure is a symbol of royal power, for which real heroic figures fight bitterly, in the *Nibelungenlied* it is only shadows of power that try to win it. For what is Kriemhild without Siegfried? And similarly, what is Gunther, the king of semblance, without his retainer? The lack of power in both originates from the murder of Siegfried. His shadow falls over the whole final part of the epic.[1]

The poet of the *Nibelungenlied*, then, did not merely want to repeat an old legend. He was posing a problem that was acute in his own day. By placing the Siegfried of unbroken, mythical, prehistoric times in the world of semblance that represented the Worms of about 1200, he has pronounced judgement on the latter. There can be no doubt that to him the world of Siegfried meant an ideal of inner genuineness and solidity. Heroes of the old days perish when they lose their way in the false pretence of courtly life. But why, then, bring back once more to the court of the Staufen that old heroic material from the centuries of the Migration? Is it merely the nostalgia of an over-refined age for the strong primitive life of old? Is it the same nostalgia which was to make Western European man in the eighteenth century dream of an unspoilt natural savage, who is in-

[1] For this view I refer to the essay by W. J. Schröder, 'Das Nibelungenlied', in *Paul und Braunes Beiträge* lxxvi, Halle 1954, pp. 56–143.

wardly more genuine and civilized than he himself? Certainly this was partly so, for in the course of the thirteenth century the great epic poems sprang up like mushrooms: *Kudrun*, the poems of Ortnit and Wolfdietrich, and many others from the cycle of Dietrich of Bern. It is a renaissance of the old heroic epic, such as France had witnessed a century before; a slow-motion film, as it were, now shown in South-East Germany. But let us remember that such a revival of an old tradition is not merely a matter of fashion, it springs from the very real needs of such a period. Did thirteenth-century Germany want to pull itself up by these old heroic figures? Did the poet of the *Nibelungenlied* wish to point the way?

He certainly had more in mind than merely to make a new song of old and, at the time, surely well-worn material. His devastating criticism of the world of pretence at Worms is really aimed directly at Vienna, where Etzel is in residence and the fall of the Burgundians takes place. With the posing of the problem of nature and civilization, doubts also arise about the value of civilization (in Rousseau at the end of the eighteenth century no less than in the poet at the end of the twelfth). Schröder goes so far as to suppose that this antithesis, which here appears in the modern dress of the thirteenth century, is really only a repetition of what had happened much earlier in the kingdom of the Merovingians: the old kings of this family had relied on power only and created the Frankish kingdom, the younger Merovingians lacked this power and appealed to authority. If this is so, then the poet of the thirteenth century brought this antithesis to light again out of the old legend, which certainly no longer showed it openly, with admirable flair. Moreover, he made it subservient to the posing of the problem of his own time. We need only think of the years in which the epic was written, the reign of Philip of Swabia. The struggle between Guelphs and Ghibellines had flared up again in all its violence. Although officially elected in 1201, Philip still had to contest his real power against the Guelph Otto IV of Brunswick, the son of Henry the Lion. The coronation could not take place in Aachen till 1205. In 1206 Otto's army was definitely defeated.

One wonders if the murder of the emperor in Bamberg in 1208 is reflected in the epic. At any rate, it was the aftermath of a struggle which revealed only too clearly how inwardly weak the Holy Roman Empire had become. Philip of Swabia is depicted as a mild and pious man who strove to make his court the centre of civilization; another Gunther of Worms, therefore, placed in a time that was hard and ruthless. Could the *Nibelungenlied* have been a warning to the emperor, or a covert criticism of him? Possibly both. Here the poet held up a mirror to his time, i.e. to the rulers of his time, in which they could recognize themselves. What did they want? To be Siegfried or Gunther? But these are mere conjectures that will never be proved. Suffice it to stress that this poem did not originate by accident, but that the time cried out for it and found the poet who was able to illustrate the essential problems of the period.

Let us return to more literary considerations. For, granting that the *Nibelungenlied* as it has come down was prompted by the needs of its time, can it be called a masterpiece? Can we be allowed to consider this culmination of Germanic epic tradition a sound and successful work? Frankly, we hesitate to place it beside the *Iliad*; perhaps the *Song of Roland*, too, has to be put above the German epic. Aesthetically it is an almost insuperable drawback that neither inwardly nor outwardly does the epic possess a real unity. The poet may have purposely placed two worlds in sharp opposition to each other, but has he managed to solve the antithesis in a higher unity? In this he does not seem to have been quite successful. In reading it, we regret the many weak places and consider many an *aventiure* as a stopgap. The preamble to the action proper is too long; the transition from the first to the second part is too flat. But we should not forget that what is indifferent to us—the long drawn-out scenes of banquets and tournaments—enchanted the Middle Ages. It is not the poet who should be blamed for this, but we ourselves. How many people do really feel, in the endless descriptions of daily life to which the realistic novel treats us, something of the charm of seeing that small world, in which we feel ourselves at home, illuminated in a poetic lustre? That is what makes us feel how beautiful life really is, though we so often live in a humdrum way. But what one can enjoy in the present day fades when one reads about it in a poem of far-off days. It does not live for us. We experience at best a second-hand enjoyment of the beautiful splendour that is gone beyond recall. It is precisely these descriptions of the details of milieu which date a work of art most quickly and irrevocably. Therefore we are only satisfied when we come to the parts of the *Nibelungenlied* that are full of fierce action; to the overheated tension at Etzel's court. But then we are richly rewarded for our severely taxed patience. From the crossing of the Danube to the deaths of Gunther and Hagen, what a tremendous succession of really stirring moments!

In this second part the poet undoubtedly rises to the height of his powers. It may be said that he is borne along by a long tradition, which in some places he follows so faithfully that an Old Norse heroic song is discernible behind it. In other places, it is an insignificant detail of description that turns out to have a truly symbolic meaning. The graphic description of the crossing of the Danube reveals with what impetuous strength Hagen is rowing:

> To turn the boat he held the oar in the water,
> Until the strong oar broke in his hand.
> He wanted to go to his comrades on the shore,
> To mend the damage, he bound the pieces together.

More forcibly it is said in the second *Lay of Atli*:

> Full stoutly they rowed,   and the keel clove asunder,
> Their backs strained at the oars   and their strength was fierce;
> The oar-loops were burst,   the thole-pins were broken
> Nor the ship made they fast,   ere from her they fared.

That violent strength, which breaks the oars, is the expression of the grimness of the heroes when they realize that they will not come back from their journey to the land of the Huns. Yet they refuse to shun the danger and return. What a perspective of tradition opens up here! On the one hand this little scene found its way into a lay said to have been made in Greenland, on the other it found its way, so many centuries later, into the Austrian epic. Neither time nor space have been able to obliterate the deep notches in the epic wood-carving.

Yet it would not be right to praise the poet of the *Nibelungenlied* for preserving so magnificently what was old and, at the same time, to blame him for sometimes failing in his own additions. If the character of Rüedeger is his own creation, which I would gladly believe, it proves his mastery. And if he took it over from a predecessor, he still put something of his soul into it. When the Burgundians enter Bavaria they know from the prophecy of the mermaids in the Danube that they are heading for their downfall. The air is heavy with disaster. They arrive at Bechelaeren and are received by the margrave Rüedeger, and suddenly the gentle sun of idyll shines through the stormy clouds. What a cordial and carefree reception, crowned by the engagement of Giselher to the margrave's daughter! What perspectives of happiness are opening up! We think that this tender happiness will not be broken: will the heroes return from Vienna safe and sound? The reception in Vienna is full of pomp and splendour. But Kriemhild is brooding on revenge. When the battle for the hall, where the Burgundians have ultimately entrenched themselves, is raging, Etzel summons his retainers, one after the other, to throw themselves into the fight with Gunther and his men. Finally Rüedeger's turn comes. He appeals to the recent ties of kinship with the Burgundian princes, but in vain: Etzel reminds him of the other and much stronger ties that bind the retainer to his lord. Rüedeger has the same inner conflict as Hagen in the *Waltharius*. In both cases the retainers' oath turns the scale. Uneasy in mind, Rüedeger proceeds to the entrance of the hall. The Burgundians see him coming and can only suppose that he comes to offer peace. How dreadful it is for the margrave to have to say that he has come to fight against them. It shows the poet's exquisite tact that he has not made him fall in a duel with Giselher, but with his brother Gernot with the sword that Rüedeger himself had given him.

Such a scene reveals the true poet. In him the feeling for the old heroic poetry had indeed not been extinguished, for he could sympathize with the old heroes, even though he was enough of a modern man to turn the inexorable pathos into an inhuman cruelty which almost mars the end of the poem. Inner uncertainty of later generations towards the ideals of the old heroic days often reveals itself through an exaggeration in two directions: either in that of a weak sentimentality or in that of pushing the stark tragedy to extremes.

The poet of the *Nibelungenlied* was compelled to his creation by an inner urge of vocation. How else could he, in the century of the playful love-song and of Celtic romanticism, have blown so resolutely on the Nibelung bugle? Were people still willing to listen to such fierce sounds at that time? Was there still an interest in those far-off legends? But every truly great poet is both an end and a beginning. This is that last poem that celebrates the story of Siegfried and the Burgundians, but at the same time, as we have already seen, it stands at the beginning of a short, flourishing period of German literature in which the old legends, in rejuvenated form, were once more to enchant large circles of attentive listeners.

Thus we have surveyed just over six centuries of development and growth, and the variety of forms of Germanic heroic song is rich. Short lays like the *Lay of Hildebrand*, the Eddic lays, but also the *Waltharius*, *Beowulf*, the *Nibelungenlied*, and *Kudrun*: all centuries and all tribes have contributed to their form. And even if there were times when the heroic song disappeared from sight, we know that even then it remained alive, growing and gathering strength to open up into new and unexpected beauty.

4

IRISH AND ICELANDIC PROSE SAGAS

WITH the heroic legends of the Celtic nations, conditions are considerably less favourable than in the case of the Germanic legends. Of the early and completely romanized Gauls nothing has been preserved; what has come down from the insular Celts dates from later times, many centuries after their conversion to Christianity. Fortunately, the Irish clergy were not too narrow-minded in respect of the old heathen traditions. There is an anecdote which tells us that Saint Patrick asked the angels whether God was not angry with him because he liked to listen to the stories of heroes, to which the answer was: let them be noted down with the stylus of poets and in the words of scholars—since for a long time to come it will be a pleasure to the people and to good men to listen to these stories.[1]

In Wales we do not know of these types of legends till fairly late. They have been given the name of *Mabinogion*, which may probably be described as 'lore of the disciple poet'. Their nucleus consists of the four so-called 'branches' of the Mabinogi, like the story of Pwyll, the prince of Dyfed, or that of the Children of Llŷr. A well-known story is also that of Kulhwch and Olwen. The Welsh legends especially have aroused a great interest, because they have provided material for the so-called 'Breton' romances which arose in France in the course of the twelfth century and spread from there throughout Western Europe.

We shall here limit ourselves to the Irish legends. Two large cycles of legends are to be distinguished: that of the heroes of Ulster, chief among them Cúchulainn, and the so-called Finn cycle. What is remarkable about the Irish heroic legend is that it has come down to us in prose, but the story is embellished with various stanzas written in a difficult language. Their content is either a

[1] Cf. Acallam na Senórach, *Irische Texte* iv, p. 3.

lyrical outpouring prompted by the story, or an ingenious dialogue between two persons. The oldest story written entirely in poetic form, *Tochmarc Ferbe* or the Wooing of Ferb, dates from the tenth century, but this form of heroic tradition is not found again. The prose story remained the favourite form. It has been suggested as an explanation of this Irish peculiarity that the Irish verse-form of four-line stanzas with ingeniously rhyming lines was hardly suitable for an epic story.[1] However, one may wonder whether a way out would not have been found by choosing a simpler verse-form, if a real need for poetic treatment had existed. The Irish had developed lyrical verse with great skill—it also served for songs of praise and satire—so that it competes with the complicated technique of the Old Norse scaldic poetry. Thus, they did not think it necessary to turn the oral heroic legends, which were of course told in prose, into poetry, when they were raised to the level of literary form. As an explanation it may be suggested that the oral legend itself had already obtained such a perfection of form that it appeared worthy of being passed unchanged into the more literary treatment of artists who recited at the courts of princes and the nobility.

The Ulster cycle, of Northern Irish origin, has as its central point the royal court of Conchobar, situated at Emain Macha. As, in the ninth century, a few ruins were all that was left of this palace, the historical core of this Ulster legend must be of much earlier date, probably of the third or fourth century. Conchobar appears in this cycle in the same function as Charlemagne in the French one or Dietrich of Bern in the German. He is the centre of a circle of heroes of whom Cúchulainn is the most famous. Cúchulainn is supposed to be a son of the god Lug, begotten in a miraculous way with his mother Dechtire, a daughter of Conchobar. Like a true hero, he gives proof at an early age of his exceptional strength and courage. When he is five years old he goes to the playing-field of Emain Macha where 'three times fifty' boys are playing. But he is not, as was usual, recognized by them as their playmate and taken up in their circle, so they try to chase him off the field. But he is much stronger than any of them, and drives them before him to Conchobar's palace. When he is six years old he has an adventure with

[1] Cf. R. Thurneysen, *Die irische Helden- und Königssage* (1931), p. 59.

Culann's dog. His own name means 'Dog of Culann' and this strange name requires an explanation. Now Cúchulainn originally really meant 'the hero of Culann', and Culann was supposed to have brought him up. However this may be, the legend had to give an explanation for his name, which characterized him as a dog. This is told in the following way. Conchobar has been invited with all his heroes to a banquet by the smith Culann. Conchobar asks Cúchulainn if he would like to accompany him, but he refuses. But as soon as the king and his retinue have departed, Cúchulainn gets ready and follows the track while passing time with a ball and stick. The smith had let loose his watchdog on Conchobar's arrival, after the king had assured him that nobody else was coming. So when, some time later, the boy arrives at the house, he is attacked by the fierce animal, but has no difficulty in killing the beast and smashing the body to pieces against a stone pillar. The howling of the dog is heard inside, and the smith, fearing that someone has fallen victim to the dog's thirst for blood, comes rushing out. Cúchulainn, however, stands unharmed before him, and is now admitted. The smith complains that he has lost his faithful watchdog. In his magnanimity Cúchulainn declares that he will serve as his guard until another dog has grown up to the stage where he can take over that task.

When Cúchulainn receives his armour, he shows, like so many heroes, that not every cuirass fits him and not every sword is good enough. Nothing brought forth from Conchobar's store-room fits his enormous hero's body, and in the end the king has to present him with his own armour. On this occasion the druid Cathba admires the young hero's tremendous strength, but he prophesies that, although he will become a famous hero, he will die young. We know the same about Siegfried and Achilles: a hero's life is like a meteor that rises glittering into the sky, but is suddenly extinguished.

At the age of seventeen he performs the heroic deed that is the high point of his life. On account of a quarrel with her husband Ailill, Medb, the Queen of Connacht, decides to steal the Brown Bull of Cualnge. This is the beginning of the tale which is told in detail, the *Táin bó Cualnge*, i.e. the Cattle-Raid of Cualnge. We find here a motif that is widespread in Indo-European heroic legends.

Naturally cattle-stealing is an everyday fact among warlike nomadic tribes that live on cattle-breeding. But the motif preserved its attraction even after agriculture had tied a man to a fixed home. We know several such legends from the Peloponnese. Thus we are told that the son of Pterelaus drove away the oxen of Electryon, the King of Mycenae, and Heracles does the same with the cattle of Geryon.[1] The Odyssey tells the story of Neleus who will only give his daughter, contested by many suitors, to that man who will take the oxen of Iphiclea away out of Phylace.[2] In *Works and Days* by Hesiod we read that part of the heroic race created by Zeus will perish before the seven gates of Thebes, in a struggle for the herds of Oedipus.[3] That this motif was also known in India is shown by the myth of Indra, of whom the *Veda* tells us repeatedly how he stole the heavenly cows of the dragon Vṛtra and with them made the rain pour down on the dry earth. Thus the motif of cattle-stealing reached far back into the past of the Indo-European nations and preserved its attraction for a long time. Evidently it was still worth while to steal one's neighbour's cattle even after agriculture had become the chief livelihood. In heroic legend, cattle-stealing continues to play an important part well into historic times.

But let us return to the story. When Medb is approaching with her army, the men of Ulster are in a condition that makes it impossible for them to defend themselves: a taboo rests upon them that in times of distress they are for five days and four nights as weak as a woman in labour. Cúchulainn is the only one that is not affected by it, and he alone can take upon himself the task of resisting the enemy.

Before Ailill and Medb marched out, they had inspected the army. The allies had marched with their hosts before the princes. When the first body of soldiers marched past, dressed in green mantles with silver clasps, girded with precious swords and their shirts embroidered with gold, people called out that this must be the hero Cormac. Medb denied this. Whenever a following troop, attired in even more splendid array, approached, this scene was

---

[1] Cf. B. Schweitzer, *Herakles, Aufsätze zur griechischen Religions- und Sagengeschichte* (1922), p. 153.

[2] Cf. *Odyssey* xi. 288 ff.   [3] Cf. *Odyssey* xi. 163 ff.

repeated. Then the last body appeared, in long silk shirts and purple mantles with gold clasps. Medb then admitted that this was Cormac.

This somewhat primitive technique of reaching a climax is an old survival from epic poetry. Franks and Persians, Greeks, Russians, and Scandinavians all used it. When Charlemagne marches into Italy with his army, Desiderius, the King of the Longobards, sees him approaching from afar. When the train of the army goes slowly by, he asks a Frankish nobleman who had come to him as a fugitive whether this is Charlemagne's army. 'Not yet,' answers the knight Ogger. Then the reserves, the army, and another train march past in succession, and at last Charlemagne himself appears, surrounded by bishops and abbots. Desiderius is overwhelmed by this spectacle.[1]

Here is another example from the North. The Norse King Olaf, son of Tryggvi, comes sailing up the Öresund from the South. On the beach the Swedish and the Danish kings are waiting to attack him in the narrow sound. With them is the Norse jarl Eric who has joined Olaf's opponents. When the first dragon-ship appears, the two kings ask the jarl whether this is the famous royal ship the *Long Dragon*. Eric denies this. Thus one ship after another comes into view, and each is bigger and more splendid than the last. Again and again the kings repeat their question, and every time the answer is that this is not the royal ship. At last a mighty dragon-ship comes along under full sail. The gracefully carved dragon-heads on stem and stern are decorated with gold, and the ship's sides are shining in vivid colours. Then the jarl, who cannot conceal his Norse pride at this sight, calls out: 'Even if King Olaf had no bigger ship than this, King Sveinn [the Danish king] alone could never win it from him with all his manpower.' [2]

It has been assumed that this Norse story derives from that of Charlemagne.[3] Yet there can be no certainty about this. Such a motif belongs to the subject-matter of heroic legend. It is so widespread that it is impossible to decide whether one example is derived from an older one or whether it turns up again and again in a given

---

[1] Cf. Monachus S. Galli II, 17, and Grimm, *Deutsche Sagen* No. 447.

[2] Cf. Snorri Sturluson, ed. F. Jónsson i, pp. 435–7.

[3] Cf. Alex. Bugge, in *Aarbøger for Nordisk Oldkyndighed og Historie* (1910), p. 34.

situation. Perhaps it belongs to the very oldest motifs of heroic epic poetry. Is the scene in Firdausi's *Book of Kings*, in which Sohrab is told to whom the variously coloured tents of King Kaus's army belong, derived from elsewhere? It is certainly remarkable. Naturally Rustum's tent is the most splendid of all, but when Sohrab asks whose tent it is the informant is silent and thus evokes the disaster, for the fact that Sohrab does not learn that his father Rustum is the leader of the hostile army inevitably leads to the tragic fight between father and son. It will be seen how the motif appears in quite a different context and, moreover, how it has obtained an entirely new motivation. It does not now serve to express the overwhelming power of the enemy, but is a motif that has become part and parcel of the story and has taken its place in the development of the action. These few examples will suffice. They only serve to show to what extent the Irish *Táin bó Cualnge* has the character of a true heroic legend.[1]

The story continues as follows. With his charioteer Cúchulainn takes up his station at a ford. We have here the same situation as in the *Waltharius*. One hero can control superior forces if the fight has to be man to man. So Queen Medb sends out her bravest heroes, one after the other, against Cúchulainn, who slays them all. Like King Etzel in the *Nibelungenlied*, again and again she has to send into the fight men that are particularly dear to her.

It is striking that the situation of margrave Rüedeger is found again in the Irish epic. Medb summons Fergus to her and charges him to fight the next day against Cúchulainn. Fergus, however, is an exile from Ulster who fled to Connacht and entered the service of King Ailill. No wonder that Fergus should try to avoid the fight against his famous countryman. He excuses himself by saying: 'It would not be fitting for me to take up arms against a young, beardless boy, especially as he was my own foster-son.' But Medb continues to urge him to fight, and in this conflict Fergus can only act like the margrave of Bechelaeren. The next day he goes to the

---

[1] Cf. J. Carney, *Studies in Irish Literature and History* (1955), p. 307, who points out that this motif occurs in the *Iliad*, Statius's *Thebaid*, *Beowulf*, Eilhart's *Tristan*, and other sources. On p. 313 he thinks that the Irish scenes (in the *Táin*, in *Mesca Ulad*, *Fled Bricrend*, in the *Vita Kentigerni*) derive from *Iliad* iii. 161 ff.

ford, and when Cúchulainn sees him he says mockingly: 'My master Fergus is coming along with a weak defence, as he has in his sheath no sword but a stick.' It is an old custom in epic poetry, undoubtedly based on real life, that before the fight two combatants incite each other to the utmost rage with mocking and even insulting words. Cúchulainn's mocking words were like a cutting lash to Fergus, for in fact he no longer had his sword. A year before, when Ailill had caught Fergus in too great an intimacy with Medb, he had drawn Fergus's sword out of the sheath and replaced it with a wooden one.

Fergus, however, restrains himself and says: 'It is all right as it is, for even if my own sword were in its sheath, it would not strike you. But be mindful of how I brought you up, and flee today from me in the sight of the men of Connacht.' This is indeed an impossible request to a boy who takes such pride in his honour, and so he replies: 'That is a repugnant idea to me, that at the Táin bó Cualnge I should run away from one single adversary.' This answer clearly reflects the fame of the legend. It is as if Cúchulainn realizes that one day his feats of arms will be sung by the poets of Ireland, and, in these glorious songs, such a dark stain would mar the radiant picture of his heroic deeds. Fergus is the older and the wiser of the two. He understands that the fiery boy must reject such a proposal, and he offers him compensation for it. 'There is truly no reason for rejecting my proposal, for one day, in the fight of the Táin, you will stand before me full of wounds and stained with blood, and I shall then flee from you. And as soon as I shall run away, I alone, all the men of Ireland will flee after me.'

Cúchulainn then mounts the chariot and orders it to be turned. He does indeed hastily flee from the men of Connacht. When they see this, they call out, mad with joy, 'Fergus, he has fled from you.' And Medb gave the order, 'Fergus, pursue him! Do not now allow him to escape from us!' But Fergus turns back and refuses to pursue the fugitive. He will meet Cúchulainn once more, but then, as he has promised, he will flee from him.

A repetition of this episode is that of Fer Diad, probably an originally independent story but later inserted in the *Táin*, which was a happy thought of the poet's for, although a parallel, it also forms the climax of the *Táin*. Fer Diad is a tremendous hero; like Siegfried, he has a horny skin and so is invulnerable. When Medb asks him to fight the next fight at the ford, he says, 'Never shall I fight against my friend, my comrade, and my foster-brother.' For both had learned all the arts of warfare from Scáthach, a female creature, whose name points to her being a goddess in the underworld. But Medb will do anything to gain her ends. She sends all the druids and magicians to him in order to conjure up lumps on his face by means of their satires. These are intended as a token of his shame, in case he should refuse to come to Medb and comply with her wishes. To save his honour Fer Diad has to yield to her request. He is given a festive reception and promised the largest presents. With a heavy heart he goes to the ford, but he arrives so early that the day has not yet dawned. He orders his servant to spread blankets and skins on the ground, because he is overcome by a heavy sleep. On his part, Cúchulainn gets up as soon as the sun has risen and orders his charioteer to harness the horses. He knows whom he is going to meet, for Fergus came to tell him the day before. There follows a lengthy description, interrupted by poems, of how they prepare themselves. Then comes the meeting. 'Welcome Cúchulainn,' says Fer Diad, to which the boy replies: 'Little does it befit you to come to fight against me. It would have been more fitting for me that I should have come to you for the fight.' Fer Diad therefore answers, 'All right, Cúchulainn, but what would be the inducement for you to seek battle with me? When we were with Scáthach you were my servant who looked after my spears and made my bed.'—'I did that because I was still young and inexperienced. But now I am standing here and need not yield to any hero in the world.' Then in a long series of stanzas they reproach each other for having broken their friendship. After that the fight begins: a tremendous fight, for both have acquired mastery in the art of fighting from Scáthach. So the struggle ends in a draw: when evening comes, they throw down their weapons, go towards each other, embrace and kiss each other three times. This also happened on the second day and again on the third. When they broke up in the evening, they parted like two sad, severely tried men. Then, the next day, comes the most terrible fight. Cúchulainn now employs his very best powers, and his distortion of face, his *riastrad,* which will be discussed presently, comes upon him. The fight rages ever more furiously. Then Cúchulainn seizes his most dangerous weapon, the *gae bolga.* He throws this spear, and it cuts through the firm, thick, iron armour of Fer Diad, who is mortally wounded. He calls out:

> Oh Cú of the beautiful art of war,
> It was not good of you to kill me!
> On you the guilt which clung to me,
> On you my blood has fallen.

Cúchulainn rushes towards him, embraces him, and carries him with his weapons and his armour across the ford, so that north of it, in the land of the men of Ulster, the triumph will be celebrated and not with the men of Connacht. Then he mourns the death of his friend,

> Oh Fer Diad, treason has conquered you,
> Sad was my last meeting with you!
> You are dead and I remain alive,
> Eternally sad is our eternal separation!

This fight forms the climax of the *Táin.* We are reminded of the scene in which Rüedeger is forced to join battle with his Burgundian friends. That was a conflict between kinship and vassal's duty. In the *Táin* the conflict is between honour and comradeship. It depends on one's point of view which of the two counts is the more tragic. But this point of view is not determined by the ethical standards applied by us, but by those of the legend itself. Naturally the conflicts of the soul at the time of the Staufen are of a different nature from those of eleventh-century Ireland.[1] I have the impression that, in the end, the Irish problems lie closer to those of heathen mentality than those of Rüedeger. It is certainly true to say that the relationship between feudal lord and vassal shows points of resemblance to that of the Old-Germanic lord and his retainers. But the latter consisted of young, unmarried men, bound moreover by an oath of allegiance, which obliged them to follow their lord even unto death.

---

[1] Thurneysen, op. cit., p. 219, dates the Fer Diad episode at this time. It remains uncertain whether it is older. Thurneysen thinks that it has been freely composed from other motifs from the *Táin* story.

Rüedeger's conflict does not really belong to that kind. But, however varied according to time and circumstances, again and again we find that extreme situation in which the warrior's code of honour conflicts with the obligations of comradeship or kinship, and always prevails.

After the fight against Fer Diad the struggle takes a different turn. No further climax is possible in the duels at the ford. Cúchulainn cannot come up against a more terrible adversary. The men from Ulster, however, are now no longer in a condition of weakness. Cúchulainn's father, Sualtam, warns King Conchobar as to what is happening at the ford. The men of Ulster arm themselves for the battle in which the Ulster army is about to oppose the entire army of the rest of Ireland. Here Fergus appears in the foreground once more; he fights against King Conchobar himself, but when Cúchulainn comes to relieve the king, Fergus flees from him, as he had promised his friend, and in his flight he is followed by the entire army of Queen Medb.

However, during the Ulstermen's period of weakness, the men of Connacht succeeded in stealing the Brown Bull. Medb, protected by Cúchulainn, has to withdraw from the battle. She has already had the Brown Bull led away, and when he arrives in Connacht he finds the White-horned Bull of Medb. They rush at each other and in a terrible fight the Brown Bull gains the victory. Thus the victory of Ulster is underlined once more—in a symbolic way. In its fury the Brown Bull rushes all over Connacht, spreading terror and destruction, until at last he falls down dead. Medb has not gained her end. The struggle has now become useless and the parties make their peace. Richly laden with booty, the men of Ulster return home.

The origin of this story, it has been suggested, belongs to the seventh century. Parts of the old tradition have undoubtedly been preserved in the later text, but as a whole this text is really a reconstruction of the old heathen past, written with a good deal of creative imagination, in the form and the style of the curiously blended culture of early-Christian Ireland. The clergy's wide knowledge of classical literature suggests that the author or the successive redactors of the Táin legend also drew on it for their motifs. For the whole of medieval West-European literature is permeated with classical motifs. The story of the *Táin bó Cualnge* shows this influence in the careful drawing of the characters, in the dramatic beginning of the fighting, and especially in the description of various earlier events, which—with the technique so well known from the *Odyssey*—seems to overtake the events in the course of the story. It is possible that classical influence is also shown in the strongly rhetorical dialogues, which for that matter are among the most favoured stylistic devices in Irish literature.[1]

The *Táin bó Cualnge* can therefore be compared with the *Nibelungenlied*, in so far as they are both literary works that show all the characteristics of the time in which they were written. But both spring from an oral tradition which reaches far back into the past. For if Conchobar lived in the third or fourth century, the cycle of legends which developed around the Irish Charlemagne cannot have grown up so very much later.

But who is Cúchulainn? We have already seen that he received this name on account of his heroic deed, the killing of Culann's dog, or rather, originally, because he had been brought up by a certain Culann. When he faces the 'three times fifty' boys on Emain Macha he introduces himself in these words: 'I am little Setanta the son of Sualtam; I am the son of your sister Dechtire.' Now the name Setanta recalls the name of the British tribe of the Setantii, who lived in the present region of Lancashire. His father-in-law Forgall Manach preserves in his name the memory of the tribe of the Menapii who had come from Gaul to the east coast of Ireland. Moreover, the name of his magic spear, the *gea bolga*, seems to be the same word as the name of the Gaulish tribe of the Belgae. All this leads to the conclusion that the figure of Cúchulainn is not of Irish origin. If it is correct that we should think of Gaul as the country of origin, this would take us back to the time before the beginning of our era.

Can one go still further and say that the legend itself, at least the oldest features of it, also derives from Brittany and Gaul—which would mean that it was common to all Celts of the West? There are indeed other indications which favour this view.

We have mentioned the strange distortion of the hero's face when

---

[1] See J. Carney, op. cit., p. 322.

he is attacked by furious rage in battle: the *riastrad*. The *Táin bó Cualnge* describes it in the following fantastic way[1] (I omit the deformation of his limbs): His hair stood on end like the branches of a red hawthorn round a hole in an old hedge. If an apple-tree should be shaken above him an apple would stick to each of his hairs. From his forehead the *lón laith* rose up, thick and long like a fist (probably a ray of light), but a spout of dark blood, long, thick, and strong as the mast of a large ship, shot up straight from his skull. One eye he pulled so far inwards that a heron could not have pecked it out of his head, but the other eye sprang out so far forward that it came to rest on his cheek.

What does this strange description mean, which shows us the un-bridled and somewhat abstruse imaginative power of the Irish at its most? It is a remarkable fact that we have what look like pictures of this on Armorican coins. It is true they are copies of the coins which Philip of Macedonia had minted, so that they imitate the die of these coins. But, as we can see from the Scandinavian bracteates, the bar-barian artist introduced all kinds of motifs from his own tradition into the classical example, so that a curious, schematic figure of the head pictured on it remained. Moreover, he often added native symbols, like the runes or the sign of the swastika on the bracteates. This was also done by the Armorican artificer. On these coins we see a head out of which a kind of flame seems to shoot up. Often hair standing on end is depicted on them, between which small bul-lets have been inserted, and this naturally makes us think of the Irish hero's hairs with apples on them. On many coins the face has a monstrously large eye situated below its normal position. Could not this allude to Cúchulainn's eye which came to rest on his cheek?

Our first thought is that an Irish story-teller had seen these coins and that he then used these strange motifs for his description of Cúchulainn.[2] But that is really not very likely. It can hardly be believed that these coins were so common in Ireland that they should have served as examples for the description of a hero. And what could have moved the story-teller to apply the motifs of these pictures in such a curious way and yet with so much relevance

---

[1] See the edition by Windisch, pp. 374 ff.
[2] See L. Sjoestedt-Jonval, in *Études Celtiques* i (1936), pp. 76–77.

to the *riastrad* of Cúchulainn? We would have to assume that with these coins had come also an explanation of the mythical meaning of these pictures. That is to say that an originally Gaulish legend must have come to Ireland, and in that case the coins could at best have played a secondary part.

Such an explanation is only acceptable as long as the peculiar features of the *riastrad* are considered merely as the strange creation of an unbridled imagination. But these features are far from being a poetic invention: they are in fact full of sense, if properly understood. There is even a parallel to them in a story from an Icelandic saga. The Viking Egill Skallagrimsson had similar berserk fits of rage. When he sat down he pulled one eyebrow up to the roots of his hair and the other down to his cheek. He had black eyes, and eyebrows which met above his nose.

The effect of the facial distortion of Egill and Cúchulainn is the same: one eye is hidden, whereas the other protrudes and seems extremely large. How is this coincidence of Irish and Icelandic tradition to be explained? Ireland lies close to Iceland, so there may have been influence of the one tradition on the other. And if so, it is clear to which priority should be granted: Irish influence has also been assumed in another field of Old Norse culture.

Yet the explanation is not as simple as that. Even if we only consider the Icelandic description, it can be explained entirely from North-Germanic tradition. By his *riastrad* Egill makes himself resemble the god Odin, who is always depicted with one eye. Odin is the god of the bersek warriors; in Valhalla he is the lord of the Einherjar. He is the god of frenzy in battle, and it may be assumed that the warriors devoted to him made themselves resemble him. Odin's one eye has a magic, paralysing effect in battle, it might be compared with the 'evil eye' of later superstition.[1] Now one can certainly say that this mythological feature was not limited to the Germanic North, and there are indeed other examples. Claudius Civilis, the Batavian hero, before battling against Rome, swore a terrible oath in a sacred wood, an oath surely sworn to his god Wodan. Tacitus tells us that Civilis was particularly proud of having only one eye. If it was an injury received in battle, there

[1] See G. Dumézil, *Mitra-Varuna* (1948), pp. 172–3.

would be no reason to glory in it so much: the heroes in *Waltharius* may joke about their wounds; they do not take any pride in them. But if the loss of one eye made him look like the god Wodan, it could be, so to speak, a consecration as Wodan's warrior. And the question even arises: did Civilis sacrifice one eye to Wodan in order to be one with the god?

There is every reason to suppose something similar in the case of Cúchulainn. His *riastrad* too means making himself one with a divine figure. We can no longer speak of a borrowing here. Evidently the Celts and the Germanic tribes each knew this mythical feature from their own tradition, and it is very possible that this tradition went back to Indo-European times. Cúchulainn is, therefore, a semi-mythological hero who was also known in Gaul. If he came to Ireland with immigrants from the tribe of the Setantii, this Setanta took root there very quickly. I would think that this can be ascribed to the fact that the Irish already knew such a figure, and that therefore Setanta became a more richly developed personality in the tradition of Brittany than the Irish knew at the time. But how richly did Setanta develop? The legend about him first spread among the population, ethnically strongly mixed, of Leinster, where (as we saw) the Belgae and Menapii had landed. Gradually the hero became widely known in other parts of Ireland. He even became the favourite hero of Ulster and overshadowed all the other characters of Irish heroic legend.

There are still more indications of Gaulish origin in the Irish story. As one of his weapons Cúchulainn uses a sling-stone, just as his divine father Lug did; and Caesar tells us the same about the Gauls.[1] The descriptions of dress and armour in the Irish stories reveal a strong preference for striking colours and precious ornaments.[2] It is remarkable that the *Táin* still talks about the sickle-wagon, which is mentioned by classical authors as being a very dangerous instrument of war. The conclusion may be drawn that in the medieval Irish stories memories have been preserved which reach back into the Celtic past before the beginning of our era. No wonder that in such a long period of time the original legend of Cúchulainn was

[1] See *De Bello Gallico* ii. 62 and vii. 81.
[2] See *Táin bó Cualnge*, p. 365, *crommsciath* with a *torc taisselbtha*.

very much modified. The *Táin bó Cualnge* as we have it now is of course the product of modification, expansion, and adaptation that went on for centuries. We are left with a typically medieval Irish story, but underneath it lie the traces of much older versions of the legend.

The legend of Finn shows an entirely different picture. Its main character is Finn mac Cumaill; the surname can be compared with that of the Gaulish god Cumalos, and perhaps this is more than a superficial resemblance.[1] This hero is in charge of a host of warriors, the *fianna*, who have entered the service of Cormac mac Airt, who was Supreme King of Ireland in the third century A.D. If this statement is correct—and there is no reason why we should doubt it—this cycle of legends goes as far back as that of Ulster, but it had a considerably longer life: at the end of the eighteenth century the Scottish poet Macpherson gave new life to the characters of this cycle of legends and even made them famous in Europe. How much the poetry of Ossian meant to the generation of the young Goethe!

The remarkable thing about the Finn legend is that it lived for such a long time, as it were, beneath the surface. Whereas the legend of Cúchulainn and other heroes of Ulster remained alive in the consciousness of poets and the people from the time of their origin, this was evidently not the case with the Finn legends. When they appear in written texts they make the impression of having suddenly arisen fresh from the soil of Irish narrative art. They contain various features which recall events of the Viking Age, and this gave rise to the view that the Finn legend did not emerge till the Viking Age.[2] But the appearance of features of the Viking Age is better explained as the susceptibility of legend to events of daily life. Also we shall see that the nature of the Finn legend was such that it could easily derive new material from the events of the time of the Norsemen and that it was this very Viking Age which must have quickened interest in the Finn legend enormously.

---

[1] All the more so because the figure of Finn arose not only out of this Finn mac Cumaill, but also out of other figures, such as Finn mac Nuadat, in whom we undoubtedly have to see the Celtic god Nuadu.

[2] See H. Zimmer, in *Zeitschrift für deutsches Altertum* xxxv, pp. 1 ff.

The *fianna* are a typical example of the units of warriors which already existed among the Gauls at the time when classical sources shed the first faint light on them. Caesar tells us that the Gaulish prince has a retinue of *soldurii* who had sworn permanent allegiance to their lord; there were numerous examples of retainers not wanting to survive their lord when he had fallen in battle. Tacitus gives the same information about the Germanic *comitatus*. The *fianna*, then, are units of warriors bound in allegiance to their lord. When the Vikings (who themselves were bands of warriors grouped round a 'sea-king') invaded Ireland and spread terror there, the memory of the *fianna* of the legend was bound to emerge again, and perhaps even the thought that these Irish units, when once aroused to new life, would be able to resist the attacks of these robbers from overseas.

It is therefore probable that the stories, as they have come down to us, must have been of fairly late origin. At any rate they have an entirely different character from the Ulster legends. After all, they flourished in a different part of Ireland, in Leinster, where the Conchobar cycle also had its origin before it moved to Ulster. The difference is first of all to be seen in the atmosphere, which is not as one would expect. Although it is naturally one of heroic courage and fondness for display, there is also a remarkable tenderness of feeling. Moreover, even more than the Ulster legend, the Finn legends show a tendency towards the miraculous and the supernatural.

Naturally the backbone of the Finn cycle is the fight, which has its origin in a feud and is therefore handed down with great pertinacity from generation to generation. The starting point is the fight of Cnucha, in which Goll, one of the leaders under King Conn mac Airt, kills another leader, Cumall, who was the father of Finn. As soon as Finn is grown up he considers it his first duty to avenge his father's death, and eventually he succeeds in killing Goll in Connacht. After this, however, the nature of the struggle changes. Where such units of fighters exist, they can be very dangerous to the established power of the king. An adventurer, who can rely on the devotion of a host of warriors hardened in battle, soon turns his thoughts to seizing a crown. Thus the *fianna* also come into conflict with royalty.

When there is no fighting to be done, the *fianna* amuse themselves with hunting, which is therefore a favourite theme in the stories of later origin. As well as Finn, other figures appear who are more in keeping with the spirit of a later age and therefore aroused fresh interest in the eighteenth century. First of all there is Oisin, the prototype of the famous Ossian in Macpherson's poems. He is a paragon of magnanimity, and practises the art of poetry. Then there is his son Oscar. These figures are probably fictitious, for no historical prototypes have been found for them. The first part of these names is the Irish word *oss* which means 'hart'. This may point to the widely known motif of the hero who is brought up by animals as a child, for instance Romulus and Wolfdietrich.

As an example of the entirely different, one might say 'romantic', atmosphere which is a characteristic of the Finn legends and which differs so much from that of the Ulster cycle, we might mention the very popular story of Diarmuid and Grainne. Grainne is the daughter of the Supreme King of Ireland, Cormac mac Airt. When Finn, the leader of the warriors in his service, sues for her hand, she refuses his love. At the banquet she offers Finn and his men a cup of drugged wine. Now she reveals herself as the typical Irish maiden; like Deirdre in the no less famous Ulster story of *The Sons of Usnach*, she forces the hero of her choice to abduct her. She has chosen Diarmuid who is thus placed in a dilemma: the allegiance to his lord as against the love of his lady. But in Irish legends the power of woman is great and irresistible. Three times Diarmuid implores her not to make this demand; but she forces him by her magic power and so they flee.

Diarmuid is enchanted by her beauty; when Grainne is tired he carries her in his arms. But in the meantime Finn has woken up from his sleep, and realizes what ignominy Grainne has offered him by preferring one of his vassals. He decides to pursue the fugitive pair. He sends his men out, but in vain. Their friendship with Diarmuid has the reverse effect, and they help him in his flight. In the end Finn sets out himself.

Again and again he comes close to them, but every time they escape from him. On one occasion he even sees how Diarmuid kisses Grainne three times. But he persists all the more in the pursuit. The lovers flee far into the woods and there build themselves a hut. But in the end they are discovered here too. Diarmuid performs miracles of bravery against Finn's superior power, which is of course too strong for him. Finally there is a reconciliation, and Finn agrees to leave Grainne to Diarmuid.

But Grainne's magic power has a complete hold over Finn. He must possess her, and, assuming an amicable disposition, he broods on revenge. Once, when hunting, Diarmuid is wounded by a supernatural boar. He asks Finn to bring him a drink of water to quench his burning thirst. Finn goes away to scoop some water from a brook with his hand, but on his way to the wounded man he allows it to run through his fingers. He goes a second time with the same result. The third time, when he really feels compassion and takes a handful of water to Diarmuid, the latter has died from his wounds. Finn then shows his lack of nobility and forces Grainne to become his wife.

This story of a fatal love which holds Diarmuid in its spell makes a romantic impression on us. It reminds us of the Welsh story of Tristan, who through a magic drink falls in love with Isolde. And is not the scene of the two lovers living together in the privacy of the wood to be compared with a similar scene in the legend of Tristan? Even if, owing to the curious idea that underlies this story, the scene of the lovers living together has an entirely different character in the Tristan legend, where the sword that lies between the two is the symbol of the chastity that Tristan has imposed upon himself.

It would, however, be far from true to say that the story of Diarmuid and Grainne is merely the story of a romantic love. It is a story of fighting and adventure. The pursuit of Diarmuid by Finn and his men recalls that other fight in the Vosges, when Waltharius has to defend himself against the superior power of Gunther. One may even wonder if there is any question here of a love that might be called 'romantic'. The Ulster story of Deirdre can give us an idea of the true nature of such a love. In the Irish stories this love is indeed no romanticism, but a tragic reality. Woman has here a frightening power; she forces the man to love her, and thereby brings about his end.

D

Woman plays a remarkable part in Irish literature. The initiative in the love intrigue comes from her. It is noteworthy that something similar occurs in the French and German literature of the thirteenth century; the woman, formerly chosen, now chooses. This new conception is often ascribed to the Breton romance which at this time develops by the side of the old Carolingian epic poetry. But, as the name indicates, this Breton romance comes from across the Channel. Its subject-matter and characters, the figures of Arthur and the Round Table, have been taken over from Welsh stories such as those of the *Mabinogion* and of *Tristan*. The *amour courtois*, the subservient love of the man in regard to the woman, which in the love lyrics assumes such a remarkable form, has its origin in the Breton tradition.

What, then, was woman's significance in her original environment? We have already discussed the figure of Queen Medb in the *Táin bó Cualnge*. She is far superior to her husband Ailill. At her instigation the cattle-stealing is undertaken; she is always the driving force in this enterprise. She is a mother who offers her daughter Finnabair to all men who want to fight for her against Cúchulainn. It is even said that she was not the wife of Ailill only, but also of Conchobar.

This privileged position of woman had led to the supposition that there are traces of matriarchy here. This seemed to be confirmed by classical sources which speak of woman in a position resembling matriarchy among the Picts in the North of Scotland. Especially at the time when ethnology assumed matriarchy was everywhere a phase of culture which preceded patriarchy, this explanation seemed eminently to fit the phenomena found among the British and the Irish. Yet the correctness of this view may be doubted. It is the figure of Medb which may give us more information. She is the wife of two kings, of Ailill as well as of Conchobar. There is another Medb of whom tradition tells that she is the wife of Fergus. This name means 'male strength'. And the name of Medb herself? It has been linked up with the Welsh word *meddw*, which means 'drunken'. These names are meaningful. Are they really the names of ordinary historical people, or is something else hidden behind them? Not long ago an entirely new light was thrown on the personality of Medb.[1] Medb is the woman who chooses kings and heroes as her consort. But this is where she reveals herself as a more than mortal woman: she is a goddess in whom sovereignty is personified. But hand in hand with this goes the fact that the man she chooses must subject himself to her will, and this he gladly does, as it is the condition for his acquiring kingship. There is undoubtedly behind this an ancient rite known among all Indo-European peoples—the rite of *hieros gamos*, the holy marriage between the god of heaven and the goddess of earth. In other words, the land of Ireland marries the prince that will rule over it. It need not be pointed out that, as elsewhere, kingship in Ireland possessed a sacral character.

Stories such as that of Grainne and Diarmuid do not therefore demonstrate a certain dissolution in Irish morals, or a particular position of authority for woman, but they reflect the myth of Medb, the goddess of earth, who chooses the king as her consort. As a goddess she remains his superior. If the king later shows himself unworthy of her, she abandons him and chooses another *ard-ri*, or supreme king, in his place. It is understandable that in the course of time the memory of this old myth was lost. But the stories which demonstrate it have remained. Transferred to the profane sphere, the position of woman assumed an entirely different meaning. She is no longer a goddess, but a woman thirsting after power and love, who with demonic power chains men to herself and seems to play with their fate. The sacral relationship was degraded into a sensual love, and the power of woman, which now seemed inexplicable, was supported by a means that had magic power at its disposal. Perhaps it is because this relationship of man and woman was so entirely different from real life, that these old stories gained such an attraction; what is impossible in real life takes place in the realm of the imagination. But the power of imagination is great; it can also influence life itself. From the Franco–Breton romances that used the motif, this conception of love penetrated into man's consciousness. A new form was given to reality under the influence of this fascinating literature. A straight line stretches from the *amour courtois*, treated as a polite game in the medieval love lyrics,

[1] In two essays by T. OMáille, in *Zeitschrift für celtische Philologie* xvii, pp. 129–46, and by R. Thurneysen, in the same periodical xviii, pp. 108–10, and xix, pp. 352–3.

to the *amour passion* which as the ideal of true love reigns supreme up to the modern novel.

Irish 'heroic epic' poetry can hardly be discussed without a glance at the Icelandic *saga*. Both are, in regard to their form, so remarkably similar that the thought at once arises that there must be a close kinship, perhaps even a close connexion. For both are prose stories in which stanzas have been inserted, which have the character partly of lyrics, partly of dialogues. In both cases the almost obvious view that the prose stories have been dissolved from an older poetic form, the remnants of which are still scattered throughout the story, can be considered to be correct. These poems were inserted later and do not always have the same function. In the Irish stories, as in some younger sagas, the stanzas serve as ornament. What has just been told in prose is once more elaborated in lyrical verse in an ingenious, at times even mannered form. We saw examples of this in the *Táin bó Cualnge*. In the older Icelandic sagas, the stanzas seem to have a different function. They belong to scaldic poems which the saga writer knew and used as his sources; so here a stanza that is quoted can serve as confirmation of the truth of his statements.

Why is it among these peoples of the extreme West that this peculiar form of heroic legend occurs? Could it be a relic of an epic form that was once also known to the other Indo-European peoples? That is not very probable, as everywhere poetry precedes prose and not the other way round. It may be pointed out that Ireland and Iceland lie in each other's vicinity and, what is more, that there have been close historical relations between the populations of both islands. And these relations are closer the farther back we go in time. The settlers who populated Iceland in the ninth and tenth centuries were for a large part Vikings who had lived for a long time in Scotland, the Orkneys, the Hebrides, and in Ireland. They often came with their Celtic wives and especially with slaves to their new fatherland. At a time when the great significance of Irish culture came to be realized more and more, people could not but conclude that everything that agreed in the cultural phenomena of Ireland and Iceland had to be considered as a borrowing from

Ireland. And even if this was greatly exaggerated, it remains certain that numerous impulses from Ireland have had their effect on Iceland. But is this also the case with the art of the Icelandic saga?

Opinions still differ very much on this point. At any rate, objections can be raised. As we have already remarked, the function of the poems inserted in the two forms of narration is entirely different. With this an important support for the connexion between the two forms of saga disappears, for it is precisely this curious mixture of prose and poetry which first of all and most of all suggested a necessary connexion. If the stanzas are excluded the similarity of the Irish and the Icelandic prose story is really not very great.

We are here up against a problem which in recent years has been the subject of a lively scholarly debate. The Icelandic saga is a story in which are described the adventures of people and families who in general belong to the first generations of the settlement of the island at the end of the ninth century. The saga itself, however, was not written down until the end of the twelfth (mainly in the thirteenth) century. As the saga on the whole tells the events in a matter-of-fact, almost sober style, it makes the impression of being particularly credible. For that reason it was considered as historical writing rather than as a romanticized story of a far-distant past. Scholars were so firmly convinced of this that the facts given in the sagas were provided with a date and noted down in the annals of history; even the very dark history of the Viking period was scrutinized more closely with the help of the data of the sagas.

But the faithfulness of an oral tradition that had firmly held the thread of events of the ninth century for nearly three centuries after would then indeed be admirable. On this basis people were fully convinced that popular tradition could hand down stories in unchanged form for many generations, and they found confirmation of this in examples of a remarkable historical memory among some primitive peoples. The strikingly fixed character of epic poetry was also referred to; did not the *Nibelungenlied* likewise tell of events of about twenty-four generations ago?

One condition, however, had to be fulfilled before such a view was possible: the material had to be moulded in a fixed form which could easily be retained in the memory, and thus handed down true to the word. So this view entailed that the extant sagas were considered as the written fixation of a tradition that had existed in a fixed form for a long time before.

A closer investigation could not but reveal great differences between the sagas. There were some that contained a fairly rambling and disjointed story. Others related in a sober style the facts of long-standing feuds between a few families. Others again gave the impression of being tales dressed up very romantically. The obvious conclusion was that a distinction had to be made between older and later redactions. The more adventurous and romantic the tales were, the later they must have been put down in writing. In a few the traces of the literature of chivalry of Western Europe could clearly be demonstrated. Thus the writers of these sagas could not with any justification be represented as chronicle writers whose aim was to record a 'true' history. They were artists who, to put it in modern terms, composed an historical novel. And yet, if the obviously later features could be taken away, a core might remain which could be used for historical investigation as a fairly clear reflection of the history of those days.

This was perhaps a somewhat naïve view. The saga is undeniably a literary form. In essence it has nothing to do with real history, even if it is, of course, right to state that in its own way it tries to give a picture of the first centuries after the settlement. If such a view is taught in all universities it tends to become canonical; then the time has come for criticism to make itself heard. And this is what has happened frequently in the course of this century. Icelandic scholars themselves, for whom the study of the sagas was a matter of national concern, raised objections. They were unwilling to sacrifice the honour of a very original literature to the illusion of a remarkably faithful oral historical tradition. In their endeavour to give, on the other hand, a clear and fully justified history of their nation, they had to apply the most severe methods of historical criticism to these texts. The texts could not stand this test. The facts did not tally; the chronology did not always fit; the family relationships could differ from saga to saga; the characters were partly fictitious. To extract history from an heroic epic mostly leads to disappointment, and the same holds for the sagas. Thus the conviction was gaining ground that anyone who wished to gain true historical knowledge from these stories was building on sand. But if nothing remained of factual credibility, then at least a native national literature had arisen all the more gloriously, one which does not have its equal in medieval Europe. Instead of being faithful chronicle writers, the authors of the sagas revealed themselves as great artists of narrative prose.[1]

This view did not merely have all the attraction of being new. It was convincing especially for the reason that it is so much more gratifying to discover a genuine artist than an accurate historian. One is reminded of the overwhelming, if short-lived, success of Bédier, whose theories of the French heroic epic seemed so easily applicable to the Icelandic saga. His treatment of it conjured up a *Song of Roland* which was a spontaneous work of art that towered far above the literature of the day, whereas formerly it had been considered as the end of a long tradition in which an obscure series of elusive *jongleurs*, redactors, interpolators, and writers had succeeded one another. But we have seen that this conception of the *Song of Roland* soon changed. It is true that the view was gratefully accepted that the *Chanson de Roland* was the work of an individual artist, but it seemed impossible to ignore the whole of the tradition preceding it. Similarly, I believe that there is every reason not to detach the Icelandic saga from a basically oral tradition.

Sometimes it would indeed seem possible to prove convincingly that a saga in its entirety is a fictitious story for which the author had used only a few names and particulars from historical writings. But it could be that this is a border-line case. When somehow or other a form of prose story has come into existence in which historical facts are given more or less accurately, it is not very difficult for a clever writer to create a similar story out of his imagination. But does the *Oera Linda Book* prove that the medieval chronicles were really fictitious stories?

Much depends on what value is attached to oral tradition. It is indeed not everywhere and not always equally reliable. But the circumstances under which oral tradition is transmitted should be

[1] A clear summary of this view is to be found in W. Baetke, *Über die Entstehung der Isländersaga* (1955).

taken into account. The Icelanders were a nation whose core was formed by a number of aristocratic families of farmers. The first centuries of their life on Iceland were full of violent feuds and of bitter struggle for power and authority. When later the names of the ancestors were written in the family Bible they were imprinted on the memory. That knowledge was indispensable. Judicial claims which a family wanted to assert were based on former transferences of property, on marriage contracts, on sharing out inheritances. Hence an accurate account had to be rendered of the rising family, even on both sides.

There is more. A nation of settlers in a previously uninhabited country begins with a blank register on which it has to fill in its deeds and its fortunes. Every family is proud of the row of its ancestors who have established and enhanced the prestige and the power of the family. Naturally one would wish to remember these. Winter nights on Iceland are long, and when the icy storms swept over the snow-covered land people were confined to their homes for months on end without any work. What could be more pleasant and useful to beguile the time than to tell stories, and what better stories could they tell one another than those about the past of their own families and district?[1]

Nor should it be forgotten that these were the glorious years of a young nation. In the thirteenth century the old glory had disappeared. The nation was subject to the Danish crown. Trade, once the main means of subsistence, was subject to regulations and largely monopolized for the benefit of Denmark. Life had become poor and depressed. Meanwhile, the feuds between the families flared up with renewed vehemence: society was of a rough and cruel nature. No wonder that people now considered the lives of the first settlers with greater attention and wanted to write them down. Thus the legend, which up to now had lived in the memory, grew into the *saga*.

But this is not all. André Jolles has counted the saga among the *einfache Formen* (the simple forms), that is, among the primary, pre-literary forms of literature.[2] This is important. Even if, in the light of more recent theories, he might perhaps have shifted the stress

---

[1] See my *Altnordische Literaturgeschichte*, 2 vols., 1941-2, passim.
[2] Cf. *Einfache Formen* (²1956), pp. 50 ff.

here and there, the fact remains that such an astute scholar could consider the saga as an 'archetype' of literature. Is it, then, a real tradition after all? And why? It seems to me that, when it has been impossible to argue satisfactorily in favour of an oral tradition contained in the stated facts, the form in itself has been sufficient to imply such an oral tradition as a necessary link. For the saga is unique in style. It tells the events in a sober and matter-of-fact way. It does not strive after rhetorical embellishment. It does not reveal the pen of a monk who wants to show how beautifully he can write. In the works of the Icelandic clergy we have many unpalatable examples of this. But the style of the saga is simple and clear, like that of oral delivery. The characters have a sharp profile and, though tending towards being standard types, are yet sufficiently alive. The narrators appear to be people with a good knowledge of human nature, who know how to gauge what their characters feel and think. They do not take sides too pronouncedly, even if they are human enough to divide light and shade according to their own preference or interest.

The dialogue is admirable. The words spoken are brief and to the point. Sometimes the sentences follow one another in quick succession, like blow upon blow in a duel. They seem to convey little, but they are pregnant with meaning. Humour and satire give them an unexpected, fierce glitter. For the saga writers, the dialogue is the means of conveying to the reader the hidden intentions of the characters. They are not expressed directly; they have to be read between the lines. I cannot see this style of narration otherwise than as polished by the technique of many generations of ardent and experienced narrators. It was certainly not born in the monastery. One has to come down to the novel of the nineteenth century to find such realistic prose, such living conversation.

Such prose does not come out of the blue any more than epic verse does. Attempts have been made to show that this terse, living saga style can be found in the typically medieval, half colourless, half bombastic prose of the monastic writers.[1] Such an undoubtedly clever argument does not convince me. This style reveals an originality which cannot be acquired by those who are imprisoned in the

[1] Cf. G. Turville-Petre, *Origins of Icelandic Literature* (1955), p. 25.

tradition of saints' lives and monastic chronicles. And if, here and there, an Icelandic monk uses a fresh style, he found it not in his cell, but because he was a son of his people and as a child had hung upon the lips of the good story-tellers in the circle of his family or in his district.

All these exceptional characteristics—lively dialogue, simple but striking characterization, straightforward style—are the things that develop in oral delivery. This has been convincingly demonstrated by the investigation into the art of telling fairy-tales. It may be right to abandon the illusion that the saga is an historical document, and to stress the fact that the writer of each saga is an individual artist, but I maintain that this artist received his style of story-telling from a long line of oral reciters.

The saga cannot be compared with the heroic epic, though there are points of similarity. It seems to be detached, but it is very much in touch with real people and not heroes. It tries to depict everyday life, no matter whether it is that of the ninth or of the thirteenth century. It does not move in an idealized world.

Yet it does not escape a certain tendency to the heroic. Its figures, at least the main characters, however much they are drawn as human beings, are no ordinary people, but the great figures of a great past. They have more or less become types. Their lives are directed towards a tragic downfall which they meet like true heroes. Fate hangs above these Icelandic farmers as inexorably as above Sigurd and Helgi in the Eddic lays. And when the decisive moment arrives, they stand just as upright and undaunted.

5

THE EPIC OF INDIANS AND PERSIANS

THE products of Oriental culture often make a bizarre impression upon Western man. This applies to Indian plastic art no less than to Indian thinking and Indian literature. Everything tends to assume the most luxurious forms of a tropical forest. The images of the gods, strange and grotesque, with their many arms, their demoniacal faces, their strange attributes; the temples with super-abundance of ornamentation and their symbolically thought-out structure; the finely spun speculations on the nature of man and God which eventually fade away into a nirvana without thought; all this bewilders us, and, in order to discern the beauty undeniably hidden in it, we Westerners must abandon many of our ways of thinking if we are to feel at home in this different world.

The epic poetry of the Indians, too, strikes us as strange. We feel at home in the *Iliad*. There we find a fine sense of proportion. There we find a sense of restraint and beautiful order which seems to us to be the essence of all genuine classical art. But when we read in the *Mahabharata* it seems as if we wander through the many galleries and turnings of a Barabhudur, and we get entangled in the multiplicity of detail and digressions.

In size, the *Mahabharata*, the most important Indian epic, is tremendous.[1] In its present form it comprises about 107,000 two-line stanzas or *slokas*; if one places these more than 200,000 lines beside the almost 16,000 hexameters of the *Iliad*, one realizes the difference between excessiveness and wise restraint. An Indian collection of fairy-tales is called *Kathasaritsagara*, i.e. the ocean of fairy-tale rivers. Indeed, the Indian thinks in terms of oceans, whereas the Greek sees before him the picture of the Mediterranean.

Naturally an epic of such a size is the result of a long development.

[1] Translated, among others, by H. Fauche, in 10 vols., Paris 1863–70, and K. M. Ganguli, ed. by P. Ch. Roy, in 11 vols., Calcutta ²1930.

The poem itself has something to say about this, as it tells us with amusing precision that it used to have only 24,000 *ślokas*, but that this poem in its turn was an expansion of an older epic of 8,800 stanzas, i.e. the size of the *Iliad*. This expansion is due chiefly to the insertion of numerous episodes: first, all kinds of other heroic legends which are told as *exempla*, but in later times also of long digressions of a philosophical and didactic nature. The sixth book of the *Mahabharata* contains the famous *Bhagavadgita* or the 'Song of the Exalted', which attempts to make a synthesis of the various metaphysical systems. The way in which it is inserted is remarkable: when the hero shrinks from shedding the blood of so many relations, the god who has changed into a man opposes this momentary weakness by pointing out that all living things must go the circular course through death to a new life.

The thirteenth book contains a series of legal treatises. Long digressions on worldly wisdom and politics, also on the *mokśa* or the liberation from the chain of regenerations, give the epic poem the character of a *dharmasastra* or a treatise on divine and worldly right. It is therefore easy to understand that in the temples devoted to Vishnu and Shiva and in the places of pilgrimage the *Mahabharata* is still read aloud to this day.

If one asks when this gigantic work was made, the answer is: in the course of about eight centuries. The final version belongs to the fourth century of our era, but the origin of the epic may certainly be as far back as the fourth century B.C. At that time it will still have been a purely epic poem. In the course of time and in the hands of Brahman priests it became the vessel which collected from all directions the streams of Indian thought. But the fact that theological and legal digressions especially could so easily find a place in it may be an indication that Indian tradition never considered it as a secular heroic poem in the narrower sense, but that the poem had a certain affinity with religious-philosophical literature.

The core of the epic may be briefly summarized in this way. Pandu, the prince of Kuru, situated in the basins of the upper reaches of the Ganges and the Jumna, leaves five sons after his death who are called Pandavas, after their father. The most prominent of these sons are Yudhishthira, Bhima, and Aryuna. They are brought up by their blind uncle Dhritarashtra. But jealousy springs up between the sons of this prince and their five cousins. The eldest son, called Duryodhana, finally succeeds in prejudicing his father against the Pandavas, in spite of the opposition of the uncle of King Bhisma, the warrior-Brahman Drona and the judge Viduera.

The sons of King Dhritarashtra manage to obtain the support of the famous hero Karna, the son of a charioteer. Duryodhana then makes an attempt to kill his cousins by luring them into a house of inflammable material which is then set on fire. This treacherous method is also found in Irish and Germanic literature. It recalls the burning of the hall in the legend of the Burgundians. But it also took place in real life; the Icelandic sagas give several examples of *brenna inni*, the burning of the enemy in his house.

The Pandavas, however, manage to escape with their mother Kunti through a subterranean passage. But the ground has become too hot underfoot, so they hide in a wood, while Duryodhana is under the reassuring impression that they have perished in the flames.

Dressed like Brahmans, the brothers live in the wood. The extraordinarily strong Bhima kills two huge monsters or Rakshasas, a feat which is almost obligatory for a hero and may be compared to Beowulf's fight with Grendel. The king of the neighbouring people of the Panchala, called Drupada, decides to hold a *svayamvara* for his daughter Krśna, usually called Draupadi. This means that she may take a husband of her own choosing from the princes that come from all sides. The five brothers, begging and dressed as Brahmans, also go there. As a test of their strength the suitors have to bend a huge bow and shoot an arrow at a certain target. None of those present is able to do this. Only Karna has the strength for it. But Draupadi rejects him as husband because he belongs to a lower caste. Then Aryuna comes forward and accomplishes the task.

The bending of a bow as a test of strength is also told in the other Indian epic, the *Ramayana*; it is evidently an old relic from a distant past, for we are reminded of Odysseus, who bends a bow in the hall of his house where the suitors are gathered, and thus initiates the denouement.

Aryuna is now accepted as husband, in spite of the protest of many of the princes present, because he is a Brahman. Then the Pandavas reveal who they are, and moreover demand that in accordance with an old ancestral custom Draupadi shall marry them all.

Drupada succeeds in making peace between Dhritarashtra and the Pandavas. Yudhishthira is made ruler of half the kingdom. Aryuna purposely breaks the agreement between the brothers regarding their relationship to Draupadi, and as a penance goes into exile for twelve years and lives the life of a recluse. But this does not prevent him from going through a series of adventures of war and love. When finally he returns to his brothers, their power has grown continuously; they have attained a dominant position in Northern India, and Yudhishthira now makes the famous king's sacrifice, known as the *aśvamedha*.

Presently, however, fate will turn against them. The sons of Dhritarashtra invite Yudhishthira to a game of dice with Sjakuni, their mother's brother. Carried away by the game, Yudhishthira stakes everything on the last die; he loses all his possessions and, finally, his own freedom and that of his brothers. In the famous story of *Nala*, which is one of the episodes of the epic, the *svayamvara* and the game of dice also occur, which proves how important these were in Indian tradition.

Tacitus also mentions the passion of the Germanic peoples for the game of dice in which everything is set at stake. If the player loses he allows himself to be bound and sold. 'Such an obstinacy prevails among them in a foolish cause. But they themselves call it fidelity.' The Roman author could not surmise what lay behind this. The *Edda* likewise tells us that in ancient times the gods played the game of dice. But this game is more than a simple pastime. It is a questioning of fate, and hence also a determination of fate. That is the reason why the loser never opposes the issue of the game: *alea locuta est*.

The Pandavas, then, have lost their kingdom, and for another twelve years they have to seek refuge in the forest. At the end of this time they remain for a thirteenth year in the service of Virata, king of the Matsya, a nation that lived south of the Kuru.

The time has come at last to reveal themselves. When the

Kauravas, the princes of Kuru, undertake a large-scale cattle-raid, they are beaten by Aryuna. The Pandavas are to be restored to their kingdom, but the sons of Dhritarashtra refuse this, and on both sides preparations for the battle are made in which all the princes of North India will be involved.

The battle is described in great detail. The poet here makes use of the frequently occurring motif of the messenger. From time to time Sanyarya leaves the battlefield to keep Dhritarashtra abreast of the course of the battle. There are many victims of the fighting, among them all the sons of Dhritarashtra. The end is a lament uttered by the mother of the dead.

Such an ending to the poem shows a similarity to that of the *Iliad* and *Beowulf*. The climax of the epic has been reached in this tremendous and decisive battle; lamentation and funeral are the satisfying final chord. But the epic continues, without however maintaining its heroic character. We are told that Yudhishthira discovers only now that Karna, the son of the charioteer, who also fell in the battle, was his own (half) brother. In order to atone for the sin unwittingly committed by him, he makes a grand sacrifice of horses. In the end Yudhishthira gives up his kingdom, and is taken to heaven with his brothers and Draupadi.

Though very brief, this summary cannot but give the impression of a genuine heroic song. Just as in the *Iliad* the struggle for Troy is told as a series of duels between the leaders, so also in the *Mahabharata*. Naturally the typically Indian features, such as the *svayamvara* or the game of dice and especially withdrawing into the wood for many years in solitude, must be put down to the social and cultural conditions in which this poetry came into being. Yet there can be no doubt that the characteristics which we mentioned in our discussion of European epic poetry are present here too. This applies not only to the subject-matter, but also to the elements of style in general.

A look at the contents may easily lead to the conclusion that this is a story of a real event embellished by a strong imagination. It is, however, noteworthy that older sources of the earliest history of India, as we know them, do not mention the Pandavas nor the Kauravas. The time of the recorded facts can be determined from the poem with some degree of certainty. For the *Mahabharata* is said to have been recited by Vaishampayana to King Yanameyaya, going back, therefore, to about 800 B.C. From the fact that the grandfather of this Yanameyaya is supposed to have fallen in the great battle of the epic, it follows that the poem deals with events of the ninth century B.C.[1] But is this sort of information, which can so easily have been made up at a later date, really reliable?

The very fact that the Indians treat history very freely at once forces us to exercise the utmost reserve. With so many gaps and uncertainties it seems impossible to pin down the Pandavas and the Kauravas to one or other century. This does not mean that in the *Mahabharata* no memories of a far-distant past have been preserved. We have already discussed this. The use of chariots recalls those early times when the Indo-European people had taken over this method of fighting from the steppe tribes in Central Asia. They used it for a long time. In the Gaulish graves of the La Tène period chariots are still found. We have seen that in the Irish legend Cúchulainn fights on his chariot. The Greeks of the *Iliad* did so too.

A very old feature, too, is that the Indian heroes fight with bow and arrow. This is also known of the Hittites in Asia Minor and of the Egyptians of the nineteenth dynasty. But in addition the heroes also swing swords and battle-axes.

There are indications enough not to deny the poem an historical core; the Chadwicks believe that this will now be accepted by most scholars.[2] As far as the external elements are concerned, one can agree. But what about the core of the story itself? In this respect opinions have certainly changed in the last ten to twenty years. If one uses the term 'historical' in connexion with unhistorical India, one should be clear about its real meaning. Naturally the feudal structure of society is an historical fact. The battle which the Aryan tribes had to wage against the indigenous tribes in their invasion of Hindustan was too important not to leave traces in later literature. But it was no longer felt as pure history. Instead it was transposed into a different environment. Hence the answer to the question of what is the real core of the story should be in mythological rather than historical terms. One should not look for political history in the story, but

---

[1] See H. M. Chadwick and N. K. Chadwick, *The Growth of Literature* ii (1936), p. 514.　　[2] Cf. ibid., p. 516.

for tradition; no powerful princes of the past, but real heroes.[1] In due course we shall try to determine what this means in greater detail. Here it may suffice to quote a few sentences from Charles Autran: 'This tradition is always carried on more or less by the fame of the legend or the more or less contradictory fantasies of the myth. It has its divine or human figures which it likes to embody as ethical or cultural ideals. It worships these as leaders. It sees in them incarnations of common memories, of protectors on the ever uncertain path of time. It jealously defends their memory against the continuous threat of oblivion. It also rescues some impressive names from that past, either religious or magic, folkloristic or heroic. But among all this abundantly rich material one can hardly point to names or facts that could be fixed chronologically with any accuracy.' [2]

How true this is appears from a closer inspection of the character of the five Pandavas. As in all genuine epic poetry, they are types, unchanging, fixed. One is either a hero or a traitor. There is no progression or retrogression in regard to man's inborn nature. When we consider Virgil not as the end of classical epic poetry that goes back to Homer, but as the forerunner of all epic poetry which appeared later, modern literature included, then it is precisely the characterization of *pius Aeneas* that is developed in the course of his poem, because he becomes conscious of his vocation.[3] In the *Iliad*, however, as in the *Song of Roland* or in the *Mahabharata*, a hero is given the character he will have throughout the whole poem from the outset. Thus the action is sharply outlined owing to this clear characterization, and creates a situation in which the reader always knows how the characters will act in the various circumstances in which they are placed.

How are the Pandavas drawn? Yudhishthira is the chief of the five brothers. He is described as a more or less passive personality, who respects the law and is true to his word. He is the incarnation of the idea of *dharma*, and for that reason he is the son of the god Dharma. Bhima, on the other hand, is a furious fighter. Armed with

[1] Cf. Ch. Autran, *L'Épopée indoue* (1946), p. 386.   [2] Cf. ibid., pp. 387–8.
[3] See concerning this W. Warde Fowler, *The Religious Experience of the Roman People* (1911), pp. 411 ff.

his club, he undertakes the defence of the five brothers and saves them in the most difficult circumstances. Aryuna is no less brave a warrior, but he is armed with bow and arrow. He is considered as the son of the god Indra. Then there are the two youngest brothers, Nakula and Sahadeva. They remain entirely in the background. They are supposed to be twins, and so it is no wonder that tradition should take them to be the sons of the twin-gods: the Aśvins.

The Swedish scholar Stig Wikander was the first to realize the true significance of this remarkable characterization,[1] basing his inquiries upon Georges Dumézil's investigations into the structure of the world of Germanic gods.[2] For Dumézil observed that the relationship between the chief gods corresponds with the social groupings in the world of men, where we find, descending in the scale of social importance and status, first of all the king and on the same level the Brahmans. Then follow the caste of warriors and, as the lowest group, the farmers and artisans. For the latter the main emphasis lies in fertility, and various gods are active in this field: particularly a series of goddesses, apart from the twins, the Aśvins. The awe-inspiring Indra appears as the god of the warrior-caste. But the upper layer—and that is the unique feature of the Aryan system—has two facets, for kingship has a double aspect: it is the guarantee of social order and of its laws, but it also takes the initiative for reform when matters have come to a standstill. In other words: on the one hand it has a sacral–religious character, but on the other it is of a dynamic–magic nature. It should be borne in mind that this apparent antithesis resolves itself in an unbreakable unity: thus among the Indian gods there is the inseparable pair Mithra–Varuna.

When we compare the five Pandavas (why five?) with this scheme—which is preserved in a more or less pure form among all Indo-European nations—they appear to be in complete accordance with it. The wise, almost passive Yudhishthira and the frenzied fighter Bhima together correspond to the pair Mithra–Varuna. The noble and brave Aryuna represents the caste of warriors, and it goes

[1] See 'Pândâvasagan och Mahâbhâratas mytiska förutsättningar', in Religion och Bibel vi (1947), pp. 27–39.
[2] Cf. his books Jupiter, Mars, Quirinus i–iii, and Les Mythes Romains i–iii.

without saying that the twins Nakula and Sahadeva who stay in the background are a replica of the Asvins.

This detailed correspondence between the five Pandavas and the Aryan system of gods cannot, of course, be accidental. As we have already remarked, scholars in the past tried hard to uncover an historical core in the *Mahabharata*. The same applies to the history of prehistoric times about which Livy speaks in his first book. The kings Romulus and Remus, Numa Pompilius, Servius Tullius in fact never existed except as mythical figures. If one looks more closely at their characterization and their actions, the typical features that we have indicated for the five Indo-European main gods appear at once. Hence it is not really true to say that everything that is mythical is a later addition to the Indian epic. This is proved by the fact that an entirely different world of gods exists in the epic: here the much younger gods Vishnu and Shiva appear. Behind them another world of gods lies hidden, namely that of the gods that are worshipped in the hymns of the *Veda*, but now as it were camouflaged as mortal heroes. Stig Wikander is therefore right when he concluded that the mythical core is the oldest part, and everything that is historical or pseudo-historical is merely an enrichment with motifs that were necessary to give action to the epic.

The marriage of Draupadi with all five brothers has indeed given much offence and caused much difficulty. It was thought to be a typical example of polyandry, and the actual establishment of this form of marriage among some primitive tribes of Hindustan seemed to prove the point. With the bold imagination that sometimes also carries scholars away, the thesis was propounded that the five Pandavas did not belong to the royal family of the Kurus at all but were in fact of non-Aryan origin.[1] Did then this powerful and very popular Indian epic prefer to have for its heroes representatives of the hostile and despised primitive inhabitants of Hindustan? Did the classic epic of the Indians, in which they liked to find the traces of their war of conquest for the peninsula, really place the main heroic figures in a conjugal relationship which ran counter to all Aryan customs and was bound to appear in the highest degree

[1] Cf. Chadwick, l.c., p. 519.

offensive? There is no question of a conjugal relationship between a mortal woman and a set of five mortal brothers, but rather of a mythical symbol. Draupadi—as has now become plain—is the goddess of fertility, who herself belongs to the lowest and third level and so comes to be closely associated with the Aśvins. In mythical terms, she is the wife of both of them, their sister or their temptress, for in this varying form the myth can attempt to give shape to what can only be sensed as a mythical symbol. Perhaps I may recall the Irish representation: the direct relationship between king and country finds its expression in the marriage of the king to Medb, the goddess of earth. Hence Draupadi likewise has a relationship with the two persons symbolizing royal power. But the more or less fluid figure of the earth-goddess Draupadi, reduced to suit the rigid scheme of an heroic epic, in her (mythically) natural relationship to the other gods becomes part of a form of marriage in which she is the wife of all Pandavas. This is a remarkable result of a *svayamvara*, in which an extremely brave charioteer is rejected as husband and a marriage with five men is accepted. In considering this enormity, one wonders whether the Indian audience still had any idea of the mythical background. At any rate it proves with what almost religious reverence the epic was accepted by the Indians.

This surprising result throws light not only on the genesis of the *Mahabharata* but also on that of the heroic epic in general. We shall come back to this later on. We shall now try to show that a similar origin is also very probable for the second large Indian epic, the *Ramayana*.

Tradition ascribes the *Ramayana* to the poet Valmiki, which probably means that he was the final author of this epic. The present version of about 24,000 *ślokas*, a quarter of that of the *Mahabharata*, is no more than the result of the enrichment of the old epic core (especially at the end) with much non-heroic, partly antiquarian subject-matter.

The poem begins with the story that King Dasharatha of Ayodhya has two wives. The one, Kausalya, bore him his elder son Rama, the other, Kaukeyi, a second son Bharata. When the king grows old he decides to hand over his government to Rama. But Kaukeyi, spurred on by her foster-mother, asks the king to honour a former promise. He had promised her to fulfil any two wishes. She now utters these: Rama must go into exile for fourteen years and Bharata will reign in his place. The king falls in a faint, overcome by grief. When Rama hears about all this, he insists that the king must keep his promise. He therefore decides to withdraw into the wood. His only companions are his faithful wife Sita, the daughter of Janaka, and his younger brother Lakshmana. Soon afterwards the king dies; Bharata, convinced that he has obtained the succession in an unjust way, visits his brother in the wood and tries to persuade him to return and to be king of Ayodhya. But Rama will not violate his father's promise and firmly refuses. Bharata returns, but in order to show that he is only reigning in his brother's stead, he places Rama's sandals on the throne.

The further adventures of Rama and Sita form a typically romantic story. We shall recount it briefly. A Rakshasa abducts Sita when Rama and Lakshmana are absent and takes her to the capital of the island of Lanka, which was later taken to be Ceylon. Rama wants to try and free his wife from the power of the monster, and in this attempt he secures the help of an army of monkeys. The wise councillor of the monkeys, Hanuman, makes the success of the dangerous undertaking possible. The monkeys build a bridge to the island, and, in a fight that is described in copious detail, the Rakshasa is killed. Rama is now united again with Sita, who in the meantime has shown herself steadfastly faithful. The period of his exile has now expired. He returns to Ayodhya, where Bharata joyfully hands over the government to him.

Leaving aside the long fight with the Rakshasa and considering only what may be called the core of the story, one gets the impression that it has not a very heroic character. The tone is noble and lofty. Rama's exile, undertaken out of a sense of duty, as well as Bharata's refusal to make use of his mother's ruse, give evidence of a high moral standard, but this does not make for exciting action. The hearer is compensated, however, by the story of Rama's adventures during his exile.

The poem was very successful. Not only did it become a source of inspiration for the whole of Indian literature, but it laid the foundation for Hinduism. It penetrated far beyond the Indian peninsula: for preference, the *Wayang*-play in Java still shows the adventures of Rama and Hanuman.

Because there is so little action in the original story of Rama and Bharata, one wonders whether one is justified in speaking of an heroic legend in the accepted sense of the word. A king's son who for years has to give up the throne, a brother who has the magnanimity not to make a use of the fortune that is thrown into his lap, all this does not really contain the subject-matter of a genuine heroic action. It is more an example of high morality. Naturally people have tried to establish an historical background for it, and the epic was thought to reflect the struggle of the Aryans for the possession of the southern part of Hindustan, or even, which is still less acceptable, the struggle of the Brahmans against the Buddhists in Ceylon.

Chadwick remarks: 'The story of Rama is of special interest as illustrating the growth of mythology.' [1] However, the conception of Rama as the incarnation of Vishnu cannot be part of this growth, for it appears only in the latest parts of the epic. It is true that the later gods Vishnu and Shiva tried to get a firm hold in the older epics, both in the *Mahabharata* and in the *Ramayana*, but they did not penetrate much beyond the periphery. Chadwick also holds that the equation of the heroine Sita with the goddess of agriculture of the same name is of later origin: a folklore element that was added later. But I cannot agree with this. First of all it is a very striking coincidence, that 'accidentally' the heroine and the goddess of vegetation bear the same name. And in addition that name is a word meaning 'furrow', and so is a name which fits a goddess of agriculture perfectly. How would the wife of Rama have obtained this strange name?

Scholars have often made conjectures about the mythical background of this poem, and have often tried to prove too much by wanting to explain everything. When the German scholar Jacobi alleges[2] that, according to Indian tradition, Sita as goddess is the wife of Indra and then deduces from this that therefore Rama equals Indra, I feel bound to make a reservation. As the epic pictures the

---

[1] Cf. Chadwick, l.c., p. 525.   [2] Cf. J. Jacobi, *Das Ramâyâna* (1893), pp. 130 ff.

hero, he is certainly not an incarnation of Indra. On the contrary, he is, like Yudhishthira, the typical representative of the *dharma*. Also he is a pronounced royal type and not at all a *ksatriya*, a member of the warrior caste, whose patron Indra is. If I had to point to a mythical background, I should like to see in the marriage of Rama and Sita a parallel to that of the Irish king with Medb. Behind this we can still discern the ritual marriage of the god of heaven with the goddess of earth which must be solemnized ritually by the king in the furrow. In popular customs this rite survives for a long time: in the spring the farmer and his wife tumble about together in the field, a mild form of sexual intercourse which at one time took place on the sown field.

If, then, we take Rama to be the Mithra-half of the two gods of royal authority, we would expect Bharata to represent the Varuna-half. Was he originally the usurper who pushed his brother off the throne? But in the epic he is equally admirable as a model of the *dharma*: the sandals on the throne of Rama are the striking symbol of this. Right is above might.

Thus we leave the two Indian epics with the feeling that they are a remarkable variant of the general Indo-European type. *Iliad, Chanson de Roland, Nibelungenlied*, these belong to a different world, the Western world, while in Hindustan an Oriental mentality gained the upper hand in the epic. How, then, do matters stand with the second Aryan nation, which pitched its tents on the plateau of Iran?

Firdausi has come down to us as the poet of the mighty Persian epic: the *Shah-nama* or the *Book of Kings*. He is an historically well-known figure; Firdausi is the pen-name of Abu 'l-Kasim Mansur, who lived from about 932 to 1021. The epic contains no fewer than 60,000 couplets (here too we are struck by the gigantic size of the poem) and was dedicated to Mahmud, King of Ghazni (999 to 1032), who, however, did not apparently reward the poet for it as much as the latter expected. Yet it was a great honour that was done to the king. The Mohammedan dynasties which ensconced themselves on the Persian throne thought it of great value to be considered as the legitimate descendants of the old royal generations. In the splendid figures of pre-Mohammedan tradition, Mahmud liked to recognize his own ancestors.

However much epic material is included in the *Book of Kings*, it is fundamentally the history of a dynasty which reaches far back into the Persian past. The history of Persia up to the death of Khosru II in 628 had been written down in the *Kwadhainanamagh* or *Book of Princes* which was probably written during the first years of Yazdgard III's reign: after the year 632. After the conquest of Persia by the Mohammedans in 638, i.e. very soon after the composition of the *Book of Princes*, many translations of it were made into Arabic, several of which have now been lost. In the middle of the tenth century the *Shah-nama* was made, written in New-Persian prose. Tradition has it that Dakiki, the court poet of Bokhara, made a poetic version of it between 977 and 997, which, however, he did not complete himself. That was done by Firdausi, who, it is assumed, completed it in about 1010.

This purely literary and written text is therefore mainly historical in character, and is not to be put on a par with genuine heroic epic poetry such as we have encountered so far. The *Book of Kings* deals with the history of Yamsed up to the fall of the realm of the Sassanids, and so stretches from mythical times up to the end of Persian independence. But out of this series of kings there arises the true hero, Rustum the faithful servant, who cannot die but gives successive generations of rulers his indispensable help. His origins lie in the district of Seistan in South-East Iran, and he first plays a part in the reign of Minutshir. The war with the Turanian tribes in the North begins to assume a threatening character, and their King Afrasiab succeeds in putting an end to the Persian dynasty. Then Rustum brings Kaj Kavad from Elburz and has him crowned. This king lives for a hundred years and becomes the founder of the dynasty of the Kayanides. His successor is Kaj Kaus, an ambitious ruler, of whom the myth is told that he tried to fly to heaven with trained eagles: a borrowing from the Babylonian Etana myth, which is also reflected in the well-known story of Alexander's flight to heaven. He is succeeded by Kaj Chosrev, who was brought up in a secret place and, like Hamlet, had to feign madness. The war with Turan flares up again, in which Rustum plays a large part. With King Lohrasp a new generation of kings begins in Balkh, the capital of Bactria. His son is Vistasp, in whose reign Zarathustra proclaimed his doctrine. Under his successor Isfandiar, Rustum appears once more on the scene after having to hand over his function of leader of the army to somebody else for a time. Isfandiar is invulnerable, except in the eye. Rustum has to flee from him, but he hears from the bird Simurg that there is a plant with which Isfandiar's life is bound up. From this plant he makes an arrow and shoots Isfandiar in the eye. With this story we are entirely in the epic–mythical atmosphere. A hero's one vulnerable spot where he can be killed is also known from the legends of Achilles and Siegfried; we are reminded particularly of the Irish legend of Balor, who likewise can only be killed in the eye, and the deadly plant is known from the Norse myth of Balder and the Finnish legend of Lemminkäinen.[1]

The episode of the fight between Rustum and his son Sohrab is justly famous. We have already met the same motif in the German legend of Hildebrand and Hadubrand, in the Irish story of Cúchulainn, and we shall see it again in the Russian heroic legend of Ilya Murometch. It is undoubtedly an ancient motif, but the view that it was handed down from nation to nation and so would have spread from the Persians to the Irish via the Russians and the Germans[2] is subject to serious objections. It is especially the early appearance of it in Irish heroic poetry that is inconsistent with this view. I would be inclined to think rather of an Indo-European tale preserved by some, but not all, separate nations. Moreover it is evident that its origin was a myth.[3]

Pressed into a royal genealogy and drawn out over several generations, the heroic legend of Rustum was never completely rounded off. Or perhaps it would be more correct to say that the original unity was broken up kaleidoscopically as a result of this treatment. At any rate, both in Persia and in India we find book

---

[1] See A. Christensen, *Les Gestes des Rois dans les traditions de l'Iran antique*, Paris 1936.

[2] Cf. G. Baesecke, 'Die indogermanische Verwandtschaft des Hildebrandliedes', in *Nachrichten von der Gesellschaft der Wissenschaften zu Göttingen*, vol. iii, No. 5 (1941), and A. van der Lee, 'Zum literarischen Motiv der Vatersuche', in *Verhandelingen der Kon. Nederl. Akademie van Wetenschappen Afd. Letterkunde*, NR. LXIII, No. 3 (1957).

[3] See my article in *Germanisch-Romanische Monatsschrift* xxxiv (1953), pp. 257–74.

epics, that is, written works of gigantic size such as the West has never produced. There is no doubt that this is the end of a very long development which must have had its origin in oral popular epic poetry. This epic activity can be assumed to have gone on for about a thousand years for the *Mahabharata*. For the *Ramayana* it went on for at least eight hundred years. The tradition of Persia may be estimated at about four hundred years. It has justly been remarked[1] that narrative poetry must have already existed before Dakiki, from which the *Shah-nama* derived not only its metre but also its fixed formulae and stylistic elements.

No less remarkable is the story of Artachsir i Papakan.[2] Artachsir is the grandson of Papak, governor of Pars. When he is fifteen years old he is called to the court by the king of Iran, Ardawan. Although he is there brought up honourably at first, he is degraded to stable-hand status as a result of a quarrel during a hunt. But one of Ardawan's concubines discovers him and falls in love with him. She tells him of a dream the king has had which indicates that the throne will be transferred to a servant, who will escape from him within the next three days. Then the pair decide to flee. They take great treasures from the palace with them and ride away on horseback. This reminds us vividly of the story of Walter and Hiltgunt, who flee from the court of Attila in a similar fashion.

On the way two women hail him as the future ruler of Iran and advise him to ride westwards in the direction of the sea. When Ardawan discovers the flight the next day, he equips an army to pursue them. In the afternoon the king learns from the inhabitants that Artachsir passed that way at sunset. At the next resting-place he is told that the fugitives passed there in the afternoon and that a ram walked behind them. But on the second day Ardawan learns from a caravan that they are twenty *parasangs* ahead of him and that a ram was sitting behind one of the riders. Ardawan now realizes the futility of his pursuit. For the ram which had joined Artachsir was the symbol of the majesty of kingship. It had turned from Ardawan to the young hero.

This story, which can already be found in a middle-Persian

---

[1] Cf. Th. Nöldeke, *Das iranische Nationalepos* (²1920), p. 22.
[2] Cf. Th. Nöldeke, in *Paul und Braunes Beiträge* iv (1878), pp. 22–69.

manuscript and which also occurs in Firdausi's *Book of Kings*, has as its main character the founder of the middle-Persian kingdom of the Sassanids in A.D. 226. Nöldeke observes in connexion with this legend that it is remarkable that such romantic tales were current about the founder of the realm whose history was known with such accuracy.[1] Certainly remarkable, but no more so than in similar cases which will be mentioned later. Here we touch upon the problem of the transition of history to heroic legend which will be discussed more fully in Chapter 10.

[1] Cf. Th. Nöldeke, *Das iranische Nationalepos*, p. 10. It is noteworthy that in the Greek legend of Atreus and Thyestes a ram with golden wool also symbolizes royal power.

6

THE SLAVONIC FOLK-EPIC

THE Slav nations have a rich epic tradition, but it is noteworthy that it has never developed into a full-scale literary epic. They do not possess such grand creations as the *Song of Roland* or the *Nibelungenlied*. The epic does not grow beyond the stage of a short lay comprising some hundreds of lines. Perhaps the reason for this is that it became typical folk-poetry too early and remained thus to the end. A second remarkable fact is that this epic poetry existed up to (sometimes beyond) the threshold of modern times. Thus it gives us an opportunity to observe the reciter and draw conclusions about the way in which the art of epic poetry in general lived on the lips of the singers.[1]

In a discussion of the Slavic art of epic poetry, that of the Great-Russians and that of the South-Slavs most deserve our attention. They are in many ways similar, both in form and in delivery.

Great-Russian epic poetry is in the form of *byliny*. The metrical form of the verse is very simple and does not show the somewhat rigid structure of Western epic poetry. The number of syllables in the verse is not fixed. Normally it has from ten to twelve, but it may come down to seven or eight, or rise as high as sixteen. The line has a caesura in the middle; the distribution of accents is usually in accordance with the normal stress of the language. Thus because of this natural and loose structure the verse lends itself admirably to the purpose of a free and easy delivery.

A point of similarity with Old-Germanic verse is that the number of lifts in the line is four, but an unlimited number of unstressed syllables can group themselves freely around these lifts. Moreover, we find here too that the line may have an anacrusis of one to three syllables, though this may also be absent. There is therefore no ques-

[1] We shall return to this in ch. 8.

tion of a monotonous regularity; the line is perfectly free to conform with its contents.

A second feature of this poetry is that it stands half-way between formlessness and a very strictly controlled fixed form. Rhyme
often occurs, but not always. Sometimes one finds the beginning of
stanza formation. As often in the style of epic folk-poetry, the
bylina has a preference for parallel lines whose content is the same
but which differ in the wording. This is especially the case in
descriptions, as in the following example of a banquet:

> Princes and boyars came together,
> Mighty, powerful heroes,
> And all brave women warriors;
> Half the feast was over,
> Half the meal was eaten,
> The boyars had almost had enough to eat.
> The boyars had almost had enough to drink.

This technique, which the Finns also use, has great advantages for
the reciter, similarly in the fixed formulae with which various
frequently recurring elements are described, such as arming oneself,
jumping on horseback, deliberating.[1] They are to be found in all
epic poetry, in Homer as well as in the *Nibelungenlied*. The Russians
and the Finns, however, make use of this stylistic feature with
such regularity that one may assume a function of duplication here.
In general the formulae make the delivery of a text easier; as soon
as the singer has come to them the lines go automatically, and he
has time to think of the next part of the narration. But when the
recitation becomes a kind of improvisation, the automatic duplication of lines becomes almost necessary in order to give shape to the
content and form of the next line.

In modern times the bylina has retreated into an outlying district
of the Great-Russian territory. It is still very much alive in the district of Olonetz, between the White Sea and Lake Onega and in the
area of Archangel. But I derive this statement from sources which
date from before the Russian Revolution. It is to be feared that the

[1] For more particulars see R. Trautmann, *Die Volksdichtung der Großrussen* i, *Das
Heldenlied* (1935), pp. 56–61.

economic changes in the country have not been favourable for the preservation of this popular tradition. So much is certain: once people began to collect them, it was this area which yielded the greatest harvest. Some parts of Siberia, too, had a remarkable wealth of byliny. Obviously, we have here the last stage of the Russian tradition. The bylina has been pushed back into the periphery, where modern culture, always hostile to old, deep-rooted popular tradition, has not yet been able to make its influence felt. One may speak of reserve areas, where a doomed popular culture can still survive for a time. The same can be seen in Finland: here the *runot* still exist only on the eastern border in Karelia and Ingermanland. We have evidence enough, however, that in the eighteenth century the byliny still flourished in many other places of Great-Russia. A clear proof of this is the fact that it was taken over by the Cossacks and penetrated with them to the north border of the Caucasus: the bylina must at one time have had great spreading-power. It is all the more striking that it is wholly absent in the Ukraine.

This survival among the poorest population groups living in the merciless tundra climate of North Russia has naturally had an unfavourable influence on this tradition of heroic poetry. Formerly the bylina extended to the highest strata of society and was even the almost exclusive property of the nobility. But this will be discussed later. It can be established everywhere; heroic poetry, the form of literature which is, as it were, the literary mode of expression of the martial spirit that prevailed among the warlike nobility, descends from this level to the people, first to middle-class circles, finally to the farmers and the artisans. At any rate, to put it more cautiously: they preserve it, while higher culture, which finds its expression in personal and original art, starts its triumphal march from the top level of society. The *jongleur* in France and the *Spielmann* in Germany are also the somewhat vulgar heirs of the poet-reciters who were once welcome guests in the knights' castles.

In regard to the Russian bylina a distinction can be made with the subject-matter used, according to several locally circumscribed areas. Kiev, Novgorod, and Moscow, in this order, also indicate a progressively later type.

The largest and most important cycle is that of Kiev, the town that was once inhabited by the founders of the Varangian kingdom, the Swedish Vikings, the Rus. Penetrating even farther inland along the network of rivers in Russia, they settled down there, because they found the place most suitable for further commercial relations. From Kiev they traded as far as Byzantium and the Arabian East.

The Grand-Duke of these Vikings, Vladimir I, who was baptized in 988, plays the same part in this cycle as Charlemagne plays in French epic poetry. He himself usually remains in the background, or at least does not always play an honourable part. Yet he is also glorified as the *Solnysko*, the 'Sun' of the host of heroes, gathered about him. It is the boyars who perform the heroic deeds that are sung in the heroic songs. They form the *druzhina*, i.e. a retinue of warriors who have, of their own free will, placed themselves under a lord to whom they are bound by an oath of allegiance. This is undoubtedly a Scandinavian tradition, comparable to the Germanic *comitatus* described by Tacitus. These boyars take part in the prince's expeditions, but in particular they have all kinds of personal adventures, and, when they return triumphantly to Kiev, they sit down at Vladimir's well-appointed table. Here they have an opportunity to boast of their courage and listen with pleasure to the singers who glorify their deeds. In such powerful people, this self-assurance often leads to an over-confidence that expresses itself in an attitude of disrespect towards their lord.

Now it appears that a later namesake was mixed up with this Vladimir who bore the byname of Monomach, and died in 1126. This man also played a glorious part in early Russian history. Whereas Vladimir lived in perpetual war with the Petscheneges, Monomach's particular enemies were in the tribes of the Polovtsi. But in the byliny these old and long-forgotten tribes have naturally been replaced by the hereditary enemies of the Russians in later days, the Tartars, just as in the *Song of Roland* the Saracens have taken the place of the Basques. The destruction of Kiev by the Mongols in 1240 finally ended the glory of its once magnificent greatness. This means therefore that the Kiev cycle of bylina must have been completed long before that time. As far as we can judge, it stretched from the tenth to the twelfth century and during this period it was continually enriched with new characters. This, then, is still the period of a creative art of byliny. Later it became purely a carefully preserved tradition.

Among the main heroes are Dobrynya Nikititch, Djuk Stepanovitch, and above all Ilya Murometch. The latter is the favourite of the singers; his nicknames 'farmer's son' and 'old Cossack' reflect the circles in which his heroic deeds were later sung. His fame even spread beyond the frontiers of Russia. In German epic poetry such as the *Ortnit*, and especially in the Old Norse *Thidreks Saga of Bern*, a prose compilation of North German songs, a Russian hero Ilias appears who is closely linked with a prince Waldimar, by whom, of course, Vladimir is meant. In spite of contradictory opinions sometimes heard, I see no reason at all to separate this Ilias from the Russian hero.[1] If it is true that the German story of Brünhild has become part of the Russian store of fairy-tales—on this point, too, scholarly opinion is divided—this would also show that in the Middle Ages various connexions existed between Germany and the Slavonic East: one can imagine singers from both sides who crossed the language frontier and recited their songs.

Ilya is the hero of a legend we have already met several times in discussion of the *Lay of Hildebrand*, in the Irish legend of Cúchulainn, and in the Persian poem of Firdausi: that is, of the fight between father and son. On one of his expeditions Ilya met a beautiful girl and begot a son by her. When this son, Sokolnitchek (Falconer), is growing up he goes to seek his father. The twelve-year-old hero is a mighty warrior: he rides on an excellent horse which jumps the length of a verst; a flame shoots out of its mouth, sparks fly from its nostrils, smoke curls out of its ears. At the left stirrup a dog runs fast as the wind, on the right stirrup sits a young grey-blue eagle. A hawk flies from one shoulder to the other and passes messages from one ear to the other. The hero throws his club up as far as the clouds, and as it falls down he seizes it with his white hands and does not allow it to fall on the damp earth.

The song continues in this somewhat hyperbolic style, often met with in epic poetry. Sokolnitchek finally meets Ilya, and his defiant attitude starts the fight. The old hero jumps up on his swift feet,

[1] Cf. Chadwick, *The Growth of Literature* ii, p. 118.

throws his adversary on the damp earth, loosens his mail-shirt, wants to cut open his white chest and gaze upon the fiery heart. Then he sees a wonderful cross on his chest, once his own property.

The father now asks him who he is and, in insulting words, the son refuses to tell him: it would be a token of cowardice to be forced to do so. Not till the father has asked him for the third time, does he tell him who he is. In his joy at recognizing his son, Ilya tells him how he had met his mother in the fields and had begotten him, the glorious son, by her. He tells him to ride back to his mother. The boy goes, but is angry about his illegitimate birth, of which his father has told him, and in his wrath he kills his mother. But now he is thirsting for revenge on his father for dishonouring his mother. He returns, finds his father asleep in his tent, aims and thrusts the sharp lance at his breast in order to pierce his fiery heart. But the lance glances off a wonderful, heavy cross. The old hero awakes, his fiery heart is inflamed, he broadens his mighty shoulders, raises his white hands, and seizing the evil-doer by his brave head, breaks him into two pieces and throws them far away into the fields.

The Russian song is not as free from blemishes as the *Lay of Hildebrand*. The poem is an accumulation of atrocities. Also in this respect it is not very satisfactory that in the end the brave young hero wants to murder his father in his sleep. It seems that the poet thought the motif of the sign of recognition so important that he duplicated it. But the cross on Ilya's chest plays an entirely different part from that of Sokolnitchek. And finally, one would have preferred to see the son die in a man-to-man fight rather than as a victim of an outburst of wrath on Ilya's part.

The Novgorod cycle has a different character. Instead of the warlike nature of Vladimir's Kiev, here there is the rich commercial town of Novgorod. It is no longer the members of a *druzhina* who play the main part, but Sadko the rich merchant, and Vasili Buslaev the son of middle-class people. No wonder that the contents are different in many respects. The atmosphere is more like that of the medieval ballad than that of the old heroic song. We are told in a bylina how Sadko has gathered his riches. This Sadko has been drawn as the minstrel's ideal. Playing on his *gusli* Sadko goes from banquet to banquet, until at last he is no longer accepted anywhere.

E

He withdraws to the shore of Lake Ilmen and there, sitting on a stone, he sings his songs in solitude. Suddenly, one day, the *tsar morskoi*, the lord of the lake, emerges from the water and thanks him for his delightful music. He will reward him: he is to lay a wager with the inhabitants of Novgorod (staking his head against all their riches) that he will catch fish of pure gold in Lake Ilmen. With the aid of the god of the lake he succeeds in doing so, and thus he is able to build up his commercial fleet of thirty 'dragon-ships'.

The third cycle is that of Moscow. The development of the powerful Muscovite state in the fifteenth and sixteenth centuries provided a new impulse for the old bylina poetry. The old songs with the ever beloved Dobrynya and Ilya were given an entirely new form, so much so that the old background is hardly recognizable. From other parts of the Russian realm, from Middle Russia to the steppes as well as from the Volga district, all sorts of byliny were added to enrich the already large stock.

Before describing the development of this epic poetry we might cite another example in order to illustrate its nature. The bylina is always built up in a fixed form: it consists of an introduction, then comes the middle part in which the story proper is told, and the end is a kind of brief epilogue. As an example let us take Dobrynya's fight with the dragon.

The introduction is as follows. Dobrynya's mother says (Nikita's son was taught by the little mother): 'Do not ride far in the field to the mountain of the Saracens, do not tread on the snakes' brood, do not free the Russian prisoners, do not bathe in the Putshay river. For wild is the Putshay stream, in the middle it splashes like fire.' But Dobrynya does not heed his mother's advice. Her request to avoid the dangers spurs him on to seek them. He rode far on the mountain of the Saracens, trod on the snakes' brood, and freed the Russian prisoners.

This opening recalls the Irish stories in which likewise various *geasa* are imposed upon a hero, a kind of taboo which he is not allowed to transgress, but which, being a hero, he is forced to ignore, thus bringing misfortune upon himself. Yet the difference is very great too. The Irish *geasa* are to a certain extent magic; the hero does not want to transgress them, but the circumstances lead him to do so, thus bringing about his ruin. In the bylina advice to be careful is scorned by the hero. By acting contrary to it he achieves heroic fame.

Then begins the main section: his heroic heart was bathed in perspiration, his heroic heart was thirsty; he spurred his excellent horse to the Putshay stream, he leapt from his excellent horse, took off his gay-coloured garb, bathed in the first stream, bathed in the middle stream, and said: 'To me Dobrynya, my little mother said, little mother advised me: "Do not ride far in the field on the mountain of the Saracens, do not tread upon the snakes' brood, do not free the Russian prisoners, and do not bathe in the Putshay stream, for the Putshay stream is very wild, the middle stream splashes like fire." But the Putshay stream is quiet and gentle, it resembles a pool of rain.'

Dobrynya had hardly spoken the words; there was no wind, but like a thundercloud it came rushing on; no cloud in the sky, but rain poured down, then the rain stops and only the thunder rolls along and the lightning whistles—when the dragon Goryntshishtshi flies aloft, the dragon with the twelve claws.

Dobrynya is frightened by the dragon, the cursed one, who says to him: 'Now Dobrynya is in my power; if I so desire, I shall drown Dobrynya; if I so desire, I shall now devour Dobrynya; if I so desire, I shall now take Dobrynya in my claw and carry Dobrynya to my lair.'

The dragon pounces down upon the swift-flowing river, but Dobrynya is a good swimmer; he dives under to yonder bank, dives under this bank. But Dobrynya does not have his excellent horse, does not have his gay-coloured garb. Only his Greek hat is lying there, which weighs more than three poods. He seizes the Greek hat, throws it at the cursed dragon, knocks off all his twelve claws. Then the dragon falls on the grass of the steppe.

Dobrynya is swift of foot, he jumps on the dragon's white breast, takes his steel knife, is about to cut open his white breast. Then the dragon implores Dobrynya: 'Oh Dobrynya, son of Nikita! I will make a pact with you: you shall not ride over the wide field to the mountain of the Saracens, you shall not tread upon the snakes' brood, not free the Russian prisoners, not bathe in the Putshay stream. And I shall not fly to Holy Russia, not seek out men, the Russian men, not gather for myself the Russian prisoners.'

Then the hero lets the dragon go from between his knees, and the dragon flies up as high and far as the clouds.

The bylina then goes on to tell how the dragon breaks his promise. He flies to Kiev, there sees the niece of the prince walking in the street, seizes her and carries her off to his lair. Dobrynya decides that he will rescue her. He goes home full of sorrow; there he asks his mother's advice.

He rises very early, washes and dresses himself in beautiful clothes, takes the bridle in his hand, takes the excellent horse of his grandfather, gives the bay horse a honey-sweet drink, feeds him with Indian corn, on the sweat-blankets he puts more sweat-blankets, on the sweat-blankets he puts felt-blankets, on the felt-blankets the Tcherkes saddle, and pulls all twelve straps tight. The thirteenth he takes because of its strength, so that the excellent horse shall not leap away under the saddle, nor throw the young hero on the wide field. The strap was made of silk, the clasps of steel, the saddle rings of red gold. The silk does not tear, the steel does not wear, the red gold does not rust; on the horse sits the young hero who never grows old.

In farewell his mother gives him a whip and speaks thus to him: 'When you are in the wide field, on yonder high mountain, tread on the serpents' brood, free the Russian prisoners; when that young serpents' brood twists round the horse's legs so that the bay cannot jump any more, cannot shake off the serpents' brood, take the silken whip, lash the bay between his hindlegs, between his ears; he will then jump again, shake off the serpents' brood, and trample them all down.'

And thus it happens. Then the dragon rushes out of his lair, and a fight begins which lasts three days. When Dobrynya is about to give up the fight, a voice from heaven urges him to go on for three more hours. And after three hours he slays the dragon. The blood pours from his body, and again a voice from heaven proclaims salvation: he must thrust his Tartar lance in the ground and ask Mother Earth to open up. Little Mother Earth does so and all the dragon's blood disappears down below. From the lair Dobrynya frees forty tsars, forty kings, forty kings' sons, and countless ordinary people.

With the princess, Dobrynya rides back to Kiev, to the gentle prince Vladimir.[1]

The dragon-fight is one of the most common heroic deeds. It occurs among the Indians and the Greeks as well as the Teutons and the Celts. Usually it does not pass off so smoothly as in this bylina. Even the hero of the fairy-tale often finds that on a cut-off head three new ones grow again and that the monster becomes ever more dangerous. Dobrynya only has to swing his hat once and all the claws are struck off the dragon's legs.

With this motif we have entered upon the field of the fairy-tale, or rather, as will be shown later, that of the myth. That does not mean that Dobrynya cannot have been an historical figure, just as one need not doubt the historical authenticity of Theoderic the Great because of him, too, a dragon-fight is told.

Who, then, is this Dobrynya? In looking for an historical proto-type we encounter the same difficulties as in the case of Guillaume d'Orange, where we have the choice of sixteen historical claimants. The name Dobrynya, too, frequently occurs in the history of Russia. Thus a Dobrynya, an uncle of Vladimir I, is frequently mentioned in the annals, and must be considered in this connexion because he played an important part in an expedition organized by the prince of Novgorod, Mstislav the Great, against the Polovtsi. In the catas-trophe at Perejaslavl, Tugar Kan, the leader of the Polovtsi, fell. This Tugar Kan occurs as Tugarin the son of the dragon in some byliny, and moreover as the opponent of Dobrynya Nikititch. The name of the father, Nikita, which was very common in Novgorod, has taken the place of that of Raguilov in the byliny.

This Dobrynya, a contemporary of Vladimir Monomach, takes us to the beginning of the twelfth century, and that is near enough to the time of the supposed origin of the byliny to make his iden-tity with the hero of the dragon-fight plausible. Cannot, then, this dragon also be linked up with that Tugarin, son of the dragon, in whom we may then recognize the Tugar Kan with whom the historical Dobrynya fought?[2]

A great difficulty, however, in establishing the historical persons who became the heroic figures in the byliny, is that the old Russian

[1] Cf. Trautmann, l.c., pp. 129–34. [2] Cf. Chadwick, l.c., pp. 108–12.

chronicles are so unreliable. Often they even assimilate the contents of the byliny as historical facts in their account. Examples of this are also to be found in the chronicles of Germany and France. But as the heroes themselves, or their names, do not just appear out of the blue, one may safely assume in the case of the Russian epics too that they are a distant echo of historical events.

Perhaps they are an echo of very distant events. For if Vladimir I appears as the centre of this epic poetry, it must go back to the Viking Age. Are there perhaps still traces of this period of Russian history? A Danish scholar assumed that he had found evidence for this.[1] Thus the bylina of Solovey Budimirovitch opens as follows:

> From the island of Kadolsky
> From the Dunay Sea
> Thirty ships came sailing,
> And on board of these ships
> Were thirty brave warriors;
> The ships were splendidly equipped
> The ships were splendidly adorned:
> Prow and stern were like an aurochs,
> The broad ships' sides like elks,
> Sails of closely woven linen,
> Anchors of the hardest steel,
> Anchor-chains were made of silver,
> Ropes of seven kinds of silk.
> And on board this ship
> Was young Solovey.

When one reads this description, one gets the impression of a fantastically described Viking ship. But when medieval ballads describe ships, we hear likewise of the most precious equipment which does not lack gold, silver, and silk. For that matter, there were examples of this in real life which were not inferior in splendour to the poetic description.

Solovey's ship makes for Kiev. When, disguised as a merchant, he has come to Vladimir's hall, he offers gold, forty bundles of black ermine, forty bundles of red fox-hides, and he is joyfully received. Then the traditional tale of the abduction of a young maiden de-

Cf. Stan Rožniecki, *Varægiske Minder i den Russiske Heltedigtning* (1914).

velops, which was a favourite theme of the minstrels in the late Middle Ages: an example is the German poem *Rother*, in which knights disguise themselves as merchants, lure a young maiden to their ship, and abduct her.

At first sight one will perhaps be tempted to think of a Viking expedition from the Baltic up the Duna to the famous Kiev of prince Vladimir. But appearances are deceptive. This song does not belong to the cycle of Kiev, but is a typical Novgorod song about a merchant, which is only outwardly connected with the well-known formulae of the Kiev songs. Everything therefore points to the song being of late origin. The description of ships is also found in byliny of Western Siberia: it is a traditional element of style. In fact the image of the falcon for the swift-sailing ship is also known in Scandinavia, and may originally have come from the sea-loving nations of Sweden and Denmark. But this does not mean that the song itself will have preserved a memory of the time when the dragon-ships sailed from the Baltic up the Russian rivers.[1]

It would be strange however if, in the Kiev cycle which arose in the Varangian milieu of Vladimir, no memories of it should have survived. The hero Ilya Murometch may perhaps be considered as a Viking who played a part at the court of Vladimir. For the Murman coast received its name from the Norsemen who sailed there regularly to buy or steal fur. The surname Murometch then may likewise preserve the memory of the Viking Age. But such an isolated name cannot, any more than the Russian loan-words from Old Norse, serve to prove that the songs, both in form and in content, arose in the Viking entourage.

If we now try to sketch the development of the byliny, it is advisable to keep to the picture that R. Trautmann, the greatest expert on this art, has drawn of it. He starts from a poetry which in the heyday of Kiev (i.e. from the tenth to the thirteenth century) played an important part at the courts of the princes and the feudal lords. In accordance with a view that has also been expressed for Romance and Germanic epic poetry, the original type of this court poetry was the song of praise, that is a glorification of the prince and his boyars. So it is easy to understand that this praise is apt to

[1] Cf. Trautmann, l.c., pp. 214-15.

assume parabolical dimensions and that even mythical elements were absorbed. Especially in the case of princes who had long been dead but whose fame still survived and who were remembered with reverence by their descendants, a human being easily developed into an heroic figure. So the singers recited their songs amidst the *druzhina*; we are still in a wholly aristocratic milieu.

After the fall of Kiev through the invasion of the Mongols, this poetry was deprived of its means of subsistence, but still did not die out. On the contrary, in the course of the fourteenth and the fifteenth centuries it was transformed into the real bylina. This need not of course preclude the possibility that even in the older, feudal times the song of praise had not remained purely dithyrambic. He who praises the prince must talk of famous deeds he has performed, and so an epic element is added from the outset, just as may be observed in the Homeric hymns. But after the fall of Kiev, another change takes place in the old court poetry. The place of the old rhapsode is now taken by another type: the *skomorokh*. He may be compared to the Middle High German minstrel, a reciter of songs for an entirely different audience. The *skomorokhi* formed a kind of guild to which belonged all those who appeared at public amusements: actors, singers, dancers, wrestlers, and clowns, who flocked together in Great-Russia wherever weddings and other festivities were celebrated. We shall see later that this was also the case with the French *jongleurs* and the German minstrels. It can still be seen from the existing byliny that these *skomorokhi* played their part in the propagation of the byliny. They do not fail to put themselves repeatedly on the stage in these poems. Thus Dobrynya, disguised as a *skomorokh*, appears at the wedding of his own wife Nastasya.

These *skomorokhi* are found not only in Novgorod but all over Middle and North Russia. The bylina gains in strength and also in form in the course of the sixteenth and seventeenth centuries. The nature of these singers differs very greatly from that of the earlier ones who appeared in the *druzhina*; the *skomorokh* can do much: he not only sings byliny, but also historical and religious songs, and he tells fairy-tales and legends. That explains why the old heroic subject-matter came to be enriched with all kinds of motifs which ultimately derive from international short-story literature and which we encounter in the Indian *Kathasaritsagara* as well as in the French *fabliaux*. It is now clear why the Novgorod cycle also, instead of using the old and perhaps somewhat antiquated boyars, yields a place in these stories to citizens, merchants, and farmers.

In the course of the eighteenth century the *skomorokh* disappears from the scene, but not till he has handed over his store of byliny to the people themselves. The singers are now ordinary people who have a talent for learning and reciting such songs. They are few and far between in any village but they sometimes have a remarkable talent. Since a beginning was made with investigating how fairy-tales are told in a village community, a greater knowledge of conditions prevailing there has been gained. It is not only, not even mainly, grandmother, sitting by the fire, who hands down fairy-tales to younger generations. Telling fairy-tales is an art like any other art. It needs a natural talent which consists not only of a good memory, but also of a lively delivery, telling mimicry, and lively gesture. The teller learns his art from an older one who is highly esteemed as such in his village. And every teller of fairy-tales, if he has a natural talent for it, can recite these stories entirely in his own way: the personal element is not by any means lacking in this art. The Russian investigators report with what astonishing skill those simple farmers and artisans from the poor northern part of Russia recited the byliny, how much they were poets no less than reciters.

Naturally the tradition eventually became predominantly conservative. The formal elements were treated with greater rigidity and became more and more frequent. They are the crutches on which a moderately talented singer likes to lean. New creations are rare, and usually stay within narrow limits. They are not much more than imitations of songs known of old. There is now also a tendency to combine various byliny into a cycle. Nevertheless, there are excellent singers here and there with a fabulous memory, who keep thousands of lines in their heads. But the bylina is coming to the end of its existence. It has been relegated to the extreme corners of Russia. It is a relic and will share the fate of all relics of the old peasant culture: modern civilization ruthlessly destroys them. In these days of wireless, singers and reciters are anachronisms.

The epic poetry of the South Slavs likewise did not develop beyond the lay. The *narodne pjesme*, the 'songs of the people', survive among the people to the present day and they were still made after such disturbing events as the Balkan Wars or the First World War. When in 1840 the feudal lord of the Hercegovina, Smajl-aga Tchengitch, was killed in an attack from Montenegro, his standard-bearer improvised a song on the way back from the battlefield which dealt with this tragic event.[1]

It was not till the nineteenth century that these songs became the subject of thorough investigation. At present we know more about the manner of delivery and even the way in which these Serbian songs have come into being than we know about any other epic tradition of any Indo-European nation. The pointers which they give for the better understanding of Greek, French, and German epic poetry are therefore of extraordinary importance, but this will be dealt with in the last chapter.

The attention of the literary world was drawn to this popular poetry, when Vuk Karadzhitch, the most assiduous collector of the *narodne pjesme*, published his first volume.[2] They aroused the keenest interest of scholars like Jakob Grimm. He praises the tender and at the same time chivalrous nature of these poems. They glorify courage, loyalty, magnanimity towards friend and foe, strange adventures, dangerous expeditions undertaken for the possession of a woman.[3] The following example illustrates their special descriptive style:

> What is the white on the green mountain?
> Is it snow, or is it swans?
> If snow, it would have melted,
> Swans would have flown away.
> It is not snow, it is not swans,
> It is the tents of Asan-aga.

This poetry is heroic in content and spirit, and the heroic age lasted

[1] Cf. M. Braun, in *Euphorion* xxxiv (1933), p. 343.
[2] Cf. *Narodne Srpske Pjesme*.   [3] Cf. *Kleine Schriften* iv, p. 203.

long in Serbia with its history full of suffering. First there is the time of Serbian independence until about 1500, the completion of the Turkish conquest. Then comes the time of Turkish domination which lasted till 1700 in Montenegro, 1800 in Serbia. The wars of independence in the eighteenth and the beginning of the nineteenth centuries again provided material for new poems.

We shall however limit ourselves to the oldest period, of which the fourteenth century forms the core. That is the time of Tsar Stjepan Dushan (1331 to 1356), who succeeded in conquering the whole of the Byzantine Empire with the exception of Constantinople. After his death the power of the mighty realm he founded is lost again, mainly owing to the insatiable greediness of the feudal lords. Then follows a brief period of struggle for imperial power when Marko Kraljevitch tries to assert his claims to the throne against King Lazar who was elected by the estates of the realm. He even went so far as to invoke the help of the Turks, who fought the Christians. In 1394 he was killed in the battle of Rovina in Rumania. In spite of his siding with the Turks, which even led to a heavy defeat of the Serbs during his lifetime, he became the national hero of the Serbs.

The first battle on the plain of Kossovo on 15 June 1389 is also a favourite subject of epic songs. The Turkish Sultan Amurat tried to forestall the plan of attack of King Lazar and provoked a battle. In the beginning the battle of Kossovo went in favour of the Serbs, but the king's son-in-law, Vuk Brankovitch, allegedly jealous of the king, committed treason. At a critical moment in the battle, perhaps bribed by Amurat, he turned his horse, and his army of 12,000 fled with him. The fight had a tragic end: Lazar was captured and beheaded. But after that the Sultan himself was murdered by the Serb Milosh Obilitch.

This dramatic defeat, which struck a heavy blow at the Serbian kingdom and which was the prelude to the total conquest by the Turks in 1459, had a similar effect on Serbian epic poetry to the catastrophe in the pass of Roncevaux on French heroic legend or the fall of the Burgundian kingdom on German legend. Here too we note the appearance of a traitor who was perhaps not a traitor, for historical sources tell us that even after the peace Vuk Brankovitch carried on his bitter fight against the Turks. Tradition sometimes has a capricious and unjust way with the historical figures of a nation. Marko, who certainly was a traitor, became the chosen hero of the Serbs, and Vuk, who certainly was not, became the prototype of all traitors!

The figure of Marko and the battle of Kossovo belong to the same period. It is all the more remarkable, then, that the two cycles of legends did not blend. They have the same heroic tone, but are distinguished by what we might call a difference in culture. Marko is a crude and cruel hero who moreover lacks chivalry towards women. He is like the Indian Indra: a tremendous fighter and a tremendous drinker, evidently features which a nation at a certain stage of its civilization can appreciate. Again and again in these poems we encounter the motifs that are also popular with other nations. Once Marko goes to the famous smith Novak and demands from him the best sword that he has ever forged. For three days Novak works in his forge, for three days Marko drinks red wine. Then the smith shows him the sword and tells him to test its sharpness and its strength on the anvil. Marko then cuts right through the anvil and asks the smith whether he did not forge a better weapon once before. He confesses that he once did so for Musa when he became a rebel. Marko is infuriated and tells the smith to hold out his hand so that he can give him the sum of money that he promised him. The smith does so, and Marko hacks off his right arm at the shoulder.

The Siegfried legend also has the motif of the sword that cuts right through the anvil, it is indeed a test of superiority. Yet how differently the motif has been worked out in the German and the Serbian legends. Siegfried tests the sword that the dwarf has forged for him three times, but the smith is treacherous: the first sword proves to be unsound because it breaks on the anvil. Only at the third attempt does the sword turn out to be so sharp that it splits the anvil in two and with this weapon Siegfried is able to fight the dragon. Very different from Marko. The sword is made excellently by the smith, but his reward is a hacked-off arm, because Marko cannot bear the fact that there is another hero who has an equally strong or even a better sword.

At times the heroes are more boastful than is compatible with our taste; they like to brag about their strength, but they act accordingly. Such types as the French Rainoart *au tinel* also occur in the cudgel-swinging strong men of Serbian heroic legends. This is clearly illustrated in the song of Tsar Dushan's marriage.

Dushan asks for the beautiful Roksanda, the daughter of King Michael of Ledyen, in marriage, and she is gladly given to him. But Michael makes the condition that the two nephews of Dushan shall not come with him to the wedding, as he fears that they may disturb the celebrations when they have drunk too much. Dushan agrees to this. When the bridal procession travels across the Kossovo plain, his nephews, the two young Voinovitch, are looking on with envious eyes. Their mother advises them to have their youngest brother Milosh brought from the mountains where he tends the sheep. When he appears, they ask him to travel with Dushan's procession in order to protect it against possible evil. A detailed description follows of how he was dressed. First he had on a clean shirt embroidered with gold from the neck down to the waist; three graceful ribbons were attached to the shirt. Next came a waistcoat with thirty gold buttons, then a gold cuirass which weighed fully fifteen pounds. But then he had a coarse Bulgarian shepherd's cloak thrown across his shoulders which covered him completely. On his head they put a fur bonnet with a high peak, so that he looked exactly like a black Bulgarian. He then took a lance, cudgel, and sword. Finally, the faithful horse Kulash is brought before him and covered with bear's hide, so that Dushan will not recognize it.

Milosh soon overtakes the bridal procession, thus revealing not only his strength and skill, but also the horse's amazing swiftness. It is a good thing that he has come with them, for when they arrive at the walls of Ledyen Dushan is told that he will have to measure his strength against the strongest champion of the town. Milosh is the only one who dares to fight, and eventually he succeeds in driving his opponent back to the walls of the town where he nails him to the gate with his never-failing lance. He then cuts off his head and puts it in his horse's food-trough. Triumphantly he returns with his opponent's horse.

Other tests follow, until at last the King of Ledyen demands that Dushan shall choose the princess Roksanda from three equally beautiful girls. Who could possibly do this? Even the tsar's envoy, who had seen the girl only once before and who had been able to admire her beauty at a perfunctory glance in the mere light of a sparkling ring without obtaining a clear picture of her, is unable to make the right choice from the three maidens. Again it is Milosh who undertakes the task and carries it out. His eye is keen: once when he was guarding twelve thousand sheep, three hundred lambs were born in one night, but he was able to tell with each lamb which mother had borne it. When Milosh faces the three girls who are dressed alike, he quickly casts off bonnet and shepherd's cloak and stands before them in the splendour of his gold cuirass and scarlet velvet. He spreads his cloak on the grass and throws rings, pearls, and precious stones on it. He then draws his sword and says that Roksanda, and no other, will pick up the jewels; if either of the other girls should do so he will cut off both her hands, right up to the elbow. The girls hesitate and look at Roksanda who is standing in the middle. She takes up her silk train and begins to gather up the rings and pearls from the cloak. Milosh then takes the three girls to Dushan, who returns to his own country without taking leave of the King of Ledyen. Roksanda's father sends the mightiest of his heroes with six hundred cuirassiers after them, but Milosh has the courage to attack the champion in spite of the fact that he has three heads; one of these spouts a blue flame and the other blows an ice-cold wind. With a gentle blow of his cudgel he lifts the giant out of the saddle, he fixes him firmly to the ground with his lance, cuts off the three heads with his sword and puts them in his provision bag. Dushan thanks him and gives him a thousand ducats. When the procession on the Kossovo plain passes the castle of the two Voinovitch, he takes leave of the tsar, who recognizes him at last, and asks him why he did not at once show himself in his true character. The final moral is: woe to him who underestimates his own blood-relations.[1]

A poem like this is truly epic in spirit, even if in comparison with West-European poems it is perhaps, to some extent, more strongly

[1] See W. M. Petrowitsh, *Heldensagen en Legenden van de Serviërs*, Zutphen 1921.

romantic in character. But the later Middle High German and French poems have that too. It should be remembered that the South-Slav poems arose when West-European heroic epic poetry was already on the decline, and the Slav songs continued to live in the oral tradition of the people. But the same people also knew legends and fairy-tales. Is it to be wondered at that motifs were borrowed from this international stock of short stories and were in fact received with particular eagerness?

Several of these fairy-tale motifs are found intact in the Serbian poems. There are the speaking horses, such as Šarac, Marko's horse. But then, did not Achilles' horses also speak? What is the borderline between an ordinary fairy-tale motif and what we may consider to be a typical mythical feature? Birds speak too: a common motif are the ravens that pass on messages. But the titmice likewise spoke to Sigurd after his fight with the dragon Fafnir, to warn him against the evil intentions of the dwarf Regin. It is difficult to see in these motifs the influence of fairy-tale literature only. It can be said that the fairy-tale actually uses the motifs that formerly belonged to the myth.

This South-Slav poetry is typically heroic, inasmuch as among the people it is felt to be the great example of a noble warrior's life. The heroes are not there to amuse themselves with adventures, but to show to posterity how they behaved in dangerous moments in life. A remarkable example of this is an incident in the Balkan War. In November 1912 a Serbian army advanced towards Prilep, the castle of Marko Kraljevitch, which was then occupied by a strong Turkish army. The general ordered the infantry not to proceed to the attack before the Turkish guns had been silenced. But the troops, moved by a sudden urge, did not heed this command. They made a violent attack and conquered the castle. After the victory the general addressed his troops and said that, although they had gained the victory, their independent action might have had fatal results. Then the thousands of soldiers cried out that Marko Kraljevitch himself had led them to victory: 'Did you not see him on his Šarac?' So these soldiers had the same experience that occurred so often in ancient Greece when troops thought that the Dioscuri on their snorting horses led them against the enemy. We can learn from this example that a hero is a living reality who is really believed in, and who can indeed reveal himself.[1]

This heroic character of Serbian epic poetry can justifiably be placed beside the Greek or Old French poems. It is therefore very fortunate that it can be established precisely how the singers sang these poems and even how original poets added new ones. But this will be dealt with more closely in Chapter 8.

Finally, we will discuss the question why it is that no great epic has ever arisen out of this flourishing popular tradition. It should be noted, however, that the poetry of the South Slavs has progressed further on this road than that of the Russians.

Serbian songs can sometimes contain as many as 4,000 lines, and so are longer than *Beowulf* and more than twice as long as the *Waltharius*. Heusler's theory of expansion is proved by this up to a point; the larger size is determined by the greater elaboration of the descriptive parts which can then be varied with the aid of fixed formulae. The long poems, some of them requiring a delivery of from three to five hours, occur especially among the Mohammedan singers, and perhaps this greater elaboration may be explained by the Oriental preference for colourful detail, which works such as the *Arabian Nights* also show in such abundance.

Moreover, attention should also be given to the environment in which the poem is delivered. In the beginning it must have been recited, as everywhere else, by minstrels in the service of feudal lords at their courts. But later, just as in the case of the Russian poetry discussed above, it descended to the broad mass of the people. Now it is chiefly shepherds and peasants who play the part of singers, and it is certainly not accidental that in the poem of Dushan's wedding mentioned above the hero appears disguised as a shepherd.

Wherever we encounter the great epic we also find the great poet who lived in and worked for a more or less aristocratic milieu. That was the case with Homer, and with the poet of the *Nibelungenlied*. This is another indication that a poem like the *Chanson de Roland* is not the work of a travelling *jongleur* choosing the hosts of pilgrims for his audience. The older and surely thoroughly heroic form of

[1] See Petrowitsh, note on p. 71.

the *Song of Roland* presupposes just as much an audience that could be found only in the castles of the feudal lords at the time.

There is, however, a *kairos* for all things: the moment that is favourable for creative action. If this is allowed to pass by, no epic can arise. Sometimes one feels that the great epic is itself really the product of a second flowering. When the epic tradition is dying out, at the last moment a poet appears who gives it its great and lasting form. The epic testifies to a nostalgia, a longing for a time that is gone irrevocably. Thus, out of a misty, remote, distant past the heroic figure seems to rise up once more, to be fixed forever by the poet's words.

7

THE EPIC POETRY OF
NON-INDO-EUROPEAN NATIONS

EPIC poetry has not been the exclusive property of the Indo-European nations by any means. We have treated this poetry first of all and in particular, because it is part and parcel of our Western civilization. But this kind of poetry can arise at any time in any nation, given that a certain form of culture has evolved. This form of culture is usually indicated by the name of 'heroic age'.[1] We shall discuss later what is meant by this; here the hint may suffice that it appears linked up almost everywhere with feudal knighthood.

Of the epic poetry of the nations that do not belong to the Indo-European family only a few examples will be given. In the course of our discussion we shall meet with the people of Mesopotamia, the Finns and Tartars, the Negro tribes of Africa, and the New Zealanders. But our choice is, of necessity, arbitrary, and much will be left unnoticed by the wayside.

According to time and chronology the Babylonians certainly deserve to have priority. Excavations made in the middle of the nineteenth century near Nineveh have revealed tablets in the library of Assurbanipal (669 to 628 B.C.), on which the text is noted down of the poem that has the hero Gilgamesh as its main character. But we know much older versions of it, and the story goes back to Sumerian times. Moreover the poem was widely known among neighbouring nations also, for there are texts written in Assyrian, Hittite, and Hurrian. The latter two languages were spoken in Asia Minor. The last-mentioned texts go back to a period between 1600 and 1250 B.C., so that they are even older than the fall of Troy, which for Westerners lies at the beginning of all epic tradition.

[1] The name is commonly used in England, and Chadwick used it as the title of a book.

It is therefore not at all impossible that this Babylonian epic poetry spread from Asia Minor, which was in so many respects fruitful for culture, to the West, and eventually reached the pre-Hellenic peoples in whose midst the later Greek heroic legends arose.

In the town of Uruk, the poem tells us, there lived once upon a time the hero Gilgamesh, whose nature was two-thirds divine. He ruled over the town with a rod of iron, so that the population prayed to heaven to be delivered from him. The god of heaven commanded the goddess Aruru to create a being that would be equal to him in strength. She created the monster Enkidu, who was half human, half animal, covered in long hairs and living on grass and herbs. A hunter encountered it and told Gilgamesh about it. He advised him (which testifies to his human insight) to take a *hetaera* to the monster, who really succeeded in catching the monster Enkidu in the snares of lust.

This was Enkidu's downfall. From this moment he can no longer live with the animals in the wilderness; he goes to the luxurious town of Uruk with the harlot. Meanwhile Gilgamesh has been warned in a dream that Enkidu will come.[1] After Enkidu has transformed himself into a civilized creature, anointed and shaved, dressed and armed, he challenges Gilgamesh to a duel. They prove each other's equal in strength, and after the fight ends in a draw they become firm friends.

Then follows the story of how they set out together to seek the giant Chumbaba in the far West. They succeed in killing him. On their return to Uruk, where they are to make a triumphal entry, Istar, the goddess of love, appears to Gilgamesh, offers him her love and promises him fertile land and cattle in return.

But Gilgamesh rejects this. The hero, who previously had not left any girl in Uruk in peace, now turns out to be chastened. Unlike Enkidu, who had succumbed to a *hetaera*, Gilgamesh resists the goddess of love herself. He reminds her of the many victims of her previous love affairs, the most atrocious example of which is the myth of Tammuz or Adonis. The goddess is angered at his

---

[1] This dream is more than a thousand years older than the pieces from the library of Assurbanipal (see Böhl, p. 22).

scorn and invokes the help of the heavenly father Anu, who sends the heavenly bull down to earth to scorch all vegetation. Gilgamesh, accompanied by Enkidu, comes to the rescue, and together they manage to kill the bull.

The following night, Enkidu has a dream in which he hears his death foretold. When death does come to him, Gilgamesh is inconsolable. He has seen death close to him and is overcome by fear of his own death. He decides to gain eternal life in the underworld, where Utanapishtim, the hero who was the only one to be rescued from the Flood, now rules over the realm of the dead. Gilgamesh sails across the ocean in a boat to the island where his grandfather lives. But the latter impresses upon him the inexorability of human fate:

> Grim death is adamant.
> Should we always build houses?
> Should we always write records?
> Should brothers always share the inheritance?
> Is there always hatred of the enemy?
> Shall the flood of rivers always rise and bring
> Butterflies and dragon-flies reflecting in the water?
> Nothing was ever destined to last.

Utanapishtim then tells him the story of the Flood, which is certainly the prototype of the almost similar story in *Genesis*. Here too an ark is built for the relatives of the Babylonian Noah and the animals. Here too birds are sent out to reconnoitre the land that rises up out of the falling waters; dove and swallow return without any result, but the raven finds land and stays away. The god Ea decides to give immortality to Utanapishtim. But how will Gilgamesh attain it, the weak man who is overpowered even by sleep? In his dream he sees his whole life pass by, and when he awakes he has become an old man. He has indeed slept through his whole life. Then he is taken to the well of rejuvenation out of which he rises twice as glorious. Down below in the well there grows the herb of life and he manages to take a twig of it. But on the way back a serpent, the ancient enemy of men, deprives him of the twig in his sleep: the serpent has attained eternal life, immortality is not destined for man. The ferry-man of death ferries him to the other side, back to the land of mortals. Once more Gilgamesh raises the shade of Enkidu from the realm of the dead and once more the friends are allowed to embrace. The poem ends with a series of questions and answers about the law of the realm of the dead:

> Whose body was thrown on the field,
> Did you see? Yes, I saw:
> His shade finds no rest below.
> Whose shade is not attended to,
> Did you see? Yes, I saw:
> With the remainders from the cooking-pot,
> And pieces thrown in the street
> He has to feed himself . . .

It is a mighty poem in which fundamental problems like the life of man and the world are thrashed out. The rise of civilization, the Flood, the question of death and immortality are the main motifs that centre round the figure of Gilgamesh. Is this really an heroic epic? Should one not rather think of it as a myth? At any rate, it is a story in which mythical elements play an important part. But a closer study of the contents brings one to the conclusion that the poem fully deserves the name of heroic epic. It is the song of a hero whose life we survey from the beginning with all his deeds and adventures. One need only place beside it the legend of Hercules to realize this completely. Like Gilgamesh, he also fights with monsters. He descends into the underworld and fetters the hell-hound Cerberus. Orpheus visited the underworld in order to regain his beloved Eurydice; he was given permission to take her back. Gilgamesh likewise gathers the herb of life and with it he too probably expected to release his friend Enkidu from death. But victory over death is impossible for man. Eurydice turns away from Orpheus back to the underworld; the serpent deprives Gilgamesh of the herb of life.

There is, then, no reason at all to deny Gilgamesh the character of a true hero simply because mythical elements occur in his story. To a certain extent that is also the case in the Homeric poems, although there they are of a different nature. We shall see later how closely related myth and epic are in their origin.

But the epic of *Gilgamesh* is extremely important, because it contains so many themes that are also found repeatedly in the literature of the West. We have mentioned the Flood and the expedition to the underworld. There is, in addition, the well of rejuvenation. A man living through the whole of his life in a dream so that he awakes as an old man is a very common motif in the literature of the West: one need only mention the medieval story of the monk Felix. The representation of sleep and death as brothers can be found here. Again, the immortality of the serpent that sheds his skin and then begins a new life is also known to the West. The scorning of the love of a goddess with the resulting punishment is also known from Greek heroic legend. From the epic of Gilgamesh there emerges a stream of motifs that poured over the whole world. In it we find an unbroken cultural stream which flowed from the Sumerians via the Babylonians to the Near East, from there to Asia Minor and the Aegean Sea, found its outlet in the civilizations of Crete and Mycenae, and from there fertilized the whole of the West through Greek civilization.

The characteristic features of epic style are already visible in the Babylonian epic. Among these is the variation of one thought in two parallel verse lines, a stylistic feature that also occurs in Hebrew poetry. Likewise we find the fixed form of sentence and formulae. On the way to Chumbaba we read:

> Every two hundred miles they ate a morsel,
> Every three hundred miles they took a rest.

This is a peculiarity of style that we also found in Slav poetry and which we shall presently find again in Finnish epic poetry. I have the impression that as a stylistic feature it is particularly suited to Oriental taste. Its function will be discussed later.

Gilgamesh is not the only epic preserved in the ancient East. Among the surprisingly rich texts that have come down from the Hittites, and which were excavated in Boghazköi, there are also epic songs, such as that of the stone giant Ullikummi or of the young Kessi. Considerations of space do not allow us to give even a brief summary of these,[1] so the epic of *Gilgamesh* must suffice to give an impression of the rich treasure of epic poetry that flourished in the East thousands of years before the beginning of our era.

The epic poetry of the Finns has become universally famous through the *Kalevala*, so much so that Longfellow adopted its metre and style for his poem *Hiawatha*. But the *Kalevala* is not an epic in the usual sense of the word; it was only made at the beginning of the nineteenth century by the poet-scholar Lönnrot.

Lönnrot was a folklorist, who set himself the task of collecting the older poetry of the Finns, in particular the epic songs or *runot*. On his travels he collected an enormous quantity of material, especially in Karelia. What he noted down, however, were mainly short songs, the singers of which sometimes did not even remember their full contents. But they fascinated him very much, and he saw a connexion between the various songs that used the same characters. He was convinced that the poems which he noted down were really the fragments of a disintegrated epic. Once this thought had taken possession of him he was not able to rid himself of it, and he felt the desire to give that lost epic back to his people. In 1835 he submitted to the Finnish public a poem consisting of 32 *runot* and comprising 12,078 lines. By 1849 it had become almost twice as long: 40 *runot* and a total of 22,793 lines. This epic is thus considerably longer than the *Iliad*.

Lönnrot was too conscientious a scholar to wipe out all the traces of his work; he even gave some examples of the texts he had collected in an appendix, and he carefully preserved all his manuscript material, which is now in the Folklore Record Office in Helsinki. We can therefore follow his work closely. It appears, as was to be expected, that he took large sections of genuine folk-poetry as the basis of his work. But he tried to combine separate songs into a consecutive whole and to fill them in with other fragments where there were gaps. More than once he was even compelled to add a linking passage of his own. But he had become so familiar with the

---

[1] An extensive table of contents of this epic poetry is to be found in Th. M. Gaster, *Les plus anciens Contes de l'Humanité, Mythes et Légendes d'il y a 3500 ans (Babyloniens, Hittites, Cananéens) récemment déchiffrés et avec des commentaires*, Paris 1953.

Kalevala that his own passages compare not unfavourably with the 'genuine' sections.

The *Kalevala* aroused enormous enthusiasm. The time of its appearance has to be taken into account. In 1809 Finland, which up to then had belonged to the Swedish Crown, was ceded to Russia. At first the Finnish nation still had a semblance of sovereignty, but it was not long before the Russian government proceeded to adopt a policy of ruthless Russification, which can only be called a reign of terror. The *Kalevala* appeared as a shining light in the darkness, the symbol of Finnish spiritual independence and originality. A genuine older literature had never developed there, as the leaders of society were accustomed to speaking Swedish and certainly to writing it. But a nation starts its literary existence with an heroic epic, and here it appeared as the promise of a new awakening. Thus Lönnrot's work was a national deed of far-reaching importance.

Yet the scholar who studies the *runot* would like something that is different from the personal creation of an ardent collector. Although the *Kalevala* was a beautiful and precious treasure, although it really gave an idea of popular poetry, if the *runot* that had come down really were the fragments of a large and connected epic, then Finland would stand in the front row of nations, for even the Greeks had not produced such a poem. Or was the plan to which the *Kalevala* was composed invented by Lönnrot; and could a popular poet in the past never have had any suspicion of the interconnexion of the whole?

Meanwhile the *Kalevala* had become too much a matter of national importance for these somewhat painful questions to be passed by in silence. While the doubtful expressed their opinion cautiously, those who wanted to defend Lönnrot's conception set to work to prove it anew. Men began again and ever more intensively to note down the *runot* from the mouths of the people, in the expectation that new finds would prove that Lönnrot's creation was indeed the popular epic of the Finns. As one could have foreseen, this expectation was not realized. The *runot* increased, but no reciters turned up anywhere who really knew connected pieces of the *Kalevala*, let alone the poem as a whole. Was it then really too late and was nothing left but the shards of a vase broken long ago?

The passion for collecting has at least resulted in the manuscript material in the Folklore Record Office growing to a volume which no other country in the world can even remotely approach in the field of folklore. The Finns even proceeded to publish all this material, and after the Second World War the publication was finished in an edition of 33 quarto-volumes which contain 85,000 *runo* variants, comprising 1,270,000 lines.

Thus the material is now available with which a history of Finnish popular epic poetry can be written and with which the work of the Finnish Homer can also be assessed. The best present-day expert, Martti Haavio, has sketched the personality of Lönnrot and his work in the following way:[1] 'The collaboration between Elias Lönnrot and the *runo* singers was remarkably successful. In the pages of the *Kalevala* many singers live on, but in them the modest, gentle spirit of Lönnrot prevails. The last great *runo* singer, surpassing all previous ones in genius and extent of material, combines all the trends of the *Kalevala* in accordance with his own nature. He had absorbed the whole of Finnish folk-poetry in his mind; he was able to see it as a whole; and on the basis of this knowledge he created a masterpiece of art by arranging the available material and combining it like the different parts of a fabric. He has been called a great literary landscape gardener.

'Generations have already enjoyed the beauty of the *Kalevala*, the epic which was built up into a unity by the organizing hand of Lönnrot out of parts which from the outset never belonged together. We have enjoyed the capriciously arched lines, the richness, the gentle force, the epic abundance, but especially the lyrical, tender dreaminess that Lönnrot produced out of his own poetic nature. When in the place of this we sense the beauty of those small works of art, those relatively short original *runot*, those glistening fragments out of which Lönnrot put together his great composition, we may perhaps feel cheated. In any case it has to be stated again: those *runot* genuine in their structure that are found in the store-room of variants are at heart simple and meagre, often hard, often masculine, but at times also of a maidenly tenderness—but like archaic sculptures in which a stiffness begins to move. If our mind is adapted accordingly,

[1] Cf. *Kirjokansi ,Suomen Kansan Kertomarunoutta*, Helsinki 1952, p. 9.

we can enjoy them: their strangely distant beauty overpowers us.'

Lönnrot could not be presented with a more beautiful testimony. He was after all a poet, the last and greatest of all the Finnish popular poets. And with his ability to identify himself entirely with the poetry of his people, we believe that he struck the right note and that an exceptionally gifted national poet would probably have done much the same.

For an appreciation of Finnish epic poetry we naturally have to go back to the genuine popular poetry itself. It is obvious that Lönnrot has combined heterogeneous poems and that he has not always been able to smoothe out the resulting unevenness. The main theme may be taken to be the life and deeds of old Väinämöinen. He is indeed old, for he was born immediately after the creation of the earth. Then he finds the corn, six grains, which he sows while singing a charm. After that, young Youkahainen comes from Lapland and challenges him, and Väinämöinen lays a curse on him by singing:

> Changed his runners into saplings,
> And to willows changed the collar,
> And the reins he turned to alder,
> And he sang the sledge all gilded,
> To the lake among the rushes,
> And the whip, with beads embellished,
> To a reed upon the water.[1]

In order to free himself from this spell, Youkahainen humbles himself before the old man and promises him his sister Aino as wife. But when the girl sees the old man who desires her, the will to live fails her and she drowns herself in the lake.

Then Väinämöinen asks the way to the realm of Ahto. On the way he goes fishing, and the fish that he catches confesses to him that she is no perch or salmon but Youkahainen's youngest sister. Deeply shocked the old man goes on, but his mother calls out to him from her grave that he must choose a wife from the beautiful

---

[1] Quotations from the *Kalevala* are from W. F. Kirby's translation: *Kalevala*, Everyman's Library.

maidens of Pohja or Pohjola, the land in the North. After Väinämöinen has tossed on the open sea for eight days and nights, an eagle from Lapland comes flying along and takes him on his wings to Pohjola.

But the Mistress of Pohjola demands of the hero that he shall earn his wife. She will only accept as son-in-law the man who forges the Sampo for her from the tip of a swan's feather, from a drop of a heifer's milk, from one single barleycorn, and from one single tuft of sheep's wool. The maiden herself sets him other impossible tasks, and when he cuts his knee while felling trees, he decides to give up and go away. After an intermezzo which contains the magic formula of the origin of iron, he goes to the smith Ilmarinen who does manage to forge the strange object, the Sampo with the many-coloured lid, which like a mill of fortune can grind corn, salt, or money just as is desired.

Väinämöinen now decides to make an expedition to Tuonela, i.e. the underworld, because he needs three magic words to finish a boat. He has a narrow escape from the nets that Tuoni's son has spread for him. But he does not obtain the three words and he therefore goes to the magician Antero Vipunen, who swallows him, just as the whale once swallowed Jonah. But when the hero scratches the monster's bowels with his knife, Vipunen sings all his magic songs and so Väinämöinen learns the three words.

The boat can now be finished and, with Ilmarinen, he again sets out for dark Pohjola. Ilmarinen has the good fortune to win the daughter Annikki as his bride. The wedding-banquet is described in detail. It is obviously a favourite song that was recited at wedding-feasts, as is evident especially from the long and tearful farewell the bride takes of her parents' home. The wise counsels given to the young wife who will have to adapt herself to her new surroundings with her parents-in-law are also remarkable.

After another long intermezzo, in which other legendary matter appears (namely that of Lemminkäinen and of Kullervo), we learn that after the death of his wife Ilmarinen forges himself a bride of gold. But when Väinämöinen scorns this work of art, because a living girl is much to be preferred, Ilmarinen again goes to Pohjola to make an offer of marriage. But this time he is rejected.

Now he invokes the help of Väinämöinen who accompanies him on another expedition, the object of which is to revenge this rejection by stealing the Sampo. With great difficulty they manage to secure the wondrous object. But when the mistress of Pohjola wakes up and misses her precious object, she pursues the heroes, transforms herself into an eagle, and makes a fierce attack on the boat; with the result that the Sampo is smashed and drops into the water.

> Thence there springs the water's riches,
> And the wealth of Ahto's people.
> Nevermore in all his lifetime,
> While the golden moon is shining,
> Shall the wealth of Ahto fail him,
> Neither shall his watery honours.

Väinämöinen takes the pieces of the Sampo to the mythical peninsula so that they can provide much rye-bread and an abundance of barley-brew there.

After the description of how the old and wise Väinämöinen constructs his new *kantele*, a musical instrument, comes the story of his wonderful playing. The sun and the moon are tempted into leaving their places in the sky and sit down on a tree-top, but that gives the evil Louhi, the mistress of Pohjola, the opportunity to steal them and hide them in a granite rock. The god of heaven perceives the disaster and strikes a new flame which he entrusts to the care of the maiden of heaven, so that a new sun and a new moon shall grow from it. The maiden rocks the young flame in a golden cradle on the edge of a cloud. But Väinämöinen sets out to take possession of the flame, which meanwhile has escaped from the maiden, burned large areas to ashes, and fallen in the Alue lake where a blue trout has swallowed it. With Ilmarinen he manages to catch the fish, and finally to banish the flame, shooting out of the trout in full strength, into a little fungus of a birch. There remains the task of freeing the sun and the moon from the power of Pohjola, and, with a hymn of praise to the freed celestial bodies, the story of Väinämöinen comes to an end.

It is not necessary here to relate in full the episodic stories of Lemminkäinen and Kullervo, although the former especially is of great interest. Here too the young enamoured hero goes to Pohjola to woo a maiden and, like Väinämöinen, he has to give proofs of his strength and courage. Now he possesses a great magic power so that nothing can injure him. But the old cowherd of Pohjola is equal to this and drives a hard reed-stalk right through Lemminkäinen's heart. His body is hacked in pieces and cast into the stream of Tuonela, the river of the underworld. His mother goes along the whole length of the river with a rake, collects the pieces and joins them together, but she cannot make the dead man speak. Then a bee fetches an ointment from heaven itself which she rubs on her son, and so brings him back to life again. Undoubtedly this story is more a myth than an heroic legend. One is reminded of the Norse god Balder who was killed by a twig of mistletoe, and of the moving Egyptian myth of Isis and Osiris.

We shall, then, confine ourselves to the story of Väinämöinen. The looseness of its structure is obvious. The many travels to Pohjola, undertaken not only by Väinämöinen but also by Lemminkäinen, look like variants of one and the same legendary motif. Some songs are nothing but magic incantations, such as those about the catching of the flame, or else wedding-songs inserted by Lönnrot where he thought he could find a suitable place for them. And in the midst of all this there stands the mysterious object, the Sampo, at times described as a mill, at times as a *kirjokansi* or many-coloured lid.

It was this description which seemed to fit the starry vault of heaven and so it was naturally taken to be a myth; the myth of the struggle between light and darkness, between good and evil. This conception was understandable in the age of romanticism which liked to take nature myths as the background to the old heroic legends. One need only compare the many attempts to see Siegfried as a sun-god. Now there are undoubtedly mythical elements in the *Kalevala*, and therefore it is not surprising that recently a Finnish scholar once more stressed the mythical character of the epic.[1]

Nineteenth-century realism demanded a different interpretation.

---

[1] Cf. Iivar Kemppinen, *Johdatus muinais-Suomalaisen Mytologiaan*, Helsinki 1957, who, however, does not support his view with convincing arguments, and moreover starts from the supposition that these mythical elements had come to Finland from the East *via* Byzantium.

The poetry of so many nations shows that, essentially, the hero of an epic is an historical figure. However much his adventures have been adorned by a lively imagination, they reflect, if vaguely, the deeds he once performed. If, then, this strange Väinämöinen was once a warrior, which historical figure are we to see in him? The Finnish scholar Kaarle Krohn gave an ingenious explanation of this. He tried to trace the historical background. His investigations led him to the following conclusion.[1] All the stories of the *Kalevala* reflect the Viking expeditions which Finnish pirates made in the Middle Ages along the shores of the Gulf of Bothnia and which even extended as far as the shores of the Mälar Lake.

At times a single name tempted him to far-reaching conclusions. He saw in such a name the keystone of his argument. Thus the name *Vuojola* occasionally occurs in the Sampo song and he recognized in it the word *Voijonmaa* with which the Finns are supposed to have meant the island Gotland. Sometimes, too, he used equivocal arguments, as in the explanation of the Sampo. It had already occurred to Lönnrot that the Sampo may have stood for the idol of the gods of the Bjarmians, a colourful picture of which is given in more or less fantastic Norse sagas of Vikings who went to the White Sea for trading purposes. But when we think of the definitions 'colourful lid' and 'mill' we can hardly find these applicable to an idol carved in wood. But Kaarle Krohn took over Lönnrot's idea and made an important alteration to it: according to him the Sampo was a holy object not of the still very primitive Bjarmians, but of the North Germanic nations. For it is well known that on either side of the main seat in the hall there were two pillars which were cut into an effigy of the god Thor on the upper part; they were in fact so sacred that the Norse emigrants to Iceland took these pillars with them and cast them into the sea near the shore: where they were washed ashore Thor wanted them to settle. Now Finnish Vikings were supposed to have stolen such pillars on Gotland; it is difficult to see what kind of treasure they thought they had won, and why in Finnish poetry such a find should have been preserved as a precious object and then described in such a strange way as the Sampo.

[1] See his book *Kalevalankysymyksiä*, Helsinki 1918, translated but much revised as *Kalevalastudien*, in *FFCommunication* Nos. 53, 67, 71, 72, 75, and 76, Helsinki 1924-8.

measuring each other's strength by trying to push each other over: a well-known game of the farmers at the Yule feast. No wonder they try their hardest to pull their opponent to and fro in order to make him lose his balance. With a nonchalance hardly to be expected from an author of travel-stories who is able, moreover, to illustrate his own text, Skjöldebrand concluded that this picture, which illustrates a popular custom well known to him from his own country, showed how the Finnish *laulajat* recited their poems. But surely the strangest thing of all is that this book had such a success that Finnish scholars supposed this picture to be a faithful illustration of the recitation of the *runot*, in spite of the fact that they must have known better from their own observations. The power of the printed word is great. Even if it was no longer done in this way, the book proved how it really ought to be done; or at least was still done in the eighteenth century. The result was that the singers themselves adopted this form of delivery and so, to this day, recite in the attitude of the wrestling lads, without of course taking over the violence of their movements.[1]

This view, however, did not remain uncontested. It has been pointed out that Old Norse literature also has examples of such a way of reciting, but they occur in dreams. Somebody sees in his dream that two men dressed in black are holding each other's hands and rocking to and fro while singing a song. Elsewhere the same is told about two bleeding women. It is clear that we are involved with magic songs here, and perhaps the singing of the Finnish *runot* is originally based upon the recitation of magic incantations as well.[2]

What Elias Lönnrot was for Finland, Friedrich Reinhold Kreutzwald became for Estonia. Rittmetsän Widri, whose name was adapted in German while he was at school, was helped by F. K. Fählmann in collecting the popular poetry of his people. But when he saw Lönnrot's work with the Finnish *runot*, he realized that he owed it to his people to act in the same way; he too noted down fragments

---

[1] This has been set out very well in an investigation by Elsa Enäjärvi-Haavio, published in 1949 under the title 'Pankame Käsi Kätehen'.

[2] Cf. A. O. Väisänen in *Kalavalan Vuosikirja* (1949) and Stefan Einarsson, *Budkavlan* (1951), pp. 24-29.

which he wanted to combine into one large whole, and so create an epic. Thus he became the founder of Estonian literature. In 1857 he published the *Kalewipoëg*, or 'The son of Kalev', an heroic song in twenty cantos, comprising 18,993 lines.[1] There is no doubt that as a poet Kreutzwald is much inferior to Lönnrot, and his epic shows the same lack of inner cohesion. But it remains to his great credit that he not only undertook the noting down of Estonian songs, but also made a valuable present of them to his people. The collecting of these songs was later continued in a scholarly way by Jakob Hurt and Oskar Kallas, who succeeded in bringing together the respectable total of 75,000 variants.

We now turn to the Turkish tribes that live in the steppes of Central Asia. Among these livestock-breeders who lead a largely nomadic life we also find heroic epic poetry flourishing richly. The Kara-Kirghiz are outstanding in this respect. They live in the neighbour-hood of the lake of Istyk-Kül. They are so-called Mohammedans, but what they know of Islam is so little and so superficial that they can safely be considered as adherents to a primitive shamanistic belief. Their epic poetry shows a good deal of independence; the subject-matter belongs to their own history; the heroes are figures from their own past. But in its form this heroic poetry does not entirely correspond to the original Turkish form, which used ornament, alliteration and middle-rhyme. But under Persian influence end-rhyme, or at least assonance, came in. This is a development which can also be established in the Germanic field: the old epic metre used the alliterative line, but under the influence of Church poetry, and still more through Romance examples, the rhyming line took its place. But as far as the metre of the Turkish poems is con-cerned, they consist of short lines of three, or sometimes two, feet which are grouped together in an irregular manner by the same end-rhyme—i.e. entirely in the manner of the Old French *laisses*.

It seems to be inherent in the style of all epic poetry that it derives a particular lustre from fixed epithets, stereotyped lines, and groups of lines. The Kirghiz singers particularly like describing dress and frequently recurring situations with an abundance of words. When

[1] There is a French translation by Nora Randsep and Paul de Stoecklin, Paris 1930.

the beautiful maiden Ak Erkäch dresses herself to receive the hero
Alaman Bet we read:

> Ak Erkäch, the lovely maiden,
> Placed the finely decorated
> Gay head-dress on her head;
> Parted her hair on the right,
> Braided it on the right,
> Parted her hair on the left,
> Braided it on the left
> And she bound the golden ribbon
> To the end of the moon
> And she bound the silver ribbon
> To the end of the sun,
> Rocked sideways like a whelp,
> Whimpered like a pup,
> Laughing showed her teeth,
> Scattered odour with her breath,
> Frisked like a young lamb.
> Curls fell down upon her shoulders.
> Ak Erkäch, the prince's daughter,
> Went outside by the door.
> Alaman Bet, the powerful hero
> She went to meet half-way.[1]

Here we see once more with what obvious pleasure the audience
must have followed such elaborate descriptions, which to us are
merely fatiguing. It was in such details that the glorious heroic past
lived again in all its alluring splendour.

The greatest hero of the Kara-Kirghiz is Manas, with his retinue of
forty friends. Again we find that the typical representative of the
heroic age is what Tacitus mentions in the case of the Germanic
peoples: the *dux* with his *comitatus*; or what the *boyar* with his
druzhina was in the Russian bylinas. They form the nucleus round
which the colourful life of adventures can develop. The heroic songs
of Manas form a cycle and, with that, the starting point for a real epic
is provided. But this was never realized. These poems are separate

[1] Cf. V. V. Radloff, *Proben der Volksliteratur der türkischen Stämme und der Dsun-
garischen Steppe* v, Petersburg 1885, p. 38.

from each other; they tell of his birth, his youth, his struggle with Er Kökchö, his fights with the Kalmucks, his marriage, death, and funeral—even his reincarnation after death.

A characteristic fragment is the fight with the hero of the Uigurs, Er Kökchö. Old enmities probably form the basis of this heroic song, but as always in genuine epic poetry, they are presented as a purely personal conflict. Such a conflict need not even have a deeper meaning; it is sufficient that there are two heroes in the world, who will naturally have to measure each other's strength. In the Kirghiz song, too, the cause of the fight remains hidden. All that appears is that in the conflict Manas seeks the support of the 'White Tsar' of the Russians, probably a reflection of the part taken by the Russians in playing off one Turkish tribe against another.

Manas sets out to fight Er Kökchö in a duel. Here again the fight itself is preceded by a long introduction in which the heroes boast of their strength and courage and taunt each other. Examples of this from Western Europe, which we shall give later, will show that this was a common custom. The various successive fights are described in detail. In wrestling Manas is naturally the victor, but the hero of the Uigurs turns out to be clever in the use of more civilized weapons: he knows the flintlock and wants to try his luck with that. Manas handles this weapon so clumsily that he always misses the target; Er Kökchö laughs at him, and when he himself fires the flintlock, Manas is wounded and flees on horseback. Evidently the poet does not approve of modern fire-arms, to which even the greatest hero must fall a victim. But even if Er Kökchö, in a certain sense, uses a technique which does not belong to the old heroic fight he is still chivalrous enough to dismount and look for herbs with which to cure Manas's wound. Then Manas unexpectedly returns and treacherously kills Er Kökchö's horse. This falseness is certainly not praiseworthy, and one may well wonder at the flaw the singers have given their national hero. Perhaps ruse was valued higher among these Turkish tribes than open courage in the fight, or perhaps the poet considers the death of the horse to be well-deserved, because the Uigur had infringed the code of chivalrous fight with his gun.

We shall not pursue the epic poetry of the Turkish tribes further:

it also flourished among other tribes and reveals the same features everywhere.[1]

A remarkably rich store of heroic legends has been noted down among the Negro tribes in the Sudan. Leo Frobenius collected valuable material on his numerous travels. We shall take the epic poetry of the tribe of the Fulbe as an example.[2] It is customary among them for the knight to set out in quest of adventures accompanied by his singer, who is also his shield-bearer. The hero is indolent in his youth: a feature we also find in Germanic heroes; the boy seems good for nothing, a real *Ofenlieger* as they say in German fairy-tales, But suddenly his heroic nature awakes in him and he sets out to fight the dragon, and to conquer a princess and half a kingdom.

The role of the *mabo* or singer will be discussed in the next chapter. He is the witness of the heroic deeds of his lord. He celebrates them in an epic poem called *baudi*, in which he uses the conventional features of style that are common everywhere.

The tribe of the Soninke possesses a great book of heroes: the *Dausi*, in which the memory of a very distant past is crystallized. One can vaguely discern the traces of long wanderings that took the people from the shores of the Mediterranean to the Sahel. Their oldest kingdom attained great fame which even reached Herodotus.[3] Four times the kingdom of Wagadu glittered in power and splendour, but four times it also fell into ruin.

The heroic song *The Lute of Gassire* tells about this. Four times Wagadu stood glittering in the daylight before the eyes of the world; four times it was lost, so that people saw nothing: once through pride, once through breach of faith, once through greed, and once through discord. Four times Wagadu changed its name. First it was called Dierra, then Agada, then Ganna, and after that Silla. Four times Wagadu turned its face. Once it looked to the North, once to the West, once to the East, and once to the South. Those are the zones from which strength comes to Wagadu and to

[1] For a complete survey see Chadwick, *Growth of Literature* iii (1940), pp. 1–218. A supplementary study of the folk epic of Uzbekistan was published by W. Fleischer in *Paul und Braunes Beiträge* lxxx (1958), pp. 111–56.

[2] Cf. Leo Frobenius, 'Spielmannsgeschichten der Sahel' in *Atlantis* vi, Jena 1921.

[3] For further particulars see ch. 10.

which it is withdrawn, or which lives only as a shadow in the minds and the desires of its children. For Wagadu itself does not consist of stone, nor of wood, nor of clay. Wagadu is the strength that lives in the hearts of men and is observed at one time, because the eyes reveal it, because the ears hear the blows of swords and the clashing of shields, and invisible at another time because it has fallen asleep tired and vexed by the untameableness of men.

The first time Wagadu was lost through pride. There was a continuous war against the Burdama. King Nganamba was very old. The heart of his son Gassire was eaten up by the desire to become king himself. He sets out to perform heroic deeds. Once he hears a partridge sing: 'All creatures must die. But the Dausi, the song of my fights, will never die.' Now Gassire also wants to know the Dausi and he orders an artisan to make him a lute. But it makes no sound. The smith then says: 'This lute is made of wood. It cannot sing if it has no heart. You must give it its heart. The wood must go into battle on your back. The wood must suck up the trickling blood, blood of your blood, breath of your breath. Your grief must become its grief, your fame its fame. It must live not only with you but with your sons. Then the sound that comes from your heart will ring in the ears of your son, and the blood that wells from his heart will pour down upon your body and live on in this wood. Wagadu, however, will perish from all this.'

Then Gassire with his son goes to war, with the lute on his back. His eldest son is killed and he carries the body on his shoulders. The blood from the heart of his eldest son trickles upon the lute. Seven more times this happens with his other sons. But then the men force him to go away with his cattle. He is too much given to fighting. 'We men,' they say, 'long more for life than for fame.'

Then Gassire goes away with his youngest son, his wives, and his friends from the old kingdom of Wagadu to the Sahel. One night a voice awakens him which seems to sound as though it comes out of his own innermost heart. He hears the lute sing. It sings the Dausi. At this first song of the lute, King Nganamba dies, Gassire's wrath has gone, and Wagadu has perished for the first time. 'Ho Dierra, Agada, Ganna, Silla!—Ho Fasa!'

Every time Wagadu perished through the fault of men, it regained a new beauty, which was made even greater by its next splendour. Pride brought with it the song of the bards which all nations imitate and praise even to the present day. The breach of faith gave men a rain of gold and pearls made of stone. Greed gave them the art of writing as it is still used in Burdana and which in Wagadu was the art of women. Discord, however, will give to the fifth Wagadu the gift of being as everlasting as the rain from the South and the rocks of the Sahara, because then every man will have Wagadu in his heart and every woman Wagadu in her womb. 'Ho Dierra, Agada, Ganna, Silla!—Ho Fasa!'

Another song recorded by Frobenius, *The Rediscovery of Wagadu*, begins as follows: The first time Wagadu was lost for seven years. People could not remember where it lay. But later it was found again. After that it lay hidden once more for 740 years. Then there was a king who ill-treated his servants. Before his death he wanted to transfer his realm to his eldest son. He was blind, but he could recognize his son by his ring and his hairy arms. An old servant arranged however that the youngest son, who had always treated him well, should cover himself with a goat-skin and borrow his eldest brother's ring. The father was deceived by this and gave his youngest son advice which enabled him to obtain followers among men and to understand the language of animals and spirits. Then he had to find the kettle-drum of war, Tabele, which the Djinns had stolen; every time on his expedition he was sent on to older creatures and at last to a vulture that brought him the Tabele.

Then the legend tells of Mamadi whose beloved can only be won when the hero brings her the dragon Bida. He manages to kill the dragon, but it pronounces a curse: may Wagadu remain without rain of gold for seven years, seven months, and seven days. He then flees, his nephew has to pursue him, but he lets him escape by means of a trick, so that he comes to the town of his mother.

The girl, whose love he has now earned, wants to leave him, but her love is rekindled through a charm. Mamadi avenges himself by making a young slave sleep with her on the first night. When she discovers this she dies of shame.

No more words are needed to show that with this story we are moving among the peaks of genuine heroic poetry. A Biblical story, a fairy-tale motif, may be inserted, but does not disturb the exalted course of the tale. On the contrary, it adapts itself naturally to the rest of the legend. It is itself raised to an epic level. Genuine heroic poetry seems to possess the philosopher's stone which turns everything into gold.

If we now add a few words about the songs of Maui, the hero of the Maori, which are spread over Samoa, Hawaii, Tahiti, and Rarotonga, we do so because they tell us of the deeds of a mythical hero in primeval times.

Maui lives on raw food. His goddess-mother visits him, but she refuses to eat his food and eats from her own food-basket. Maui discovers that her food has been cooked and he now decides to learn the secret of fire. When his mother leaves him he follows her without being seen. On the way, she splits a black rock by pronouncing a magic formula: he commits it to memory. He now comes to the god Tane, whom he asks for the red dove Akaotu, whose name means 'fearless'. With this dove he goes to the underworld, and transforms himself for this purpose into a small dragon-fly. Thus disguised, he settles upon the dove. The demons of the underworld chasm through which he has to fly try to seize the dove but only get hold of its tail.

When he arrives in the underworld Maui resumes his human shape and visits his mother's house. She tells him that the secret of the fire is with Mauike the god of fire who lives in the house which is called Areaoa or the house of the banyan sticks. He asks the god for a burning piece of wood, which he extinguishes in a river. Then he asks for a second piece. But when he asks for a third, Mauike becomes angry and gives him some hot ashes on a dry bit of wood. Again Maui extinguishes it in water. Once more he goes to the god of fire who now chases him away. Maui then proposes to fight him, but the god tucks him into his fighting-belt. This does not prevent Maui from swelling to an enormous size. Mauike seizes him and throws him up in the air—as high up as a coconut palm. But Maui is not injured. Mauike again throws him even higher into the air. Then it is Maui's turn. He throws the god of fire up, catches him like a ball, and throws him up in the air again. Now the god has met his match, and has to ask for mercy. He teaches Maui the art of making fire by turning a stick in another piece of wood. Then Maui burns the god of fire with all his possessions and returns with the two 'fire-sticks'. When he has come back safely on the back of the dove, he returns the borrowed bird to Tane. Later he reveals his secret and commands men to sing the song of the god of fire when lighting a fire, so that they shall have luck in the use of the 'fire-sticks'.[1]

This song clearly has a magic function. It reminds us of the song of the *Kalevala* which tells how Väinämöinen obtained fire. Poems of this kind are called 'runes of origin' by the Finns, and they all imply that man cannot obtain power over the elements of nature until he knows how they were first forced into the service of man. In such stories there always appears a creature who is half god, and is usually called a 'culture hero'. He does not lack heroic character, as appears from the throwing match between Maui and Mauike. More important, however, is his knowledge of the magic formulae.

The motif of the bird flying through a narrow chasm and losing its tail reminds us of the Symplegades motif in the legend of the Argonauts. But fundamentally this legend too is really a myth,[2] and in many parts of the world the motif of the narrow gap through which a living man can hardly pass uninjured belongs to the image of the underworld.

[1] Cf. ch. 11.
[2] Cf. Wyatt Gill, *Myths and Songs from the South Pacific*, London 1876, pp. 51-57.

8

POETS AND RECITERS

THE Finnish scholar Martti Haavio[1] says in his discussion of the Finnish *runot* that it is our first duty to remember always that the creator of these poems was an individual poet. But he was a poet who worked on the basis of a general tradition, and his personal creation presently became part of this tradition and was transformed by it.

This is the subject that we will now discuss. What is the role of the creative artist of heroic epic poetry, and what is the significance of the popular tradition that precedes his work and absorbs it?

It is not easy to lay hands on the poet as a personality. Only when a work of art of great value has actually sprung from tradition can it happen that a name comes down to us. We have already come across the Indian poet Valmiki and the Greek Homer; but we also saw that the poets remain vague shadows. Medieval epic poetry is more sparing in mentioning the names of poets. The *Song of Roland* ends with the line: *Ci falt la geste que Turoldus declinet*, in which only the meaning of the proper name is clear unfortunately. For what is the meaning of the word *geste* in this context? It may be a Latin chronicle, e.g. the *geste Francor*, which itself mentions the poem; and even so one would have to assume that it cannot have been a source for the poet. But it may also mean the song itself, the French *chanson de geste*. And especially, what is the meaning of *declinet*? I shall not quote all the explanations that have been given of it, but shall merely mention what seems to me the most likely one: 'to elaborate poetically'. This would lead to the supposition that this Turoldus had a source in front of him, written in either Latin or the vernacular, and that he then either gave it its poetic form, or made a new poem of it in a more elaborate manner. In the search for a Turoldus who has come down to us in some writing or other,

[1] Cf. *Kirjokansi* (1952), pp. 211 ff.

a certain Turoldus de Fécamp was found, son or nephew of Otto of Bayeux, stepbrother of William the Conqueror.[1] He came over with William in 1066 and was later rewarded with the abbey of Malmesbury, which in 1079 he exchanged for that of Peterborough. He died in 1098. Could this nobleman and prelate have been the poet of the *Song of Roland*? How, then, can this Norman from Fécamp have given such a graphic description of the nature of the pass of Roncevaux? And does the poem with its loose verse structure and traditional epic style point to the work of a nobleman? This identification seems to me somewhat doubtful.

Although some of the names of poets who made *chansons de geste*[2] are known, the bulk of French epic poetry comes from poets who have remained anonymous. Germanic poetry is entirely anonymous. Neither the Eddic lays, *Beowulf,* or the German heroic epics reveal who their author was. The fact that we know the name of the poet of the *Waltharius* can hardly be considered an exception, as this is a formal Latin poem in which the young monk will have taken no little pride.

Why is all this literature anonymous? The poet of the *Nibelungenlied* can surely not have any real reason for remaining so modestly in the background, when in his own days a Gottfried of Strasbourg or a Wolfram von Eschenbach signed their work with their names. In France, Chrétien de Troyes or Thomas or Béroul did not conceal their names when they wrote about Tristan or Arthur's Round Table.

The actual poetical value of the work cannot have been the reason for the poets mentioning or concealing their names. The reason may well have been the nature of the work. The poet of an heroic epic had quite a different attitude towards his subject-matter from that of a Wolfram or a Chrétien. These men had the feeling, even if they had models in front of them, of creating an entirely new work. The man who gave the *Nibelungenlied* its final and most perfect shape knew very well that he was merely a link in the long chain of poets

---

[1] Cf. M. Delbouille, *Sur la genèse de la Chanson de Roland* (1954), p. 92.

[2] Such as Adenet le Roi as author of *Bertes aus grans piés*, and of the *Enfances Ogier*, Jean Bodel of *La Chanson des Saisnes*, and Raimbert de Paris who wrote the *Chevalerie Ogier*.

and reciters who had carried the legend through the centuries. One may therefore speak of a folk-epic if one bears in mind that it is not a spontaneous product of collective poetry-making, and that moreover (certainly in earlier times) the word 'people' meant something different from what it means today. Yet it is an epic of the people in the sense that the subject-matter, the legend, is actually the property of a popular tradition.[1] The death of Siegfried, the fall of the Burgundians, are told in the Eddic lays of the ninth century much the same way as in the German epic of about 1200. Who preserved this matter through the centuries if not an endless row of bearers of a common popular tradition, who sometimes did no more than communicate a text that they had learned by heart but who sometimes (with more or less talent) gave a new shape to a legend? *The Nibelungen* legend was put into alliterating Germanic poetry in the dim past, but the German poem made use of four-line stanzas with rhyme. This in itself presupposes that there must have been a period in which all epic poetry was given a new dress, namely, that of the triumphant rhymed verse.

When epic poetry as a living art of recitation enters our field of vision it has become the property of the people. The *jongleurs*, the minstrels, the rhapsodes, and the *skomorokhi* were reciters who recited old heroic songs in a manner that had long become stereotyped. But we shall see presently that they also played a creative part.

Heroic poetry, however, is originally an aristocratic art. It lives at the court of the nobility. Roland and Olivier were equal in rank to those who had their deeds recited to them. When in the Sudanese tribe of the Fulbe a nobleman went to war he sang, to the accompaniment of his guitar, of the heroic deeds of his ancestors, for thereby he showed what kind of a man he was himself and what obligations such a lineage imposed upon him. On the eve of the battle, we are told, the guitar went from hand to hand, so that each nobleman should be conscious of his duty towards himself and the others.[2]

The heroic song, therefore, has an important function in battle. There are numerous examples of this. Tradition has it that before

---

[1] See Otto Höfler, *Die Anonymität des Nibelungenliedes*, in *Deutsche Vierteljahrsschrift für Literaturwissenschaft und Geistesgeschichte* xxix (1955), pp. 167–213.

[2] See Leo Frobenius, *Atlantis* vi, p. 39.

describes what response such singing found in the hearts of the men:[1] 'The heart of the audience warms while listening to the songs, for in them is happiness and will-power. When the singing begins the hall is filled with *kleos* (fame): the great deeds of the past are conjured up and are present before the mind's eye; joy and strength at the same time. The hall fills with friends and relations; the dead as well as the living; the man who hears his own ancestor praised feels flattered: he knows that, when his own life and deeds sound in song and legend, he will not be dead. Indeed, when the family is praised in song the whole family is present.'

It is, then, anything but mere pastime. The heroic song has a very particular function in the lives of a warlike nobility. Cato tells us that in Rome it was customary (*mos*) that the participants of a banquet, one after the other, sang songs to the accompaniment of the flute, in which famous men were praised.[2] Later Varro mentions something similar: at the banquets boys sang old songs of ancestral deeds; sometimes a flautist accompanied them too.

The same holds true for the Germanic nations. When in 448 Priscus visited Attila, two barbarians (in this case certainly *Germani*) came forward and recited songs, which they themselves had made, about Attila's heroic deeds and victories.[3] *Beowulf* gives a colourful picture of the royal banquet where the singer is present. He may be a warrior, covered in glory, who recites not only the old legends but even improvises a song about the heroic deeds just performed by *Beowulf*.[4] At the court of the Scandinavian princes the *scald* must be present too: in ingeniously constructed songs he praises his lord; in the simple measure of the *Edda* he sings of the heroes of old.

Only very seldom does one come across a ruler who does not like to have minstrels perform at his banquet. This is sometimes mentioned with surprise and even disapproval: Theoderic II of the Visigoths, it is said, rarely allowed any minstrels at his table.[5] This evidence comes from the middle of the fifth century. Even worse is Louis the Pious who has been blamed, certainly unjustly, for ordering the destruction of the book of heroic songs made by his eminent

---

[1] Cf. *Hellas* i, *Adelstiden* (1942), p. 138.　　　[2] Cf. Cicero, *Tusc.* IV. ii. 3.

[3] Cf. K. Müller, *Fragmenta Historicorum Graecorum* iv, p. 92.

[4] Cf. *Beowulf*, ll. 867 ff.　　　[5] Cf. Sidonius Apollinaris, *Epist.* i. 2.

father. It is true that at a later age he despised the heathen song
that he had learned in his youth, and did not want to read or
hear them. But he was evidently a pious and serious-minded man;
when at a banquet everyone was laughing at the pranks of clowns
and jokers, he never revealed his white teeth in a smile.[1]

From Ireland we learn that it was customary in the *cuirmthech* or
beer-hall to listen to short stories and music in moderation.[2] This is
told in the wise lessons of Cormac. But things must often have been
more lively: when King Conchobar gives a feast, singing and
instrumental music are heard, narrative songs and songs of praise
are sung and precious objects are liberally distributed.[3]

When Firdausi tells us that Rustum (after his reconciliation with
King Kaus) partook of the banquet, he says:

> They drank from the wine-cups till midnight
> And sang the songs of the heroes of old.

Finally we mention the Serbians. At weddings and other feasts
heroic songs were always recited.[4] And where did the Russian
skomorokhi have a better and more appreciated opportunity to recite
their byliny that at such wedding feasts?

It should, however, be fully realized that the rulers themselves
also took part in this recitation. We already know that among the
African Fulbe, the noblemen sang the heroic deeds of their ancestors
before the battle. Well known is the story of the Vandal King
Gelimer. When he was besieged by the Heruli in 534 he asked the
enemy for harp, bread, and sponge: he was an experienced cither-
player and wished to sing of his misfortune in a song of lamentation.[5]

In early days, as we have seen in the case of Taillefer, the warrior
was a singer at the same time. In the oldest song of Guillaume
d'Orange we hear about his *jongleur*:

> En tote France n'ad si bon chanteür
> N'en la bataille plus hardi fereür.

---

[1] Cf. Theganus, *Vita Hludowici Imperatoris* 19.
[2] Cf. 'Teosca Cormaic', ed. by K. Meyer in *Todd Lecture Series* xv (1909), p. 11.
[3] See 'Mesca Ulad', in *Todd Lecture Series* i, 1 (1884), p. 12.
[4] Cf. M. Braun, in *Euphorion* xxxiv (1933), p. 342.
[5] Cf. Procopius, *Bellum Vand.* ii. 16.

And his repertory is not small: he can sing of Clovis, the first 'Emperor', of Flovent and Pippin, Charlemagne and Roland, Girard and Olivier, Raimbert de Paris, and Ogier le Danois.[1] Adenet le Roi says in his *Enfances Ogier* of the former *jongleurs* that their shields were their pride and their bow was the steel sword. We are reminded of the Volker of the *Nibelungenlied* who could 'fiddle' so dangerously with his sword, and we really never know of this minstrel whether he is a singer or one of the heroes in the Nibelung struggle. It is noteworthy that when Odysseus feels the bow in his hands, Homer uses the simile of the singer who takes up his lyre.[2]

That the noblemen themselves take up the lute to praise the heroic deeds of their ancestors proves clearly what these songs meant to them. The Old-French word *geste* not only means a story of remarkable events, but also of genealogy; this in itself shows that the heroic legend is to a large extent rooted in the history of the family. But it is obvious that this does not mean that the heroic song was not the song of the great noblemen only: again and again we hear of the professional singers, *jongleurs*, *minstrels*, *skomorokhi*, *dialli*.

In Greece a distinction was made between the *aoidoi* and the *rhapsodoi*. The former are considered to be the poets proper who themselves made an epic song and then, on their travels, recited it to the accompaniment of the lyre at the courts of the nobility. The rhapsode is really only the man who recites a song he has learned and who then has a *rhabdos* or staff in his hand. Hence the word *rhapsode* has been explained as 'staff-bearer', but it seems that the word is based on a different idea. For *rhabdos* really means 'shuttle', or more correctly the wooden needle with which the weft is led through the warp. This, then, presupposes a comparison of recitation with the work of weaving; it will be remembered that in Old Norse the making of poetry is often indicated by the word 'forge'. Now it is remarkable that Pindar speaks of the 'singers of the sewn words'[3] and of singing *kata rhabdon*,[4] that is, according to the seam, with which he means the end of the hexameters. While Pindar compares the form of his own hymns with variegated wicker-work, by the expression 'according to the seam' he means the regularity

---

[1] Lines 1260 ff.   [2] Cf. *Odyssey* xxi. 404.   [3] Cf. *Nem. Ode* ii. 2.
[4] Cf. *Isthm.* iv. 63, and also *Iliad* xii. 297, and xxii. 186.

of the hexameters. The epic song is therefore a work of weaving with the shuttle going to and fro. But the rhapsode can bear a staff, too, just as the king bears his sceptre or the messenger his mace. Seers like Tiresias or Cassandra can also have a staff in their hands, which is originally a branch of a tree (in particular a laurel twig) and is therefore evidently the symbol of the fruit-bearing power of the spoken word. As we know that the Boeotian singers of hymns had a laurel twig in their hands, it seems probable that the *rhabdos* has been tranferred from these to the singer of the Homeric poems.[1]

With a view to a later discussion, it is of importance to point out that there is therefore a connexion between the lyric poetry of the hymns and the epic poem. What we want to stress here is the distinction between the creative poet and the reproducing reciter. The recitation of these Greek singers should certainly be imagined as very lively, with a clear mimicry picturing the epic persons and their moods. The voice must have modulated itself according to the sounds of the lyre. The tempo probably varied a great deal, in accordance with the nature of the content.[2]

It has been assumed that there used to be poetical guilds, or poets' schools, in which the pupils competed with the master. In fact we know of these in the Celtic world where the *file* had to go through a long period of apprenticeship. This was supposed to explain the firmly fixed style of the Homeric poems: it was the style of the community. Thus the Homeric epic was assumed to have had its origin at Chios as the result of the joint poetic activity of such a society, just as the *Aethiopis* originated at Miletus.[3] But a fixed style need not be proof of a poetic community, for we find it everywhere as a characteristic of the epic. And, to choose an entirely different example, there was never a more formal kind of poetry than the sonnet of the Renaissance, and who would think of the work of poets' schools in this connexion? An epic like that of Homer is indeed not a communal product; this would lead us dangerously near to the romantic theory that the epic was sung by the

[1] Cf. Peter Corssen, *Archiv für Religionsgeschichte* xxviii (1930), pp. 95-105.

[2] Cf. Felix Bölte, in *Neue Jahrbücher* x (1907), pp. 571-81.

[3] Cf. S. J. Suys-Reitsma, *Het homerische epos als orale schepping van een dichter-hetairie* (1955), pp. 87 ff.

people, even if the theory just mentioned starts from a 'people' of professional poets. We really need not deprive Homer of the origin-ality of his *Iliad* and *Odyssey*. He thought up the contents; he made the arrangement of the scenes; but he also gave it beautiful words.

The poet knows what he is worth. He is no poetaster; he creates, rather, by divine inspiration. We know this in Greece about Homer, Hesiod, and Archilochus,[1] in England about Cædmon. It is therefore not surprising to hear them speak of the immortality of their songs.[2] The Persian poet Firdausi also speaks of it:

When this famous book is completed, the world will praise me greatly;
.Then I shall not die, for I remain alive, as I scattered the seed of the word.

It is therefore not only the heroes who are immortalized in the songs, but also and especially the poets themselves. But only the privileged few felt this, those who were conscious of having created a work for eternity: the bulk of the singers remain hidden in a modest anonymity.

Much has been written on the question whether the Homeric poems were of sacral origin. In the age of romanticism people were firmly convinced that there had been sacerdotal poets' schools, where the art was practised for generations and developed to such a technical perfection that a Homer could arise there as a final product.[3] Later, people went to the other extreme; Homeric epic poetry lived at the courts of the nobility, and that explained why it had no contact at all with an older religious poetry that existed among the original population subjected by the Greeks. But what if Greek epic poetry goes back to that of Mycenae, for which there is plenty of evidence? A whole series of words all relating to poetic technique (*dithyrambos, elegos, iambos, mythos, hymnos*) or to musical instruments (*kitharos, lyra, phorminx*) are all clearly of pre-Hellenic origin. One can only deduce from this that the poetic diction together with the instrumental accompaniment was a relic of the Aegean population.[4] We have already mentioned that the metre of

[1] Cf. K. Kerényi, *Griechische Miniaturen*.
[2] Cf. Pindarus, *Pyth.* xvi. 10-11, and Horace, *Odes* iii. 30.
[3] Cf. J. A. Kanne, *Erste Urkunden der Geschichte*, ed. 1815, p. 6.
[4] Cf. Ch. Autran, *Homère et les origines sacerdotales de l'épopée grecque* i, p. 33.

the hexameter points in the same direction.[1] Later it will appear still more clearly that Greek epic poetry at least was practised for a certain period in sacerdotal circles. At present we shall merely pose the question: what other reason would there have been to prefer the well-known themes of heroic legend for the adornment of temples, if there was not a close connexion between heroic song and the cult? Thus we arrive at the conclusion that the epic poet-singer had a long series of predecessors. On the one hand this points to a connexion with the cult, on the other to the fact that the tradition itself is lost in the Mycenaean past.

In France a distinction is made between *trouveur* and *jongleur*. The former is the finder, hence the poet; the latter the reproducing reciter. Perhaps not too sharp a distinction should be made here. At any rate the *jongleur* did more than merely repeat what he had learned by heart, he also made songs himself. Moreover the word *trouveur* originally belongs to a different type: in the eleventh century the word *trobaire* appears in Provence, by which the poetry-making troubadour was meant. If one uses *trouveur* figuratively for the poet of epic song, one may easily cause confusion, for in this case poet and reciter are difficult to separate.[2]

The word *jongleur* points to a remarkable gap in the tradition of the epic reciters. It goes back to the Latin word *joculator* which was taken over in the eighth century and which meant 'jester'. Now one can make jests in many ways, and that is what the *joculatores* did: they could leap and tumble, do conjuring tricks and perform antics, make animals do tricks; and they could also tell popular stories. Fundamentally this type of jester has nothing to do with heroic epic poetry. When in the twelfth century these very *joculatores* are mentioned as reciters, a great change must have taken place. In the thirteenth century Thomas Cabham says: *joculatores* are people who sing of the deeds of the rulers (*gesta principum*) and of the lives of the saints. And he mentions that there is no objection to their being received in the monasteries.

There was therefore a time when the old singers at the courts of the nobility had to make place for the *joculator*, who himself went

[1] Cf. Autran, l.c., p. 125.
[2] Cf. E. Faral, *Les Jongleurs en France au Moyen-Âge* (1910), pp. 73–79.

up a degree higher. One could safely call this a 'democratization' of the epic art. It appears that at a certain moment the singer of nobility disappears from the scene: the *aoidos* yields his place to the rhapsode, the Germanic *scop* to the medieval *Spielmann*. This also happened in France. When the interest in the old heroic epic poetry began to flag at the court of the nobility, these legends continued to live as beautiful stories among the people, and the *jongleurs* saw a new field for their already richly varied activity. Then however, probably in the eleventh century, the interest in heroic epic poetry rose again; the *jongleurs* now became *hoffähig* (admissible at court) and with this development not only their status but also their poetic activity must have been raised to a higher level. What gave the impulse to this development remains obscure; we shall come back to this later.[1]

In the eleventh century there is also the following testimony of Pierre de Blois: 'In the tragedies and in other poems, as well as in the *cantilenes* of the *joculatores*, a certain wise, noble, strong, amiable, and in all respects honourable man is often described. They also sing of the ordeals and troubles such men are cruelly subjected to, as those of Arthur, Gaugan, and Tristan, and the *histriones* tell of incredible things which fill the listeners with pity and move them to tears.[2] It seems, then, that the human race has become weaker and more tearful in the intermediate centuries. But perhaps it should also be remembered that the *jongleur* had learned from his experience of ordinary people how to play on their feelings to his best advantage.

Nothing is told in the old sources about the technique of these reciters. We would be limited to mere suppositions, if we did not have a good deal of evidence concerning the epic art of recitation that has, among some nations, survived to the present day. Thus the following is told of the Serbo-Croatian singers: the repertoire of the singer is often very extensive and can comprise two to three hundred songs, each containing 1,000 to 1,500 lines. How much the memory is developed as a result appears from the remarkable fact that most singers can add a song that they have heard only once to their repertoire. What we already suspected of the Greek rhapsodes turns out

[1] Cf. ch. 12.   [2] *De Confessione* (Migne Patrol. Lat. ccvii).

to be reality here: the recitation is a great mental and physical exertion, and the singer is often completely exhausted, with perspiration pouring from him. That is not only due to expressive mimicry but also to the fact that the recitation means much more than the mere speaking of a song that has been learned. That would have been beneath their dignity: their reproduction is more in the nature of improvisation. As they have at their disposal an extensive repertoire of fixed expressions and similes and, more especially, certain outlines of composition, they can easily recite a song in an entirely new way. It may therefore be safely said that each recitation is a poetic re-creation at the same time.[1]

The same holds for the Russian bylina singer. Here too the personal element is not absent from the recitation. Although the singer himself faithfully maintains that he sings it precisely as he has learned it from the 'old', in reality it appears that he frequently recites the song in a new form. Naturally it is of paramount importance whether the singer himself is a poetic personality. But the greater his poetic and musical susceptibility, the stronger the personal element. The Russian investigator Hilferding made the acquaintance of two singers who had learned the art from the same master, and he says: 'It is at once noticeable that their byliny have a certain similarity in content, but in the details of presentation and in the manner of expression they differ greatly.' [2] If this is the case in one single generation, how great must have been the change in the tradition in the course of a few centuries!

The ambition of the singers induces them to make their songs different from what they have originally learned. They do so by means of 'swelling', as Heusler called it. Stereotyped situations are treated in greater detail, episodes are inserted, either taken over from other poems or invented by themselves according to fixed schemes; this is a fusion of various poems, and then the formation of a heroic cycle. It is obvious that the bylina, which, as we have remarked, also experienced a great change in social *milieu*, had to undergo very strong alterations because of the 'faults' in the tradition.

Instructive, too, are Radloff's experiences among the Tartars. He

---

[1] Cf. M. Braun, in *Euphorion* xxxiv (1933), pp. 354–5.
[2] Cf. R. Trautmann, *Die Volksdichtung der Großrussen* i (1935), p. 27.

says: 'Any even moderately gifted singer always improvises according to the inspiration of the moment. He is not even able to recite the same poem twice in precisely the same way. It is easy for him to vary his recitation every time, for he knows by heart large numbers of situations fixed in a poetic form, and whenever he wishes he can insert these. Examples of such situations are the birth of a hero, his growing up, praise of his weapons, preparation for a fight, praise of the beauty of a bride, the description of a dwelling, a banquet, the death of a hero, the dirge, pictures of the scenery, nightfall or daybreak.'

According to his mood he can deal with such situations briefly in a few lines, or he can describe them in the most minute detail. One should also remember that he can always be sure of the greatest attention from his audience, when he describes splendour and pomp, fame, and honour. It is therefore possible for an experienced singer to improvise in verse a story of which he knows the course of the action. Another reason for the continual variation of his recitations is provided by the kind of audience that he will have. If they are poor people, he is prodigal with taunts at the rich, but if he sings before a circle of noblemen, he goes all out to praise their lineages. 'I have experienced myself,' says Radloff, 'that merely because of my presence an extensive glorification of the White Tsar was inserted.' And so he arrives at the conclusion that the singer does not recite well-known songs, but deals with well-known subject-matter. It appears very clearly that an oral tradition always fluctuates, and that within a span of ten years it can alter completely.[1]

It is now clear why Autran can say, in connexion with the Greek rhapsodes, that with a little practice, a little familiarity with the keyboard of poetic expression, one can easily say anything in verse; one can therefore improvise a song merely by using the ready-to-hand formulae in the right places, or at least the formulae that are imitations of them.[2] The Finnish folklorist Hautala goes so far as to say: 'A whole *runo* can be composed out of stereotyped lines.'[3] I may recall here that the famous scene of Hector and Andromache swarms with 'stereotypes'. We are inclined to consider all these

---

[1] Cf. *Proben der Volksliteratur der nördlichen türkischen Stämme* v (1885), pp. XVI–XXI.
[2] Cf. l.c., p. 143.   [3] Cf. Hautala, *Lauri Lappalaisen runo*, pp. 16 f.

fixed formulae as something merely accidental, or even as ballast. In reality they are the fixed points round which a song is composed.

Here a typical antithesis between the secular and the religious tradition may be observed. In the latter the greatest possible precision is expected. Magic formulae and prayers must be recited precisely as they have been handed down, for the slightest deviation endangers their effect. We are told about a secret society in Tahiti where a small error in a word or a verse was sufficient to break up the whole ceremony. And we know that in Iceland the slightest error in the law formulae had the most fatal results for the pleader. We now understand why the Druids had to imprint the whole history of the people on the memory of their young adepts in the course of years of teaching. Of the South Sea tribes it may be said in general that their great epic stories had to be learned by heart and that nothing in them was allowed to be altered or twisted; thus they were passed on in unaltered form to children and grandchildren.[1] The training of a *file* took a long time: in his first year of training he had to learn twenty tales by heart and in the seventh year he managed no fewer than a hundred and forty. Such a long training is only understandable if he was required to recite the legends in their prescribed form—and word-perfect.

A popular tradition like that of the Russians should not be put on a par with a tradition in which the heroic legend is still an integral part of civilization. If it has a more or less sacral character, this leads to rigidity. But as soon as heroic epic poetry has become an element in the culture of the nobility, such rigid rules are no longer valid. Then a gifted personality cannot be prevented from breaking the tradition. This is proved in those cases in which we can compare various written texts: variants appear in them everywhere. This holds good for the Irish heroic stories as well as the Icelandic sagas or the Middle High German epics.

It will have become clear that epic tradition is characterized by a great rigidity as well as great flexibility. As a genre, it is of an iron firmness, but each poem in itself is still a result of a personal creation. In times when new forms of culture arise, new canons of beauty, and especially a new outlook on man and the world, a complete

[1] Cf. W. E. Mühlmann, *Arioi und Mamaia* (1955), pp. 55–56.

breach with the tradition may result. It would not be right to bridge the distance between an Eddic lay, such as the *Atlamál*, on the one hand, and the *Nibelungenlied* on the other by means of a number of intermediate transitions that led gradually from the one to the other: in between there lies a revolution which produced entirely new forms of poetry and thus broke all continuity.

9

THE HERO AND THE HEROIC AGE

WHAT is a hero? The classic answer to this question is given by Glaucus: 'My father Hippolochus sent me to Troy with the instruction always to be brave and surpass all others and not to disgrace the ancestors.' [1] This is also Homer's conception, as appears from another section of the *Iliad*, where Peleus uses the same words to his son Achilles. [2]

It is the heroic ideal of the warrior to be strong and courageous, to conquer all opponents, and so to win fame with posterity. All over the world this thirst for glorious remembrance is found. It is innate in man. Many an unappreciated artist or scholar has found consolation in the thought that posterity would give him the honour that his own time denied him.

It is no longer our ideal. We have our heroes of science and technology; worse still, our heroes of sport and film. Not much is left of the old idea of the 'hero' except that he surpasses all others in a certain field, and that for a short time he comes into the limelight. Sometimes there is an echo of the old idea: the hero of science is not the exceptionally learned scholar, but the man who has sacrificed his life to science.

Our hero-worship is short-lived. A centenary may rouse it once again and journalists gratefully find in it an opportunity to fill the columns of their papers. But is that hero still alive in the consciousness of the people? Can his picture at a given moment really come to life in the hearts of men and show them the way to a better and nobler life?

For that in fact holds good for the old heroes. Their legends live for hundreds of years in the mouths of the people; poets sing their deeds; these songs are recited and no one is ever tired of listening to them; the legend is not only preserved but continually renewed.

[1] Cf. *Iliad* vi. 207-09.   [2] Cf. *Iliad* xi. 784.

The knights of the Staufen Court felt themselves related to Siegfried, although he himself belonged to a barbaric past. What did a story of Burgundian princes who perished in the fifth century convey to people of the thirteenth century? A different nation that had long since ceased to exist, a different time with which no fibre of the soul of chivalry was still in any way connected, and yet the *Nibelungenlied* continued to arouse a tremendous response in the hearts of its listeners.

The same applies to all heroes. If it is true that Pisistratus had the Homeric poems codified, how important they must have seemed to him, these stories of the heroes who, seven centuries before, fought a virtually purposeless war in an out-of-the-way corner of Asia Minor! To put it even more strongly: when Alexander the Great crossed to Asia he landed, according to Plutarch, at Ilion. He made a sacrificial offering of animals to Athene and dedicated a libation to the heroes. Then he adorned the sepulchral column of Achilles with wreaths after having solemnly anointed himself. In accordance with an old custom he had a naked running-match with his friends in honour of the dead. He declared Achilles happy because in Patroclus he had found a faithful friend and, after his death, a great herald of his deeds in Homer.

What induced Alexander to do this? There was not at that time any reporting in the press which could devote a front-page with photographs to this show. This action was certainly not calculated to spread fame. Evidently Alexander felt compelled to honour Achilles at the start of his tremendous undertaking. And did not his own life prove that in Achilles he honoured a man who was like himself: *hupeirochos allôn*, and one who died young?

When we read such an old text, do we really understand it? Can we enter into Alexander's personality and feel with him? Would we act in the same way? And we smile, perhaps somewhat compassionately, and would like to ask: 'Noble Alexander, was your Ilion really situated in layer VIIa? Are you so sure that Achilles ever lived? Perhaps you show an honourable veneration for something that is a figment of the imagination.'

These are indeed questions that Alexander could not have answered and which would have seemed to him entirely senseless.

But they are questions that we can raise only to our own shame. Reality is not what happened more than two thousand years ago in the Scamander plain, but what has lived for centuries in the memories of many generations as a precious testimony to a glorious past, and—even more important—from which these generations have come to life.

In a certain sense, the twelfth and thirteenth centuries are the zenith of western heroic epic poetry. (This applies both to the Romance and to the Germanic areas.) The end comes suddenly after that. When, at the end of the eighteenth century, this literature was rediscovered, people did not at once feel at home in it. Romanticism, however, hailed the heroic epic with joy: but as the beautiful memory of a great past. And in spite of the endless stream of editions, translations, and popularizations, it cannot be said to have become more than an antiquarian interest of certain intellectual circles. The hero and his legend are irrevocably gone.

Thus the problem has become a purely historical one. The hero is the symbol of a long period of European history, or perhaps of European infancy, but that does not make the symbol less important. In the depths of the modern soul it is still alive, in Jung's words, as an archetype, and hence indestructible. We have an unexpected force disturbing to many. Perhaps it was not the hero who came to life, but a caricature showing many signs of spuriousness. For this reason also it seems desirable to know precisely what is meant by the idea of 'the hero'.

In a society in which a warlike nobility strikes the keynote, the brave warrior is naturally an ideal image. What the saint is for the spiritual world, the hero is for the world of chivalry. The comparison perhaps points to something that is more fundamental. The saint is not only the ascetic or the martyr, as he lived and died; he has a halo of glory about him which raises him to a super-human symbol. Was the hero perhaps likewise such a symbol in which much more was expressed than merely the man who had shown exceptional strength and courage in his lifetime?

It is noteworthy that the true hero is the brave young man who dies an early death. This applies to Siegfried and Achilles as much as to Roland and Cúchulainn. When Ekkehard, in the end, allows his Waltharius to rule his kingdom of Aquitaine to a ripe old age, a happy husband, we feel this is almost an injustice, which obscures the picture of the true hero. The *moniages* of Guillaume d'Orange, Walter of Aquitaine, and Renout de Montalban are Christian distortions of an heroic life. And all the time it turns out that the heroic spirit will come out even in the monastic grave: the old man will once more reveal his indomitable courage in the splendour of his armour, but this time combined with a true Christian meekness. And still a false light of cheap humour falls on the image of the hero in his monk's habit!

A hero dies young: that is his tragedy. It has been prophesied to him. And even when protected by the horny skin of Siegfried or Fer Diad, even when almost invulnerable like the Greek Achilles, even when safeguarded by impossible conditions against death, like the Welsh hero Llew Llaw Gyffes, his fate will be fulfilled inexorably. That is perhaps what is most moving in the image of the hero: his fragility in spite of his (humanly speaking) unassailable strength. During the whole of his brief life this fate is ever present. Is it to be wondered at that he defies it in the end?

When Cathba has prophesied to the young Cúchulainn that he will become famous but will not live long, the boy answers: 'Great is the prize, should I live but one day and one night, if only the stories about me and my adventures will be remembered after me.'[1]

The hero, then, lives in order to win eternal fame. Is that ambition? Our age with the inflated vanity of its short-lived celebrities has indeed little reason to criticize the fame of the heroes of antiquity. Do we really know what was meant by heroic fame in the old days?

At any rate it appears again and again that in those days people were very sensitive to fame and blame. The former enhanced the value of life, the latter destroyed it. We will first, therefore, try to understand from some examples what part they played in the estimation of men at the time.

Hector addresses the Trojans and the Greeks in this way: 'Let us fight; I challenge any of the Achaeans. And if I should fall in the fight, let my body be taken to Troy; if I should win, I shall have

[1] Cf. *Táin bó Cualnge*, ed. Windisch, ll. 1111–13.

the body of the loser taken to the ships. When a man of a later generation will see the monument on the grave, he will say: "This is the grave of a man who died long ago, who was once killed by the glorious Hector." This is what someone will one day say and my fame will never be lost.' [1] How the hero does remain alive is told in another section of the same poem. Achilles is sitting sulking in his tent, while the battle rages outside. How gladly would he join his comrades in the fight against the Trojans, but his injured pride forbids him to do so. Nestor and Odysseus come to visit him in order to prevail upon him to put the welfare of the Greeks before his personal grudge. They find him with the *phorminx* in his hand and singing the *klea andrôn*, 'the fame of men'. [2] This warms his heart, for the fame of the former heroes will also be his; other people will be consoled and uplifted in their sorrow by hearing the song of the heroic deeds of Achilles.

We have already seen how Roland prevented himself and his companions from being saved by not blowing his horn, merely out of fear that later a *male chançun* should be sung about him. This desire for immortality is expressed tersely in an Eddic lay. The *Hávamál* or *The Lay of the High One* says in stanza 77:

> Cattle die, and kinsmen die,
> And so one dies one's self;
> But a noble name will never die,
> If good renown one gets.

But it is not only fame after death; it is fame during their lives that people long for. Posidonius tells us that the Celtic singers, called bards, express praise in their songs, [3] and so he considers this to be their most important task. Another classical author, Aelianus, remarks that the Celts strive most of all after danger; the subject of their songs is the men who have died a noble death in the fight. [4] These songs are indeed no mere ornaments to the banquet, but have a very real function. We have pointed out that by their recitation at the beginning of a battle an example is given to the men, to which they have to live up. In one fight Fidach, the son of the King of

---

[1] Cf. *Iliad* vii. 67-91.　　　　　　　　[2] Cf. *Iliad* ix. 189.
[3] Hist. xxiii, fragm. 17 in *Atheneus* vi. 49.　　[4] *Var. Hist.* xii. 23.

the Britons, says: 'Sing a song in my praise, oh Fergus Finnbél, so that, fighting against the pirates, my spirit shall be the more warlike and my fight the braver.'[1] But what does this praise consist of? The memory, of course, of the brave deeds of his ancestors.

Beowulf returns from the fight with Grendel; Hrothgar's men go to the lake to see the strange sight.

> There the fame
> Of Beowulf was told; many declared
> Full oft that south nor north between the seas
> Over the wide world 'neath the sky's expanse
> There was no other warrior in arms
> Better than he—— [2]

At the banquet the Queen comes forward with a ring and gives it to Beowulf with the words:

> For thou hast brought to pass that far and near
> Throughout the generations men esteem thee,
> Where'er the sea, the birthplace of winds
> Encompasses the cliffs.[3]

The thirst for glory can also elicit the song of praise. Of the Chancellor William de Longchamp—we are here in the England of about 1200—it is said that he lured singers and *jongleurs* from France with rich gifts, so that they might sing about him in the fairs, to the enhancement of his fame.[4] But one feels the difference from genuine heroic behaviour. In the case of this Chancellor it looks very much like a panegyric advertisement which rulers whose authority is wavering use to influence public opinion. Cormac mac Airt was once asked what sounds most pleasant, and the Irish king answered: 'a song of praise after a victory'. [5] The brave deed only becomes lasting if committed to song, as one knows it will defy time.

If fame is sought for, blame is feared all the more. It is certainly not a fanciful embellishment when it is said of Archilochus that his

---

[1] Cf. *Cath. Finntrága*, ed. K. Meyer (1885), p. 38.

[2] Cf. *Beowulf*, ll. 856-61; all quotations from *Beowulf* are from M. E. Waterhouse's translation: *Beowulf in Modern English* (1949).

[3] *Ibid.*, ll. 1221-4.   [4] Cf. Roger de Hoveden, *Rerum Britann. Scriptores.*

[5] Cf. *Teosca Cormaic*, ed. K. Meyer (1909).

lashing satire drove his victim to suicide. We have already heard how Roland feared nothing more than *que malvaise cançun de nus dite ne seit*.[1]

It is typical that the meaning of the Irish word *ainech* is both 'face' and 'honour', for the best way to injure a person's honour is to make his cheeks blush with shame. The satirical song is more than an injury, it works like a curse. In our discussion of the *Táin bó Cualnge* we pointed out that just such a satirical song caused pustules to appear on the cheek and forehead of the hero Fer Diad. This psycho-physical correlation can perhaps explain the *ainech*, metaphorically, but I believe that in those days people felt it to be very real.

In an Old Norse story, which is certainly not to be considered as historical, the poet Thorleif avenges himself on the jarl Hákon by entering his hall in disguise and starting a song about princes at his request. The beginning is indeed a song of praise of jarl Hákon, but as the song progresses the jarl's whole body begins to itch. He cannot bear it any longer and has his body scratched with combs. He suspects the poet of being the cause of this, and asks for another, better song. Thorleif continues, but now the whole hall becomes dark; presently the weapons hung upon the wall begin to move; that was the death of many a man. The jarl falls in a swoon, and in spite of the closed doors the poet vanishes unnoticed.[2]

This is of course a gross exaggeration. But there is a core of truth in every exaggeration. And in this case it is the great fear of 'losing face'. Even a mocking nickname can lead to the greatest revenge. In the Icelandic *Njálssaga* a woman says of Njáll, the old and wise, who evidently has a sparse growth of beard: 'It is strange that beardless Njáll does not rub his chin with dung to make himself look like other men; let us therefore call him the beardless man and his sons dung-beards.'[3] This insult leads to murder and man-slaughter.

It would not be difficult to adduce more examples of the careful way in which man tried to preserve his honour. Honour and fame were the pivots of man's life—of the hero's life first and foremost;

[1] Cf. *Chanson de Roland*, l. 1014.
[2] Cf. *Flateyjarbók*, ed. Nordal, i, 1944, pp. 233–4.   [3] Cf. *Njálssaga*, ch. 44.

through these he could be hurt most severely. This sounds quite modern, for even now there are many men who avenge a personal insult with their fists.

But in earlier days it was not only a question of insult. Man was not yet the individual then that he became later. He was a member of the family, the temporary link in an eternal chain. Fame and blame were transmitted to children and grandchildren, or reached back to the ancestors. The man who failed in his honour was a weak link in the chain; it could snap. He dragged his whole race down with him in his dishonour. Hence it was not only (not even mainly) for the sake of personal honour that honour was preserved so anxiously. The worst horror was that the man who did not behave in accordance with the code of honour which his lineage demanded of him cast a blemish on his family, a blemish that could not be erased. Thirst for fame is therefore not a satisfaction of personal vanity, but a duty towards ancestors and descendants.

That is the reason why the *geste* is not only a story of famous deeds but also a genealogy. When a man died in ancient Ireland, the *cépog* or dirge was sung, the contents of which were the ancestry and the deeds of the dead man.[1] This shows again how the one is inter-mingled with the other. The fame of the dead man does not die, said the *Hávamál*; this means not only that poets will ensure that it is remembered, but also that it will be continued into all subsequent generations and will give new lustre to the family. Why else should it be the task of the Indian *vandin* or panegyrist to sing to the kings about the fame of their ancestors,[2] if it was not to preserve in the consciousness of the princes the demands which fame made upon their own attitude to life?

Where is this fame sung? In those places where men are gathered together. Achilles may sit sulking in his tent and cheer himself by singing to himself of the fame of heroes. It reaches its full significance only when there is an audience to listen to it. The heroic song belongs to the hall of princes and noblemen. No wonder that a middle-class civilization like that of recent centuries finds this art so difficult to approach.

[1] Cf. Sullivan in O'Curry, *Customs and Manners* i (1847), p. cccxxiv.
[2] Cf. Chr. Lassen, *Indische Altertumskunde* i (1847), p. 630.

First of all the heroic song is sung in the king's hall. The English epic of *Beowulf* has a vivid description of this; whenever a banquet is held in Hrothgar's hall the singer appears:

> Music and song were raised together there
> Before the battle leader of the Danes.
> The sweet harp sounded, 'twas a tale oft told,
> That Hrothgar's minstrel on the banquet benches
> Must tell as entertainment in the hall,
> Of Finn's retainers.[1]

The harp is called *gamanwudu*, 'wood of joy'. This suggests the joy that arose from the 'meadbenches' when the song of famous deeds was recited. Elsewhere in the same epic we read, in Beowulf's report to his King Hygelac, of his heroic deeds at Hrothgar's court:

> There was both tale and song; the Scylding prince,
> Old and experienced, told of far off days;
> At times a warrior woke the harp's delight,
> The sounding wood; at times he told a tale
> Tragic and true——— [2]

The words are sober enough, but when one knows how to listen to the undertones of a text, one feels the power of the song. Both in Germanic and in Greek literature we notice over and again the exceptional function of the heroic song. Grönbech puts it strikingly in the following words: 'It is the *aretè*, the virtue of the poet to clothe immortal deeds in immortal words; this gift is the basis of his right to be ranked among the nobility and to occupy the seat of honour at the ruler's right hand. The great heroes fully recognize the equality of the poet. They show him their appreciation by giving him *timè* and *aidôs* (honour and fame); he sits in their hall, honoured as one of them, almost as one of their kinsmen. From him they expect immortality, for by his immortal words he gives the deeds of the heroes a lasting life in the souls of men. Sages and warriors, says Pindar in one breath, and by sages he means poets; he puts deed and song on the same level and, as always, Pindar's

---

[1] Cf. *Beowulf*, ll. 1063–8.
[2] *Ibid.*, ll. 2105–09.

words are rooted in a sober reality. Together they are the creators
of honour; the heroes bring it to life through their deeds, the
poets foster it, and in Greek that means that they renovate it every
time.' [1]

We always hear of the joy that arises in the hall. This springs from
a feeling of happiness aroused in the hearts of the warriors, not only
and not in the first place by the beauty of song, but by the response
which it finds in their manly hearts. To live up to the examples of
immortal heroes means that one day a poet will celebrate their own
deeds, and that through his song they will continue to live on the
lips of distant generations. The heroic song must have had a great
educational power. It revealed to the warlike nobility an ideal that
was bound to direct their own lives. The fame of the ancestors was
their own fame; their own fame that of their descendants.

Thus it may be said that the heroic song belongs to the retinue
or, as Tacitus would say, the *comitatus*, of princes and dukes. It has
often been pointed out that the heroic song is supranational and
that therefore the glorification of a particular land or nation rarely
occurs in it. Indeed, the spirit of the *comitatus* was far removed from
national feelings. Tacitus gives us a clear description of it in his
Germania: 'Conspicuous ancestry or great services rendered by their
fathers can win the rank of chief for boys still in their teens. They
are attached to the other chiefs, who are more mature and proven,
and no one blushes to be seen thus in the ranks of the companions.
This order of companions even has its different grades, as determined by the leader, and there is intense rivalry among the companions for the first place by the chief, among the chiefs for the most
numerous and enthusiastic companions. Dignity and power alike
consist in being continually attended by a corps of chosen youths.
This gives one consideration in peace-time and security in war.
Nor is it only in a man's own nation that he can win name and fame
by the superior number and quality of his companions, but in
neighbouring states as well.' [2]

A brave leader is like a magnet to all those who want to win such
honour and fame. A *dux* or duke gathers around him not only the

---

[1] Cf. Grönbech, *Hellas I* (*Adelstiden*), p. 137.
[2] Cf. *Germania*, ch. 13.

youths of his own nation, but also many others who have heard about his bravery. Thus the *comitatus* is in no sense a national institution, but is composed of men from far and wide. They flock together in order to perform warlike deeds under his guidance and gain fame and booty from them.[1]

The ethics of such *comitati* must have been strong and powerful. It is again Tacitus who gives us a clear picture of this: 'On the field of battle it is a disgrace to the chief to be surpassed in valour by his companions, to the companions not to come up to the valour of their chief. As for leaving a battle alive after your chief has fallen, *that* means lifelong infamy and shame. To defend and protect him, to put down one's own acts of heroism to his credit—that is what they really mean by "allegiance". The chiefs fight for victory, the companions for their chief.'[2]

These words convey clearly in what extreme tension such a *comitatus* lived. And it is not an arbitrary interpretation of Tacitus, but a living reality. Several heroic songs, such as the Old Norse *Bjarkamál*, describe how the *comitatus* sacrifices himself to the lord, even when further fighting has become completely useless. In this song, which Saxo Grammaticus rendered into Latin verse, the hero Biarco says to his comrade in arms: 'As long as life lasts we shall exert ourselves to die with honour and with our hands to win for ourselves a glorious end. Defeated I shall die near the head of my fallen lord and you will fall down dead at his feet, so that any one who looks upon the pile of corpses shall see how we have paid our lord for the gold we received from him.'[3]

It should not be assumed that this is the exalted imagination of an heroic poet: it was like that in reality. In 991 the Vikings invaded England once again and raided Essex, but here the *ealdorman* Bryhtnoth quickly gathered an army together and gave battle at Maldon. A poet, who may have been an eye-witness, shortly afterwards made a poem in which he describes the death of Bryhtnoth. In it, one of his followers, Byrhtwold, says:

[1] Cf. my essay in *Westfälische Forschungen* xi (1959), pp. 5–10.
[2] Cf. *Germania*, ch. 14.
[3] Cf. *Die ersten neun Bücher der dänischen Geschichte*, translated by Hermann Jantzen (1900), p. 106.

> Thought shall be the harder, heart the keener,
> Mood shall be the more, as our might lessens.
> Here our good prince lies, on the earth,
> Hewn to death: that man will repent for ever
> Who now thinks to turn from this war-play.
> I am old in life: away will I never,
> But bethink me to lie by the side
> Of my lord, the man I cherished.[1]

Such a contempt of death can only be inspired by the realization that a man has to follow the high example of former heroes. We now understand something of the joy in the king's hall on hearing an heroic song. The warriors gathered there know that when the hour comes they will not act differently. Literature and life merge into each other. Here one has a striking example of the hold that literature can have on life. At a time when literature has sunk to the level of a more or less aesthetic amusement of leisure hours, we find it hard to realize not only how much a poem can move us in the depth of our souls, but arouse us to deeds and give purpose and dedication to our lives. It is possible that the *Song of Roland* and the *Nibelungenlied* have come to be pure literature, although I can hardly accept this. In the old days, at any rate, the heroic song had an educative power in the lives of the warlike nobility.

The time when the heroic song originated and still had its full function is called the heroic age. What is meant by this phrase?

It is supposed to lie in the dim past. That is proved by the epic of *Gilgamesh*. In Sumeria already we hear of the *ur-sag*, i.e. the hero. He is half godlike and therefore gifted with extraordinary courage. For that he is praised in the epic stories. The Heracles of Mesopotamia fights with monsters and descends into the underworld: he reveals the features of a 'cult hero', for he wants to obtain the herb of immortality for men.

For the Greeks the heroic age is that of late-Mycenaean culture; for the Germanic peoples the period of the Migration. In a later chapter we shall see that it is the figures and events of these times that form the subject of heroic songs. But although we may call

[1] Cf. *The Battle of Maldon*, ll. 312-19.

these times in a narrower sense the heroic age, the heroic songs also find a full response long afterwards and especially wherever a war-like nobility maintained the old traditions. The feudal lords in their castles still lived to a large extent in accordance with the ethics of the heroic legend. France is a striking example of this. How over-confident are those vassals in their resistance to the weak successors of Charlemagne—one need only think of the *Couronnement de Louis*. How bitter are their feuds with the people of their own class—one need only think of the romance of the Lorrains. What fighting spirit carried to the absolute extreme, what consciousness of honour and the importance of their own race! Truly it is the heroic songs that again and again arouse in the hearts of those lords the desire for great deeds. Who shall say how often such a nobleman, after listening to an heroic song, leapt up, seized his weapons and exhorted his men to renewed fighting—to prove that he was still moved by the old spirit?

But the heroic song also preserved its educative function where the old aristocratic nobility had long since perished, or had never been fully developed. In Iceland the heroic songs were eventually noted down. They must therefore have lived there for centuries in the memory of the people. But this nation had come into being because a powerful farmer-nobility from Norway wanted to withdraw from the tyranny of King Harald Fairhair and so preferred to found a new fatherland. It consisted of a number of farmer families who lived on their scattered farms and who certainly did not collect around them a *comitatus* as the Norse jarls did (that did not happen till the thirteenth century, when it caused the fall of the free state). Hence the annual *Thing* meetings became the place where not only the literary, but also the juridical and religious traditions of the people were kept alive. Here the powerful farmers came together and here was the opportunity for scalds and saga-tellers to show their art. The same picture is seen in Ireland, where the *oenach* or the meeting of the people, held at regular intervals, afforded the opportunity for amusements both serious and gay. It has been expressed in this way: the *oenach* was the great school where the people were taught their rights and duties, where they learned the laws under which they lived, the history of their country, the warlike deeds performed by famous men of the past and the genealogies of the ruling families.[1]

For all this time and in these different circumstances the glory of the heroic age remained alive. But the age itself belonged to a dim past, a time in which men became heroes.

Is it, then, true to say that heroes are brave men who thirst after honour and fame, and is there nothing more to add? And what about the halo that glorifies them? Did they obtain it merely because they could fight and, particularly, die so bravely? No, there is more, far more, but this can only be made clear in a later chapter.

[1] Cf. Sullivan in O'Curry i, p. cclv.

10

THE HISTORICAL BACKGROUND
OF HEROIC LEGEND

THERE can be no doubt that the heroic epic bears some relation to historical events. They have evidently made such an impression that they have been, as it were, lifted out of the course of history and given a lasting glory.

The Indian epic has preserved only faint memories of the historical past. But perhaps this is our judgement only because the history of Hindustan is so little known. History was not of much interest to the Indian. He paid little attention to the course of worldly events, convinced as he was that life is only a semblance, a *maya*, which as it were enchants us, and that reality lies in the transcendental world. If man has to strive after *moksa*, i.e. deliverance from the eternal cycle of rebirth, his mind must be focused on other things than the would-be events here on earth. It is therefore difficult to establish with any certainty which historical figures are hidden behind the Pandavas or Rama; perhaps it may be said that the fights described in these epic poems may partly preserve the memory of the struggle which the Indo-European tribes had with the native population on coming from the North into the Ganges plain. Since excavations have revealed that they found the highly developed civilization of Mohenjo-Daro in the Indus valley, their invasion may be compared to that of the Dorians in the Mycenaean Peloponnese. It must have been a hard struggle, in which an old civilization was destroyed. After that a new one had to be built up slowly.

As to the Greeks, we have already discussed at length how the Homeric epic reflects the Mycenaean age. The Achaeans acted in the archipelago like freebooting Vikings. Their adventures are reflected in the legend of the Argonauts and in that of the fall of Troy. It is difficult to establish what proportion of these legends is really historical. There are several indications that the figures appearing in them are for the most part not related to historical persons. But it may be assumed that the *Iliad* represents a large-scale attack on a stronghold which had a key-position at the entrance to the Helles-pont and so was a much coveted possession for seafarers who wanted to penetrate into the Black Sea. *L'histoire se répète*. When, much later, the Norsemen took up the practice of privateering, their first aim was likewise to destroy or take possession of fixed and favour-ably situated key-points on the coasts of the seas they sailed on. Why should not historical truth be hidden behind the story of this confederation of Achaean tribes, even if the rape of Helen was not the object of this difficult undertaking.

Since Firdausi's epic is a poetic treatment of a king's chronicle, the historical figures are clearly visible, as has been pointed out in Chapter 5. In the Slav heroic legends, too, a few historical persons may be found, even if they have become very vague and the events are veiled in a mist of poetic invention.

The same applies to the Irish epic. The kings Conchobar and Cormac mac Airt, who are the centre of the Ulster and Finn legends, in all probability lived in the first centuries of our era; here too we are on historical ground, although it is covered by a rich vegetation of imaginative legend.

In France matters are clearer, for the subject-matter does not go back so far into the past. It is the time of the Merovingians and Carolingians, culminating in the figure of Charlemagne, that is dealt with in the *chansons de geste*. The *Song of Roland* treats of a defeat in the Pyrenees, the song of *Gormont and Isembart* of the battle of Saucourt. Here, then, we have an opportunity to compare the contents of the poems with that of the chronicles. The result of this comparison of the actual facts with the data of the epic poems is this: an epic account turns out to be entirely different from an historical account.

Similar observations can be made in Spain. The hero of the epic *Cantar de mio Cid* (which was written about 1140, probably as a poetic treatment of an older prose story)[1] is an historical figure from the second half of the eleventh century. Don Rodrigo Diaz de Vivar was one of the most powerful opponents of the Moors, as brave as

[1] Cf. E. von Richthofen, *Estudios Epicos Medievales*, pp. 346-7.

he was generous. His fame earned him the name of *Campeador*, 'fighter, conqueror', among his own people, whereas the Moors honoured their great adversary with the name of *sidi*, 'lord', taken over in Spanish as *Cid*. The short lapse of time between the historical events and the poem about the hero explains why the broad outlines of his life and deeds have been preserved unaltered in the epic; they have only been given in greater relief.[1]

If, however, we want to observe how history assumes a different appearance in the epic when many centuries have passed by between the composition of the epic and the events with which it deals, we turn to the Germanic epic for the fullest evidence. It has already been said that the real Germanic heroic age was the Migration period. The main personages are Ermanaric, who committed suicide in 375 when the Huns destroyed his power, which extended over a large part of Russia; and the figure of Attila, who died in 453. In his lifetime occurred the fall of the Burgundian power on the Rhine (in 436), in which the Huns played a part, although Attila was not present. Then comes Theoderic the Great, the King of the Ostrogoths, who died in 526, and finally there is the Longobardian King Alboin, who died in 572. This covers a period of two centuries.

If one surveys this period during which, in startlingly quick succession and with the greatest vicissitudes, kingdoms were founded and destroyed, whole nations were eclipsed, and others came to unexpected power, and in which the foundations of later Europe were laid, one can understand that contemporaries as well as descendants were deeply impressed by these events.

An age of great upheaval also brings forth personalities who seem to focus on themselves all world-events. Attila and Theoderic the Great were indeed men of great stature. On the other hand we also see mighty rulers crushed by the impetuous course of events. The tragic fate of Ermanaric and Guntharius cannot but leave a lasting echo.

These stirring times hardly allowed people to settle down. In later years, when medieval Europe had consolidated itself, people looked back on the past centuries to find event pressing on event, one figure jostling another. It was like looking from a distance at a

[1] See for this especially R. Menendez Pidal, *La España del Cid*, 2 vols., Madrid 1947.

mighty range of the Alps, in which the steep giants seem to stand in a row against the horizon, although in reality great distances separated them. The Migration period was telescoped so that the figures came to lie in one plane. Ermanaric, Attila, and Theoderic became contemporaries, and their relative positions no longer accorded with actual history. The *Nibelungenlied* shows us Dietrich of Bern, the poetic name of Theoderic of Verona, at the court of Attila at the time of the tragedy of the Burgundian princes, although they are almost a century apart. What is even more remarkable is that Theoderic sought refuge with Attila because he was driven from his kingdom in Italy by Ermanaric, who, in fact, lived a century and a half earlier.

Now we are inclined to attribute this historical confusion to an epic tradition which preserved only vague memories of the actual events and was not greatly concerned with them. But there is also another reason to be considered. In those days the means of communication were extremely poor: it could take a long time before an event became known to other nations. Therefore it sometimes happened that an earlier fact became known later than another— which had happened later but nearer to hand. This was only natural in the early Middle Ages, but even in our days of quick communication such confusions do occur.

However this may be, tradition strangely distorted history. This was partly the result of a foreshortened perspective, partly of the character of these centuries. When Attila suffered his first and only defeat on the Catalaunian fields, why should the Huns who destroyed the Burgundian kingdom five years later not have been led by him personally?

How opinions about historical figures change in the course of time! Attila was the scourge of Christianity, overrunning and enslaving many Germanic nations. That is why the *Edda* preserves a clear memory of the cruel Asiatic tyrant. Atli thirsts for gold and is inhuman; he lures his brothers-in-law, the Burgundian princes, to his court in order to take possession of the Nibelung hoard. He has them killed in a cruel manner: Hagen has his heart cut out and Gunnar is thrown into a snake-pit.

But the Goths, who had been the first victims of Attila and had been dragged along with his hordes from South Russia into the plain of the Theiss, later became his faithful allies; their princes were highly honoured at his court. The barbaric, nomadic ruler learned from these Germanic people the delights of a higher civilization for the first time. The excellent relations between him and the subjected tribes appear from the name they gave him: Attila, a Gothic word meaning 'little father', which survives in the German Etzel. Now the *Nibelungenlied* pictures the king of the Huns as a worthy, gentle, even somewhat weak prince. It is not he who treacherously invites the Burgundians to his court, but his wife, the revengeful Kriemhild who destroys her brothers. What a remarkable reversal of the old legend! Whereas the Gudrun of the Old Norse lay of *Atli* tries to warn her brothers and avenges their death on her own husband in the most cruel way, the German Kriemhild is a fury who drags down the unsuspecting Etzel in her thirst for revenge.

The figure of Siegfried gives rise to particular difficulty. He seems to be so unreal that for a long time he was considered to be a mythological figure. The young hero who awakens the sleeping valkyrie could hardly be anything but the sun-god who awakens the earth from its winter sleep in springtime. There may be an element of truth[1] in this representation, just as for the fairy-tale of the 'Sleeping Beauty' a similar mythological background has been assumed.[2] But that is not everything. In Siegfried's life the valkyrie motif is only a single episode.

We shall see presently that Siegfried's life as a whole is constructed in accordance with the typical pattern of heroic legend. But his curiously ambiguous attitude towards the two women, and towards his death, brought about by Brünhild, falls outside the framework of the normal heroic adventure. The name of this woman, blinded by injured female pride, recalls a demonic figure in Frankish Merovingian history. Brunehild was a Spanish princess, the daughter of the Visigoth King Athanagils. She married Sigebert II of Austrasia. After nine years of married life, he was murdered through the intrigues of Chilperich, whom Brunehild was suspected of having

---

[1] Cf. F. R. Schröder, in *Zeitschrift für Deutschkunde* (1930), pp. 443-9.
[2] Cf. my essay in *Fabula* ii (1958), pp. 110-21.

hounded into the murder. After the death of her husband she married a member of the family of the murdered man. After this a fierce feud sprang up between her and Fredegunde, whose name mocks at her terrible deeds. She contrived for Brunehild's sister, who was married to Sigebert's brother Chilperich, to be killed by him; after that she herself married the murderer.[1]

With this we are in the middle of the unsavoury history of the Merovingians in the sixth century. But it still remains problematic whether we can extract from this the data for an historical foundation of the Siegfried legend. Some points of similarity are indeed tempting. The Nibelung legend considers Siegfried to be a Frankish hero. In the race of the Ripuarian kings names with *sigi*—'victory'— are very common. The name of one of the women is the same in history and legend. The second part of the name Fredegunde may be compared to the first part of the name Gudrun, which North-Germanic tradition substitutes for the German Kriemhild. The word Nibelungs, which is often taken to mean Nebulous Ones and so would have a mythical meaning, has been connected with the place-name Nivelles. But all this is very uncertain, and there are many differences. The more strictly one tries to link history and legend, the more arbitrary become the means used for this purpose.[2]

Another explanation entirely eliminates the figure of Brünhild. She is supposed to have been the creation of the poet who wrote the song of Siegfried's death. If it is assumed that our hero belonged to the Burgundian legend from the outset, the main point of the argument shifts there. The appearance in this royal house of names like Sigismund and Sigerich, after a series of princes' names that are typically Burgundian, is easily explained therefore as the results of Frankish–Burgundian marriage.[3] But here, too, the links between history and legend are very loose. As a starting-point there are some vague similarities of names, and these are supposed to be supported by details of the story corresponding with similar historical facts,

[1] See, for this identification and other highly uncertain ones, G. Schütte, *Sigfrid und Brünhild, Ein als Mythus verkannter historischer Roman aus der Merowingerzeit* (1935).

[2] Cf. Grégoire, in *Byzantion* ix (1934), pp. 1–39.

[3] Cf. H. de Boor, in *Paul und Braunes Beiträge* lxiii (1939), pp. 250–71.

while, by really rather violent interference with the legend itself, the figure of Brünhild is eliminated.

If, however, a parallel for the full legend is desired, entirely different combinations can be made. At first sight the similarity of the Siegfried motif to the history of the Gothic hero Uraja is astonishing. Procopius gives the following account of him:[1] 'Uraja was married to a woman who surpassed all other Gothic women in riches and beauty. Once she went bathing dressed in a splendid garment and surrounded by numerous servants. She met the wife of King Ildibad, and in her pride she ignored the queen. No wonder that the queen, gravely insulted, insisted that her husband should avenge her. And it happened thus: first, Ildibad spread the rumour that Uraja wanted to go over to the enemies of the Goths, and after that he had him assassinated.'

These events, which also belong to the sixth century, reveal at first sight an almost convincing similarity to the Siegfried legend. But an objection can be raised: the names are entirely different, and, in addition, a Frankish legend has to be grafted on a Gothic story. Is there any reason to suppose, then, that Uraja's tragedy was known to the Franks, and had become such common property there that it was cast in an entirely Frankish mould? Can one assume that the name Uraja was replaced by a Frankish Siegfried, although the latter name was itself formed from Sigibert, the name of two Frankish kings?[2] Or can one perhaps draw the conclusion that in early Germanic circles such conflicts between proud women were not rare and could lead to disastrous results; and that the bathing scene was a fairly common occurrence?

These examples show that it is extremely difficult to find a really convincing historical prototype for the Siegfried legend. This is easy to understand, because legends usually handle the facts of history rather arbitrarily. Those who are good at ferreting things out will easily find some points of similarity, but the argument will not be conclusive and few will be convinced.

A view that was held very early links the Germanic hero Siegfried

---

[1] Cf. *Bellum Gothicum* iii. 1.

[2] Cf. M. Lintzel, 'Der historische Kern der Siegfriedsage', in *Historische Studien* 245 (1934).

with the hero of the *Germania*, Arminius. And indeed there are many points of contact. Arminius is a Roman name—it has nothing to do with Hermann or with names of the Ermanaric type—and the Cheruscan prince who was brought up in Rome is supposed to have adopted a Roman name, in the same manner as the Batavian Claudius Civilis. What was his original Germanic name? To answer this question one should note his father's name, Sigimerus, and also his father-in-law's name, Segestes, and this man's son Sigimundus. Names with the element *sigi-* were therefore not only popular among the Franks, but no less so among the Cherusci. It should also be remembered that the tribe of the Cherusci was one of the important components of the Frankish confederation. If, then, Cheruscan names lived on among the Franks, why should this not also have been the case with a legend of the Cherusci? One point at any rate is remarkable: an *Edda* song tells of Siegfried that he hid himself under the pseudonym 'hart', but the tribal name of the Cherusci has also been supposed to contain the word 'hart'. From all this, the very plausible conjecture may surely be hazarded that Arminius had such a name among his own people and was perhaps even called Sigifredus.[1] Tacitus tells us that Arminius was the subject of Germanic songs, and these songs, which must have been heroic epic poems, eventually gave rise to the Frankish poetry about Siegfried. It is not so strange that such a great and famous hero later assumed a more or less mythical character. We shall come back to this later.

Sometimes historical facts are altered on purpose. These alterations make the favourite heroic figures shine in an even nobler light. In his conquest of Italy Theoderic the Great cast a dark stain on his name. At the command of the emperor he went there to drive away another Germanic usurper, the Rugian prince Odoaker. His expedition did not fare as smoothly as he had expected: he was held up by the morasses that protected Ravenna. For years he had to besiege the town, and eventually it was famine that forced Odoaker to capitulate in 493. Theoderic was by then at enough of a disadvantage to agree that the two monarchs would rule Ravenna together. But a few days after his entry into the town Theoderic

[1] Cf. O. Höfler, in *Festschrift F. R. Schröder* (1959), pp. 11–121.

invited his adversary to his palace for a conference, and he is said to have slain him then with his own hand. 'Where is God?' the striken Odoaker called out; to which Theoderic answered scornfully: 'This is what you once did to my people.' Was this a sudden outburst of revenge or a political murder?

The dishonourable way in which he managed to become the sole ruler in Italy was naturally unacceptable to the Ostrogoths. Their revered king had to be whitewashed. And so we read in the *Lay of Hildebrand* that Theoderic was forced to flee from the 'envy' of Odoaker. For a long time he had to live in exile; until at last he reconquered his realm. So Odoaker was to blame, and it was understandable that Theoderic wanted to take revenge for so long an exile.

The conquest was therefore twisted into a reconquest. It is interesting that usurpers often try to falsify history by making it appear that they are not foreign conquerors, but princes returning to their legitimate property. The Arabian and Turkish conquerors of Iran have always represented themselves as the direct descendants of the Sassanids. But the Spartans also used this fiction as a means of propaganda. Later people made romances about the return of the Heraclids.

Now, how could Ermanaric take the place of Odoaker? Naturally the Rugian Odoaker had to be eliminated from the story. If Theoderic returned to his own country, then it must have been a Gothic prince who had at one time driven him away. Who could this have been? Not of course Theoderic's father, for it was too well known that he had been a vassal of Attila and had lived in Pannonia. An older king was needed. Why not the founder of the royal family of the Amali? So why not Ermanaric himself? He who loses is always wrong. Gothic tradition has not preserved a grateful memory of this ill-fated ruler. Already very early on he was said to have been killed by two brothers from the race of the Rosomoni, who wanted to take revenge on him for an infamous deed: Ermanaric had had their sister Sunilda trampled to death by horses. This is even remembered in the Old Norse *Edda* song, the *Hamdismál*.

This story gave Ermanaric the character of a cruel tyrant. Now it was he who had driven Theoderic from his realm. For this purpose Ermanaric was made into the uncle of the later Gothic king, and his now doubly infamous deed was accounted for (as happens so often in legend) by the treacherous promptings of an evil counsellor.

These examples may suffice to show how strangely legends can deal with history. It has been justly remarked that in Germanic heroic legend the great historical events assume the character of family conflicts. That is easily understandable. The people themselves have no clear notion of political relations. They ascribe what happens to the will and actions of their leaders. For it was mainly the rulers who determined the course of events, and they in turn were mainly driven by dynastic interests. By the marriages of royal children they attempted to strengthen their own authority, but these marriages often gave rise to unbearable tensions which inevitably led to war. Once it had started, the strife could go on as a feud for many generations; the romance of the Lorrains gives a terrifying example of this.

But there is more, for poetry deals with men and their fate. A poet cannot describe a fight as a clash of armies, he dissolves it into a series of duels in which the leaders and their noblemen on both sides measure each other's strength. In the French poem of *Gormont* the battle of Saucourt is made into a series of duels between the leader of the Vikings and the French noblemen; the culminating point is of course the personal fight between Gormont and the king himself. This is conditioned by the epic poem, which cannot describe mass fights. On the other hand we may possibly have here a relic of an older method of fighting in which the *dux* and his *comitatus* distinguish themselves by personal courage in fighting against their enemies, not stooping to conquer them by superior numbers.

It is, then, to be expected that in the course of the oral tradition the historical facts change out of all recognition. Eventually the moment must come when the matter is ripe for poetical treatment. For only then can the artist give a clear picture of the figures of the legend in their mutual relationships. The motivation of the events no longer lies in obscure political forces, but in the personal decisions of the acting heroes. And it is these that appeal to the minds of the listeners, who turn a deaf ear to history.

Now that we have given a few examples of the arbitrary way in which the facts of history can be changed in epic tradition, it is only fair to set against this the fact that they can occasionally be preserved with astonishing accuracy. What the Gothic historian tells us about the death of Ermanaric is found again with very little change in Scandinavian Eddic lays. His name has remained a beacon in the variable history of the Migration. Even in the poem of *De Vos Reinaerde*, in twelfth-century Dutch, King *Ermenrikes scat* is mentioned. The tragedy of the Burgundians, in itself not such an important event in the maelstrom of the events of the time, is still remembered by Austrians and Icelanders of the twelfth century. Theoderic has become the central figure of German heroic poetry: even his residence of Verona is remembered under the name of Bern.

It is striking how often the epic poetry of primitive nations will sometimes reflect historical facts from a very distant past. In New Zealand, stories are still told of the immigration of tribes which came from Tahiti and Hawaii centuries ago. I should like to quote as an example what Leo Frobenius relates of the Negro tribe of the Fulbe.[1] We have already given the narration of *The Lute of Gassire*, in which the kingdom Wagadu is mentioned, which four times came to power and glory, and four times perished. In it occurs repeatedly the chorus-like exclamation 'Ho Dierra, Agada, Ganna, Silla!—Ho Fasa!' Now Frobenius says that the tribe of the heroes is that of the Fasa, about which a great deal is told in the Sudan. Their capital is Dierra. Fasa, supposed to lie in the North and in the neighbourhood of the shores of the Mediterranean, can only be the Fezzan in which at present the ruins of 'Djermas' (Dierra) still lie: a memory of the old Garama, mentioned earlier in Herodotus, Pliny, and Strabo.

The hero Gassire set out southwards from there, and then the kingdom of Agada came into being—by which Agadez, situated in the land of Air north of the Haussa states, must have been meant. It seems very likely, therefore, that the Wagadu of the story stands for this same Agadez. A further conclusion may be drawn from this: the central sections of the *Dausi* had already been fully developed in Agadez before the foundation of the kingdom of Gana.

The *Dausi* epic goes back to an astonishingly early time. We can

[1] Cf. *Atlantis* vi, p. 50.

even turn to Herodotus for the elucidation of its historical background. For there, five hundred years before the beginning of our
era, we find the description of a tribe of Garamants who know about
agriculture, and go to war on chariots drawn by four horses. This
Garamantian civilization may go back to Phrygian-Thracean
colonies that flourished near Syrtis. This would give a surprising
explanation of the riddle of this epic that flourished in Central
Africa. Moreover, this view is confirmed by the fact that the district
in which this epic is found corresponds with the area in which
corpses are placed in huge urns: a custom that, on the shores of the
Mediterranean, can be traced as far back as 2500 to 3000 B.C.

We know that in the middle of the second century the Garamants
were still living in their old home. They were, however, already
pressing southwards and casting covetous eyes upon the Ethiopians
living farther inland. In the following centuries the Garamants begin
to withdraw and settle in the West Sudan. Taken together with
these events, then, *The Lute of Gassire* must have been made in the
fourth or fifth century B.C.

So far, then, does the *Dausi* epic go back in the past. The name of
Garama was changed to Djerma in the Fezzan, in the Sahel and in
the Sahara the first element Gara was preserved as the name of the
singers and curriers. If one remembers that in the Sudan languages *r*
can be replaced by *n*, it seems very probable that the powerful realm
of Gana is connected with the incursion of the Garamants into the
heart of Africa.

Finally, here is a remarkable example from Polynesia. In the year
1788, a fleet suddenly turned up in Guam, the capital of the Marianas, which appeared to have come from the Caroline Islands. In
order to arrive there, the seafarers had had to make a journey of
about three to four hundred miles. When they were asked by the
astonished inhabitants how they had been able to find their way
at all, they told the following story. Their ancestors had always been
accustomed to trade in Guam, but those expeditions had been dis-
continued when the whites had come to the Marianas and had
destroyed them. Now these islands were first discovered in 1521,
and the Spaniards took possession of them in 1565. It follows from
this that when these seafarers appeared in Guam the connexions

between the Marianas and the Caroline Islands had been broken for 223 years. They were then asked how they had been able to find the way. Their answer was that their songs contained several particulars about these voyages, and these had been sufficient to show them the way. Thus after more than two centuries they had been able to cross the Pacific to an island with a diameter of not more than twenty to thirty miles.[1]

Side by side with the question of a greater or lesser degree of historical accuracy in the epic tradition there is another problem, which is no less important: how long a period is necessary for the formation of an epic? The answer to this is not easy, because, to a great degree, we lack the evidence for it. The tendency is to assume a fairly long time for development, yet there are a few examples that show that it can happen surprisingly quickly.

Herodotus tells a story of the youth of Cyrus, which is a typical example of the formation of a legend. It recalls that of Romulus and Remus. A hero's child is hunted and has to go into hiding. He is brought up secretly, but his heroic character emerges clearly and his honours are restored to him later. (Chapter 11 gives several examples of this theme.) Herodotus had therefore heard the story of Cyrus' youth in this form. He travelled in Persia around 450 B.C. in the prime of his life, and if he heard such fabulous stories about the historical Cyrus they may be assumed to have been generally current there. We may at least suppose, then, that about 480 B.C. this legend about Cyrus was in circulation. Now this Persian king died in 529, so that in about half a century his history had grown into a true legend.[2]

Even more striking is the Hungarian legend of Hunyadi, the famous warrior who lived from 1385 to 1456. He was the son of a Rumanian of the lower nobility, who had received the castle of Hunyad in Transylvania from the Emperor Sigismund. Later, he fought successfully against the Turks and forced them to conclude a peace that was advantageous to the Hungarians. At last he even became regent for King Ladislaus V. But at the end of his life he suf-

---

[1] Cf. A. de Quatrefages, 'Les Polynésiens et leurs migrations', in *Revue des deux Mondes* 864, p. 865.

[2] Cf. J. G. von Hahn, *Sagwissenschaftliche Studien* (1876), p. 68.

fered several defeats. His son, Matthias Corvinus, stepped on to the throne of Hungary.

The remarkable life of a simple country nobleman whose son rose to be King of Hungary was bound to appeal strongly to the popular imagination. As in the case of Theoderic, the desire to make the dynasty he founded a legitimate one played a great part, and this could only be done by linking it to the line of Sigismund. And indeed a chronicle[1] says: One day, when Sigismund was in Transylvania, he fell in love with the beautiful daughter of a Wallachian nobleman. When on his return he learned that she was pregnant, Sigismund gave her a rich gift and presented her with a ring as a symbol, commanding her to bring the infant up properly, and to send their child to him with the ring when he was grown up. A boy was born, who received the name of Johannes. But one day, before the child was born, a raven had come and stolen the ring. She asked her husband at once to pursue the bird and get the ring back. He succeeded in killing the raven with an arrow, and so the ring came back into the mother's possession. When the boy grew up he took the ring to Sigismund, and when the latter recognized his son by this ring he gave him a large piece of territory.

This typical legend of a hero's youth is, it would seem, needlessly complicated by the fact that the ring had first to be stolen by a raven, for the final result merely means that the normal state of affairs is restored when the ring returns to the mother's possession. However, this episode served to give an explanation of the family arms. It is probable that this legend had already arisen in the years immediately following Hunyadi's death in 1456. The *milieu* in which this happened was a group of soldiers whose fathers had taken part in Hunyadi's wars under his leadership. It is therefore a legend that arose in the circle of a *comitatus*. Moreover, these warriors consisted mainly of frontier inhabitants[2] of Wallachia, so that the local origin of the legend can also be indicated here. If we compare the legend of Roland, we can conclude that this too may have received its first form among his warriors, who came from the Breton borderland.

[1] Cf. *Die Chronik der Grafen von Celli.*
[2] Cf. H. von Mžik, in *Mitteilungen der Anthropologischen Gesellschaft in Wien* lxiv (1934), pp. 213–18.

It appears, then, from the preceding observations that heroic legends are rooted in some historical fact, and also that any nation can experience an 'heroic age' in its history, i.e., an age in which historical figures who have appealed to the imagination of contemporaries and descendants can become heroes. The hero is therefore the sublimation of a man who actually lived at some time.

The question that must now be answered is: how does it come to pass that an heroic legend can arise out of a period of history in which people actually lived, and, we may add, lived intensely.

Andreas Heusler, whose great importance for our deeper knowledge of the essence and development of the heroic song nobody will deny (however much we have later come to differ from his views in many respects), once expressed it as follows: 'The heroic songs drew upon history, upon personal life, upon personal invention, and upon subject-matter at hand.' [1] This is a striking summing-up of the activity of the great poets which crowned and at the same time ended the long tradition of heroic song. This applies to Homer, to Turoldus, and to the unknown poet of the *Nibelungenlied*.

About personal life: the flowery similes of the *Iliad* come to mind; the description of the swineherd Eumaeus in the *Odyssey*, the story of tournaments and messengers' journeys in the *Nibelungenlied*, the description of the battlefield of Roncevaux in the *Song of Roland*.

About personal invention: one immediately recalls Odysseus' sojourn in the country of the Phaeaceans in the *Odyssey*; Hector's farewell to Andromache, or the grey-haired men throwing bright glances at Helen as she walks along, in the *Iliad*; the journey of Ganelon to the Emir of Saragossa in the *Song of Roland*; and the Rüedeger episode in the *Nibelungenlied*.

About subject-matter at hand to which motifs from fairy-tales and myths belong: the myths of the gods in the *Iliad*; the hero's sojourn with Circe and Calypso or the episode of the Sirens in the *Odyssey*; the motif of the Symplegades in the legend of the Argonauts; the fight with the dwarf Alberich and the winning of the *Tarnkappe* in the Siegfried legend; and the Grendel episode in *Beowulf*—all these come to mind.

[1] Cf. 'Geschichtliches und Mythisches in der germanischen Heldensage', in *Sitzungsberichte der Akademie der Wissenschaften*, Berlin 1909, pp. 920–45.

And it is all perfectly true. But it applies mainly to the great epic poems that come at the end of some development. Their poets have a positive hunger for subject-matter, and one can understand this, for out of given and fairly meagre subject-matter they wish to conjure up a comprehensive whole. But when we try to imagine how an heroic legend, the first heroic song, arose out of an historical fact, this explanation does not hold. In the legend of Hunyadi the story of the raven can easily be eliminated as a secondary motif, but what remains is a fixed scheme of heroic legend and myth which has taken the place of the historical life of the hero.

One might call it a mutation when one considers the transition of an historical person into a hero. He is placed in an entirely different sphere—a sphere much higher and more important than that of the world from which he has emerged. One should not therefore think that the addition of all sorts of elements—those mentioned by Heusler—from an event of history makes the origin of an heroic legend. Nowadays people often speak of *Ganzheiten* (complete entities): an entirely different matter from joining together a number of parts. The human body is not a structure of limbs, heart, lungs, and stomach, but it is a 'complete entity', an organism with its functional organs. The historical event and the heroic legend can be said similarly to oppose one another—as entities. What is the magic wand which effects this mutation?

To explain this it will first of all be necessary to obtain an idea of the curious structure of an heroic legend. For only then do we realize that the heroic life is a life *sui generis*, which does not belong to history and which cannot be lived by ordinary mortals.

II

THE PATTERN OF AN HEROIC LIFE

IN considering the history of various heroes we are struck by the appearance of the same or at least similar motifs. A dragon-fight as well as the liberation of a maiden seem almost obligatory for a hero. A hero's youth is usually passed in secrecy and humiliation: he is hunted and so has to remain in hiding. His birth is not like that of an ordinary mortal, there is often difficulty in having it legitimized. Gods frequently play a notable part in it.

It is not necessary that the lives of all heroes should contain the complete series of these motifs. Yet one always has the impression that a hero's life is the more or less complete reflection of a pattern in which these elements have their fixed places. Moreover, it appears that the same applies to the contents of myth as well as of fairy-tale, so that it is possible to draw up a scheme or pattern to which myth, heroic legend, and fairy-tale conform in broad and general outline.

The brilliant but often unappreciated scholar, J. G. von Hahn, who was in the diplomatic service in Greece for a long time and diligently collected and noted down Greek popular traditions, drew up such a scheme in 1876, which he called a 'complex of motifs'.[1] He distinguished three main sections: birth, youth, and then return or death. His scheme contains thirteen motifs, all or most of which he points out in the Greek legends of gods and heroes, but for which he also points out examples from Rome, Persia, Bactria, and India, as well as Germanic ones. It is a pity that so little attention was given to this view at the time of the appearance of his book.

In 1936 the English author Lord Raglan also drew up a 'hero-pattern' in a book which sometimes makes the reader suspicious because of its amateurish character, yet contains a number of fresh

[1] Cf. *Sagwissenschaftliche Studien*, pp. 240 ff.

observations and ideas perhaps precisely because of this.[1] He distinguishes twenty-two motifs. This scheme is not very consistently thought out. It has, as well as basic motifs, others which are only of a secondary significance. In spite of this, one gains the impression that a hero's life is not merely a fortuitous combination of marvellous deeds and experiences, but that it also has to be the expression of a certain idea. Finally, in 1954, in a book whose subject was really the fairy-tale, I also drew up such a pattern.[2] But this was mainly intended as a scheme for the life of the fairy-tale hero, although again and again remarkable parallels from myth and heroic legend could be brought in for comparison.

In the light of these observations on heroic legend it would therefore seem useful once more to outline such a pattern, but this time I shall naturally leave out all references to the fairy-tale. On the other hand, I shall mention a fair number of examples from myth and heroic legend. Although I shall make the pattern as full as possible, I lay no claim to completeness; I only want to show, by citing the best-known or most typical examples, how wide-spread this pattern is. I shall naturally confine myself to the area of Indo-European heroic legend, although for the sake of illustration I shall occasionally go beyond it.

PATTERN OF AN HEROIC LIFE

I. *The begetting of the hero*

A. The mother is a virgin, who is in some cases overpowered by a god, or has extra-marital relations with the hero's father. Greek examples are: Danae, the mother of Peleus; Alcmene, the mother of Heracles; Antiope, who gave birth to Amphion and Zethus; Tyro, the mother of Neleus and Pelias; Phylone, the mother of Leucastus and Parrhasius. For India, there is Kunti, the mother of Karna. For the Romans, Rhea Silvia, who conceived Romulus and Remus. In Germanic tradition we can cite Hiltburg, the mother of Wolfdietrich. For the Irish, Dechtire, the mother of Cúchulainn. Among

---

[1] *The Hero, A Study in Tradition, Myth and Drama*, pp. 178 ff.
[2] 'Betrachtungen zum Märchen, besonders in seinem Verhältnis zu Heldensage und Mythos', in *FFCommunications* No. 150, pp. 137–53.

the Hungarians it occurs in the legend of Hunyadi. In the story of the fight between father and son this is likewise an obvious starting point; cf. among the Persians Rustum, Kavad, Chosrev, and Abu Ga'far; in Great Russia the legend of Ilya and Sokolnitchek; in Ireland the legend of Cúchulainn.

B. The father is a God. Among the Greeks this is a very common motif. Thus Zeus mates with Danae, Alcmene, and Antiope; Poseidon with Tyro and Alope; Apollo with Rhoio; he is also supposed to have begotten Pythagoras with a virgin! Among the Indians we know the example of the sun-god with Kunti, among the Romans that of Mars with Rhea Silvia. In Irish tradition Cúchulainn is assumed to be the son of the god Lug and Dechtire. In Old Norse legend Odin begets a son Vali with the giantess Rindr.

C. The father is an animal, often the disguise of a god. Zeus as a bull begets Dionysius with Io, as a swan Helen with Nemesis. Kronos in the shape of a horse mates with Filyra and begets Chiron. Alexander is the son of Nectanebus who, in the shape of a serpent, mates with Olympias.

D. The child is conceived in incest. Castor and Clytemnestra are the fruits of Tyndareus' association with his daughter Leda; an Irish legend takes Cúchulainn to be the son of Conchobar and his daughter Dechtire. The Irish hero Lugaid Riab n-Derg is the son of three brothers, Bres, Nar, Lothar, and their sister. Norse legend knows Sinfjötli, child of Sigmund's union with his sister Signy.

II. *The birth of a hero*

A. It takes place in an unnatural way. Zeus brings forth Dionysus out of his thigh, Athene out of his head. It is told in India that Mamdhatr was born out of his father's side.

B. The 'unborn' hero, i.e. the child that is born by means of a caesarean section. This is told of the Persian Rustum, the Welsh Tristan, and the Russian Dobrynya Nikititch. The Russian hero Rogdai is even born out of his mother's corpse.

III. *The youth of the hero is threatened*

A. The child is exposed, either by the father who has been warned in a dream that the child will be a danger to him, or by the mother who thus tries to hide her shame.

This is said in Indian tradition of Krishna; in Persia of Cyrus, Feridun, and Artachsir. Greek examples are Aeolus and Bopotos, sons of Nestor, also Antilochus, Oedipus, Hippothous, the twins Amphion and Zethus, Pelias and Neleus, Leucastus and Parrhasius. German legend mentions Wolfdietrich. The well-known Moses motif, that the child is thrown into the sea or a river in a basket or chest, is told in Greek tradition of Peleus, Telephus, Anius, and Dionysus, in Welsh tradition of Taliesin. Romulus and Remus are cast into the Tiber.

B. The exposed child is fed by animals.

a. By a doe: the Greek heroes Antilochus and Telephus, the Germanic hero Siegfried, and the Knight of the Swan.

b. By a she-wolf: Greek legend has Leucastus and Parrhasius, Roman legend Romulus and Remus, Irish legend Cormac mac Airt. From this motif the German hero Wolfdietrich received his name.

c. By a she-bear: the Greek hero Paris and the French Ourson. By a she-wolf as well as a she-bear: the Slav heroes Valigora and Vyrvidab.

d. By a mare: in Greek legend this is said of Hippothous and the twins Amphion and Zethus, in Serbian legend of Milosh Obilitch.

e. By a cow: the Persian hero Feridun.

f. By a goat: the most famous example is Zeus and the goat Amalthea; Persian legend tells this of Artachsir; in Babylonia we have Nebuchadnezzar.

g. By a bitch: besides the Persian Cyrus, there is the Greek hero Neleus.

h. By a jackal: this is told of Nimrud.

i. By an eagle: in the Babylonian epic of Gilgamesh and, among the Persians, Achaimenes.

j. By the bird Simurg: the Persian hero Zal.

C. After that the child is found by shepherds, etc. In some cases it is found by shepherds or it is taken to them.

a. Shepherds: this is told of the Indian Krishna, of the Greek Zeus, also of the Persian heroes Cyrus, Kaj Chosrev, and Feridun; of the Greek heroes Heracles, Oedipus, Orestes, and the twins Aeolus and Boetus.

b. Fishermen: the Greek Peleus.

c. Gardener: the Assyrian King Sargon.

D. In Greek legend various heroes are brought up by a mythical figure; e.g. by Chiron: Achilles, Aeneas, Asclepius, Jason, Peleus, and Polyxenus.

IV. *The way in which the hero is brought up*

A. The hero reveals his strength, courage, or other particular features at a very early age.

While still in his cradle Dionysus reveals his god-like nature by the theft of Apollo's cattle, and Apollo kills the dragon Python when he is still very young. When only eight months old, Heracles strangles the serpents sent by Hera. As a child Paris wins back the stolen cows. The Persian heroes Cyrus and Kaj Chosrev mature at an early age. Well-known examples from Germanic heroic legend are Siegfried and Mimir. When one night old the Norse god Vali avenges Balder. Cúchulainn reveals his strength in the fight with the 'three times fifty' boys as a boy of five years. In Tartar heroic poetry we have an example in the story of the hero who breaks his iron cradle into pieces, and then at once proceeds to make arrow-point, spear and sword, to break off the horns of six ibexes in order to make a bow out of them, and to cut the string out of an elephant's hide.

B. On the other hand the child is often very slow in his development: he is dumb or pretends to be mentally deficient.

Unmanly in their youth are Percival and Starkad, also the Russian hero Ilya Murometch. This is also said of the French Rainoart and of the Fulbe hero Samba Kullung. The Old Norse saga calls such a hero *kolbítr*, the 'coal-biter'. Because he just lazes about near the hearth, this is said of Grettir, Glúmr, and Thorsteinn, the son of Thorgnýr. In the *Edda* there is the example of Helgi, the son of Hjörvard. The Danish hero Offa is dumb in his youth; the figure of Hamlet, who pretends to be feeble-minded, is famous; so is the Persian Kaj Chosrev.

V. *The hero often acquires invulnerability*

First of all Achilles, who can only be wounded in his heel. It seems that this motif, which appears first in Apollonius Rhodius, is a later addition; this is also assumed in the case of Aias, Cycnus, Meleager, and Pterelaus. The Cretan King Minos, like the Etruscan Messapus, is invulnerable. The same applies to the Germanic hero Siegfried, who is protected by a horny skin, a trait which is also narrated of the Irish heroes Fer Diad and Conganchnes (= horny skin). The Persian hero Isfandiar also has an impenetrable skin. Particularly safeguarded is the hero who can only be wounded in the sole of his foot, such as the Indian Krishna, while the Danish Frogerus can only be killed when sand is taken from under his feet. The Persian Spandiyadh and the Irish Balor are vulnerable in the eye, the French hero Ferragus in the navel. The death of the Welsh hero Llew Llaw Gyffes is subject to very special conditions. Balder can only be killed by mistletoe; the Finnish Lemminkäinen by a stem of hemlock. It often occurs that a hero can only be killed by his own sword, such as the Persian Isfandiar and the Russian Charko.

VI. *One of the most common heroic deeds is the fight with a dragon or another monster*

The dragon-fight is known from the Persian heroes Rustum, Sam, Gushtasp, Isfandiar, Artachsir, and Bahram Gor; from the Germanic heroes Siegfried, Beowulf, Wolfdietrich, and Heimir; and it is also told of Tristan (in Béroul's poem). In Greek legend Heracles is the great conqueror of all kinds of monsters, but Apollo too conquers the dragon Python, Theseus the Minotaur, and Bellerophon the Chimaera. The story of the fight with the dragon, who is the symbol of chaos, is known from the Babylonian myth of Marduk, and also from the Egyptian myth of the god Re.

VII. *The hero wins a maiden, usually after overcoming great dangers*

Thus Perseus has to rescue Andromeda from a dragon. Neleus must accomplish the task of fetching the cattle from Phylace; Pelias has to harness a lion and a bear to a chariot; Pelops has to have a running-match with Oenomaus; Oedipus solves the riddle of the

Sphinx. Siegfried and Wolfdietrich win a maiden. The same is told of Väinämöinen in the Finnish *Kalevala*.

VIII. *The hero makes an expedition to the underworld*

Gilgamesh does this in the Babylonian epic; Heracles, Ajax, and Odysseus in the Greek epic; Väinämöinen in the *Kalevala*.

IX. *When the hero is banished in his youth he returns later and is victorious over his enemies. In some cases he has to leave the realm again which he has won with such difficulty.*

This is told of the Indian Pandavas, of the Persians Cyrus and Kaj Chosrev, of the Greeks Jason and Peleus, and the Gothic hero Theoderic. Pelias and Neleus kill Siderus; Amphion and Zethus rescue their mother Antiope. The Roman heroes Romulus and Remus kill Amulius.

X. *The death of the hero*

Heroes often die young, like Achilles, Siegfried, and Cúchulainn. In many cases their death is miraculous. Romulus is taken up into heaven, Heracles has his apotheosis on Mount Oeta, Theseus is thrown off the rock on Scyros, and Kaj Chosrev vanishes into the desert.

Naturally, not every heroic life shows the complete pattern. Yet there are several examples that contain a large number of these features. Some examples, especially from Greek legend, may serve to illustrate this:

Heracles is begotten by Zeus with Alcmene, reared by shepherds, at an early age already performs his first heroic deed, has to perform his twelve labours in the service of Eurystheus, among which is the fight with dangerous monsters and the descent into the underworld to fetch Cerberus. In the end he has his apotheosis— after having met his death through the poisonous garment of Nessus.

As a result of an oracle Oedipus is exposed and found by shepherds. He kills his father, marries his mother, and finds his death in exile.

Theseus is the son of Aegeus and Aethra, slays the Minotaur on Crete, returns to Athens (where Pandion had to flee from him) and is the real founder of the Athenian *polis*; but he is thrown from a rock into the sea on Scyros by Lycomedes.

Cyrus, as a result of an ominous dream, is handed over by Astyages to servants to be killed; they expose him, he is fed by a bitch and found and reared by shepherds. At an early age he reveals his royal talents by acting with authority and power as a boy-king. In the end he dethrones Astyages and conquers his realm.

A good example in India is Karna. He is the son whom the sun-god begot with Kunti, and after his birth he is thrown into the river. He has to serve the Pandavas as a charioteer, plays a great part in the victory of Kuruksetra, and finally meets his death in a desert.

The Germanic hero Siegfried is fed by a doe and reared by a smith. He avenges his father, slays a dragon, wins the Nibelung hoard and rescues a maiden; in the end, although invulnerable, he dies young—through treachery.

Many investigators of legends are in the habit of analysing the story of an heroic life, separating younger from older elements in it, and then reducing the legend to its simplest form. Thus Bethe tried to show [1] that in the legend of Perseus the fight with the dragon, the rescue of Andromeda, and the story of his birth may be considered as later additions. From the original contents there remains only the fight with the Gorgons and the slaying of Medusa. But it is surely remarkable that the Perseus legend as a whole conforms so completely to the pattern of an heroic life, such as we have drawn up above. Are we to assume, then, that features gradually came to be added to the legend of Perseus which were part of this universal scheme which lived in the subconscious minds of poets and singers, and that this gave rise to the pattern? But this raises another question. In the life of which hero does this pattern first reveal itself in clear form, and how was it then possible that it could assert itself, so to speak, as the obligatory form for the life of a hero?

A figure like the definitely historical King Cyrus also shows very clearly that his actual life has been reshaped according to the proto-type of an heroic pattern. In this case it is useless to try and investigate the order in which the various motifs were connected with him. There has been no question here of a gradual development; at a

[1] Cf. *Hessische Blätter für Volkskunde* iv (1905), p. 135.

H

certain moment people saw in him, as the Ostrogoths saw in Theoderic, no longer an ordinary mortal but a true hero, and then his life was at once transformed in accord with the heroic pattern.

The Welsh tradition of Arthur shows a completely analogous development. He was soon thought of as the son and successor of the god Naudu. Even the story of the wounding of Naudu was transferred to Arthur, and he was therefore expected to return to his people one day from Avalon, the land of the dead. It is assumed that this transformation of the tradition of Arthur into myth began as early as the tenth century.

It is remarkable that among so many nations the life-history of a hero again and again reveals the same features. The result of this is that the heroes of virtually all parts of the world have features in common. In such cases of similarity one should not be too quickly inclined to speak of borrowing. The German scholar Dornseiff has drawn an ingenious parallel between Heracles and Samson.[1] He mentions as points of similarity the story of the birth, the first fight with the lion, death through a woman (Delilah and Deianira, but what a difference!), carrying out slaves' work (serving Eurystheus and working the mill with the Philistines), submissiveness to a woman (Heracles spins for Omphale, Samson is powerless with Delilah), losing a head of hair (but with Heracles this happens through the heat of the intestines of the sea-monster). In reading this we may easily be impressed by the large number of similarities. But when we consider them separately, the differences are often so great that we can hardly equate the two legends.

Yet Dornseiff expresses the opinion that Heracles was borrowed by the Greeks from an Oriental legendary figure. And we remember that von Wilamowitz was once struck by the great similarity between Heracles and Gilgamesh![2] Dornseiff also points to a Sumerian seal dating from about 2500 B.C. and found in Tell Asmar. This has on it the picture of a boy covered in an animal's skin and armed with club and bow; he is fighting with a hydra and crayfish in the presence of the gods. We might imagine Enkidu in his natural state as more or less like this.

---

[1] Cf. *Antike und alter Orient* (1956), pp. 351–63.
[2] Cf. *Herakles* (1909), p. 26, n. 50.

But what does this prove? That the Greeks took over the figure of Heracles and his legend from the East? Naturally. The Greeks lived in a *milieu* that was entirely influenced by the civilization of the peoples of the East. But the Greeks developed in the midst of the Aegean civilization, and so the Heracles-type may in fact go back to the period in which the Greeks began to form their civilization in direct contact with this highly civilized pre-Indo-European population. But the question assumes an entirely different aspect when we bear in mind that the same heroic pattern is found among virtually all Indo-European nations. This can surely hardly be explained by a simple borrowing from a type that is supposed to have arisen first among Semitic nations, still less when we find a very analogous structure in the life of the cult-hero Maui in New Zealand.

We must therefore try to explain why the heroic life is found over large areas of the world and why always formed in the same pattern. Several times we have come across examples in which gods reveal at least partly the same features as heroes. In several places in the list drawn up above we included Krishna in India, Zeus, Apollo, and Dionysus in Greece—and after the investigations of Dumézil we may safely add the Roman twins Romulus and Remus. It seems to me out of the question that the myth of the gods should have been extended by borrowings from heroic legend. For then the question arises: what about the heroic legend? This in itself is nothing but a poetic invention to which all kinds of fairy-tales are supposed to have contributed: the fighting with a dragon and the cutting out of the tongue as evidence (as in the legends of Peleus and Alcathous), the rescue of a maiden, Melusine motifs (as in the legends of Peleus and Thetis, Amor, and Psyche), the stepmother motif (as in the legend of Phrixus and Helle), the setting of three tasks (as in that of Jason and Theseus), the motif of the Urias letter (as in the legend of Bellerophon) and so many others.[1] And then the verdict must be: we should break with the method of deriving the details of a complex legend from an underlying mythical representation.[2]

But against this the following may be advanced. It is certainly dangerous and it may lead to false conclusions to consider every

---

[1] Cf. W. Kroll, *Neue Jahrbücher für das klassische Altertum* xv (1912), p. 170.
[2] *Ibid.*, p. 171.

detail in this way. The legends lived for centuries as handed down by many bards and poets, who exercised their imagination on them all the time. Why should they not have gathered new motifs from all directions for the further embellishment or expansion of the story? This may, for example, have happened in the case of the Urias letter in the legend of Bellerophon. But this does not follow everywhere to the same extent.

Let us take as an example the fight with a dragon and the rescue of a maiden. They belong to the central motifs of heroic legend. Are we to treat them as simple fairy-tale motifs? And the fairy-tale itself? Is it autonomous? Or did it get its motifs from somewhere else? At any rate this much has recently become clear: the fairy-tale too is built from motifs that belong to the world of myth; it is even a secularized form of the myth itself.[1]

In a discussion of the neo-Greek epic of *Digenis Akritas*, J. Lindsay made the following observation:[2] 'But if we look deeper into the meaning of *Digenis* we recognize in it the initiation-term *Twice-born* used of the second birth of the young man who has successfully passed the tests and ordeals. And we can call our hero the representative of the initiation-ritual, the youth who supremely defeats the dark forces of the crisis-moment and who therefore symbolizes his people in their death and renewal. Such an interpretation harmonizes with the many elements of fertility-ritual that surround Digenis in the ballads and the lay, and that show up in the folk-beliefs about his tomb and his Heraclean club.'

This seems to me a thought which is worth considering in regard to other heroes. But it would apparently have to be supported in a different way. Let us therefore ask first: what is the ritual of initiation?

Everywhere puberty is considered as such an important moment in a young man's life that it is connected with a complicated and significant ritual. These are in the first place what van Gennep has called the *rites de passage*. The content of these rites is not so much the symbolization of a transition as of a 'new birth'. The child dies and the man begins his life. They are, as it were, two different beings

---

[1] See my book mentioned in note 2, p. 211.
[2] *Byzantium into Europe* (1952), p. 370.

who at this moment separate within the same individual. The ritual has to provide the adequate symbol for this. The initiation is therefore a passage through death to a new life. We shall see presently how this is realized.

Naturally the initiation is much more than this. First of all it is the maturation of the male individual, the capacity to beget children. A sexual element is therefore inseparably linked up with the initiation. This often takes the form of orgiastic promiscuity; the newly-gained virility has first to run its full course in unbridled vehemence so as afterwards to be canalized, often by the strictest regulations of social life. Now is also the time that the marriageable young man must choose himself a wife, and he often has to prove himself worthy of her by giving proofs of his valour. Is it then so strange that, in the legends, dragon and maiden are so closely linked together?

Finally, from the moment of puberty the young man acts as a fully qualified member of society. He must now learn which laws and rules are valid and, especially, how they are sanctioned. Hence initiation also means a severe schooling in which the young man has to make himself familiar with the holy traditions of his tribe. So first of all the mythical traditions are taught: in particular all those things which a full male member of the tribe must know but which must be kept strictly secret from women and children. And further, everything relating to the daily life of a man as a member of his tribal community.

After the ceremony, he is a mature and informed man. It really testifies to great wisdom that the primitive peoples treat this transition period for the young man, so important and hazardous physically and mentally, as a focal point of an important communal experience. They avoid the many difficulties and disturbances attending this transition which is allowed to take its course as inconspicuously as possible in modern society, with the result that the young man finds himself in complete isolation. The old tribes seem to have realized the danger, and to have counteracted it one way or another. This was also the case with the Indo-Europeans. Sexual and mental maturity are attained at the same moment: could this be the key to the remarkable linguistic fact that the same root *gen* means both 'know' and 'beget'—a fact which we also know from the Old Testament?

But let us return to the ritual proper. The initiation, then, is a passage through death to a new life. But how is new life acquired? The oldest example of this is the way in which all organized life on earth once came into existence. The creation of the earth therefore is the obvious example for the ritual of initiation, which is only a repeated manifestation of it.

It is thus far from accidental that the heroic pattern can also apply to the gods in many respects. I may mention here the fight of the Babylonian Marduk with the monster Tiamat and of the Egyptian Re with the serpent Apep. The monsters slain by these gods are the powers of chaos, which must be destroyed so that the cosmos can be created. This is sometimes said to be created out of the parts of such primeval creatures; an example of this is the Norse myth of Ymir. Another idea is that the earth rises up out of the primeval waters and is therefore still lying in the middle of the ocean. Hence the monster of chaos is a water-monster, both in Babylonia and in Egypt.

This explains why, in the initiation ritual, the dragon or some such monster plays an important part. The creature is a symbol of chaos; he who is going to be initiated must pass through this creature to be born a new man. The monster is therefore constructed artificially, and is made to look so dangerous that it must have an enormous suggestive effect on the unsuspecting youth. It looks like a real monster; the youth is convinced that he is devoured by it, and for some time suffers hellish torments in its body.

The story of Jonah in the whale undoubtedly belongs to this group of ideas. But the same is told of Heracles. He has to fight the monster that threatens to devour Hesione, whom Laomedon, directed by the oracle of Zeus Ammon, had chained to a rock on the sea-shore. The Trojans are said to have built a high wall to protect Heracles against the monster. But when the animal rose out of the sea and opened its enormous mouth, Heracles jumped into its throat fully armed and stayed three days in the monster's belly, finally emerging from it as the victor.

We may compare the similar heroic deed done by Perseus who

had to rescue Andromeda—likewise chained to a rock on the sea-shore—from a monster. Only his fight and victory have a less archaic character than that of Heracles. Perseus, provided with the winged sandals of Hermes, flew to the place where Andromeda was chained; and when he saw the monster approach from the sea he dived down suddenly and cut off his head with a sickle.

The legend of Theseus is of particular importance in this con-nexion. This time the monster is the Minotaur who is locked up in the middle of a mountain. The approach to him is through the laby-rinth constructed by Daedalus. But the labyrinth is a symbol of the realm of the dead, or rather of the way to get there, which must be retraced in order to return again to the world of the living.[1] With-out the thread of Ariadne the hero would never have managed this. But with it he killed the monster in its lair and found his way, un-injured, back to the world of the living. Here the outline of the myth, and also of the initiation ritual, comes out very clearly. Through the labyrinth the hero descends into the underworld where the demon lives. Once he has killed it, he can be freed from death and be reborn. After his arrival on Delos, Theseus instituted the labyrinth dance, which was to be not only a memory of his heroic deed for future generations but also created the possibility of performing the initiation ceremony symbolically.

The hero can be devoured by the monster. An example of that is the Finnish hero Väinämöinen, who descends into the mouth of Antero Vipunen. The monster can also be visited in his lair, and killed there. A clear example of this is the legend of Beowulf. The monster Grendel lives at the bottom of a lake, and again we have here the combination of primeval creature and depth of water; i.e. a reference to chaos. The hero has to dive into the water, and at the bot-tom he finds a cave in which the monster lives. Here he has to kill it.

The German heroes Ortnit and Wolfdietrich fight the dragon in his own cave, to which they have been dragged by the monster; with a tragic result in Ortnit's case, for he meets his death in it. Wolfdietrich is the triumphant hero, for he manages to kill the dragon and all his brood.

[1] Cf. my treatise 'Untersuchungen über das Hüpfspiel, Kinderspiel—Kulttanz', in *FFCommunications* No. 173 (1957).

The underworld is the place where riches lie hidden—an idea based on the observation that all fecundity comes from, and is fed by, the earth. The riches of the field are a gift from Mother Earth. From the grain of corn sown in the earth grows a rich harvest. The Greek conception is 'Plutos' is 'Pluton'. This at once explains why dragons always guard hoards; as powers of the underworld they have all riches at their disposal. But another idea is also mixed up in this. From chaos spring the overwhelming riches of the cosmos: the land with its mountains and valleys, seas and rivers, plants and animals: all the treasures that man may command at his pleasure. The primeval being in his malevolence kept all these treasures hidden, the god who killed it took possession of all these treasures. The myth of Ymir puts it differently: all the elements of the cosmos come from the body of the primeval being.

That is why in killing a dragon the hero often finds an immense treasure. This happens to Siegfried. After killing Fafnir he is able to take possession of the Nibelung hoard. Odin advises him to dig three ditches at the place where Fafnir goes to drink, and there to strike him in his belly—the only spot in the scaly body where the monster is vulnerable. Would it be too bold to see in these three ditches a memory, no longer understood, of the labyrinth motif?

After having tried to show that the central theme in an heroic life is an echo both of a god's first work of creation and of its imitation in the initiation ritual, we shall now deal with another almost equally indispensable part of the heroic life: the hero's birth and youth.

Whenever gods are born we meet the same motifs as in the youth of a hero. When Zeus is born he is threatened by Cronus who (like Pelias) is afraid that his son will deprive him of the government of the world. He therefore swallows up at once every child that is born to him. But the mother is able to deceive Cronus: she has the child taken to Crete where he is suckled by a goat. There he grows up fast among the shepherds on Mount Ida. When Zeus is fully grown he returns to his mother Rhea and revenges himself on Cronus.

Apollo is the fruit of the union of Zeus and Leto. His birth is threatened by the jealousy of Hera, and so it has to take place on the island of Delos. At four days old, he asks for bow and arrow and goes to Mount Parnassus, where the Python lives who, at Hera's command, had pursued Leto. He kills the dragon in the place where sacred Delphi was later to be built.

Hermes too was a son of Zeus, by Maia, the daughter of Atlas; he was born in a cave on Mount Cyllene in Arcadia. His cradle was a winnowing-fan, but, as he did not want to stay in it for very long, he climbed out in search of adventure, and in Pieria found a herd of oxen belonging to Apollo. His resourcefulness is already shown on this occasion: he tied sandals of oak-bark under the legs of the animals, but turned the wrong way round, thereby deceiving Apollo in the direction he had driven the herd.

One may be inclined to say that the gods appear as human heroes in these stories; the poets have used heroic legends for the embellishment of the myths of the gods. But is it not rather the other way round? Are not the lives of the heroes repetitions and imitations of the lives of the gods? Is not therefore the myth the parent of the heroic legend?

We have seen that a king like Cyrus could become the hero of a real legend. How was that possible? Let us once more consider Marduk, the god who made creation possible by killing the monster Tiamat. He does this as a young boy. None of the gods dared to undertake this adventure. But he did so, and demanded, in exchange for performing the heroic deed, that he be recognized as the highest of the gods. Now in the East, the kings were the representatives of the gods themselves. We always find there the idea of the godlike nature of the king. This must give rise to the idea that the king lives the same life as the god. When in Babylonia the Feast of New Year is celebrated this is essentially the repetition, or rather the activation, of the deed of creation: the old year dies, and after a short period of chaos a new year arises. It is therefore easy to understand that it is on this occasion that the epic of creation is recited: what happens *hic et nunc* is really the same as what was once performed as a work of creation in primeval days, *in illo tempore*. So the king takes the place of the god himself. This explains how a mythical scheme can immediately be transferred to a king. If the king is considered as essentially identical with the god, then he also performs the deeds that are told of the god.

And so the question forces itself upon us: what is the relationship between hero and god? How far are we entitled to explain heroic legend from myth? I shall attempt to answer this question in the next chapter.

12

THE MYTHICAL BACKGROUND OF
HEROIC LEGEND

IN the previous chapter we gave several indications of the connexion between heroic legend and myth. When one speaks of mythical elements in the epic, as a rule one has in mind particularly the 'apparatus of gods' in the Homeric poems. But however great the significance of the gods may be for the proper understanding of the *Iliad* and the *Odyssey*, this is not the essential mythical element that I have in mind. In the Western European epics, which were handed down in Christian times, there are of course no heathen gods. In the Old Norse heroic songs Odin appears only sporadically. For that reason it has been supposed that he was only added in a more or less 'antiquating romantic' period. But however much Christianized, the epic naturally preserves here and there a memory of the rule of a god in and over the heroic life: in the *Lay of Hildebrand*, *irmingot* is invoked, which has rightly been taken to be the name of an originally heathen god; in the crusade-like atmosphere of the *Song of Roland* it is only natural that God is often mentioned.

But if these were all the indications of a mythical element in the heroic epic, we should not need to pay much attention to it. The truth is, however, that the mythical nature lies in the very core and essence of the heroic epic itself. What do we really mean by a myth? For a long time not much more was meant by this than some story or other about the deeds or the experiences of the gods; and the often not very edifying character of the Greek myths gave rise to the opinion that they were not much more than poetic inventions and had therefore little or nothing to do with real worship.

A closer investigation, prompted by experience among primitive people, led to an entirely different view. It appears to be irrefutable that the myth cannot be separated from the rite. Mircea Éliade puts it thus: the act of sacrifice is the repetition of an event that took place in primeval times. We have already seen an example of this in the ceremony of initiation: i.e., the primeval struggle between god and chaos-monster is again made real. The same applies to the blood-sacrifice. The animal that is slaughtered on the altar is not meant to be, as was formerly thought, a pleasant gift for the gods. 'How deliciously does the smell of the sacrificial animal rise up to the nostrils of the gods!' That is not the real meaning of the sacrifice; the animal—often a later substitute for a man—stands for a being that was once killed, so that through it, happiness can come to mankind.

In earlier days the consumption of food and drink was not considered as something everyday and ordinary. The animal that was consumed had to be killed first. Bread could only be made after the ripe corn had been cut. In order to live, man had inevitably to kill some living thing. Thus it may be said that man's existence in itself implies a sin and man always remains conscious of the guilt he incurs. The myth expresses it in this way: at one moment in primeval times a killing took place and this still takes place every day; at certain times this event of primeval times must be repeated in the rite, in order that the salutary effect thus gained shall continue to exist in undiminished strength.

Man lives on the fruits of the soil. How he acquired the power and the right to do so is the question that is asked on Ceram. The answer is, a female primeval being Hainuwele was once killed on purpose by a certain action, her body was divided up and buried in the ground; from the parts tuberous plants then sprouted up. Every year the death of Hainuwele is still imitated in a certain dance, or rather, through it it occurs again.

The rite illustrates what happened in primeval times; the myth tells of it. For its meaning would be unintelligible to the believer who now makes the sacrifice, if the action were not explained to him in words. Through myth as well as through the rite, the original event lives again in a meaningful reality. As Éliade puts it: what once happened *in illo tempore*, must be repeated *hic et nunc*, here and now, again and again. The words of Jesus: *hoc est corpus meum*, indicate unmistakably in what sense the breaking of the bread is to be understood in the action of the mass.

The myth, therefore, is much more than a story accompanying

the action of sacrifice like a written text to an illustration; it indicates the original and essential meaning of the sacrifice. Th. Gaster has raised objections to this.[1] He considers the myth to be no more than the accompaniment of the rite, serving to set before the eyes of the believers its various elements in their ideal aspect as events in a transcendental situation. Therefore the myth must not be regarded as the story of an event in primeval times, for then it ceases to be the ideal accompaniment of a present-day situation and assumes the character of an archetype or prototype. If it is supposed that the primary function of a myth is to legalize a traditional custom by representing it as a repetition of an action in the past, the essential point is missed: that myth and rite are parallel and do not stand in a linear or genealogical relation to each other.

This, it seems to me, is a complete misunderstanding of what Éliade means. There is no such genealogical connexion between myth and rite—both are inseparable as the activation of one single occurrence in primeval times. It is not that the myth is the story of what once happened and that the rite repeats it as action: myth and rite recreate what happened in primeval times *hic et nunc* as experienced reality. When Gaster says that the myth shows believers the events in a transcendental situation he is right, but the transcendental situation is precisely the re-realization of an action that took place in primeval times. Hence, at this moment, it is not at all a memory of what is irrevocably past, but now appears again in its full transcendentality. The ideal aspect of which Gaster speaks is therefore very much present: the action that takes place in the present is projected on to the divine plane of primeval times.

We have already seen this in the example of the fight with the dragon. It is an event *in illo tempore*, and belongs to the creation of the cosmos. Whenever in real life something is created, what happened in primeval times becomes a living reality. The creation could not even happen if one did not place oneself in the situation of the act of creation that stands at the beginning of all others. This primeval deed is also newly activated in the initiation rite. In the heroic legend the myth has been separated from the rite; here it only remains a story.

[1] Cf. 'Myth and Story', in *Numen* i (1954), p. 200.

If this is so one may ask: did not heroic legend also have the full reality of a religious act at one time? Were not the deeds of Heracles and Theseus, therefore, also of such a nature that they made divine acts again into reality and could have a salutary effect by doing so?

This can only become clear when we know what was meant by a hero in olden days. He is not only an exceptionally brave man, he has a cult. The cult of a hero, Gaster says,[1] means that people see in the hero somebody who has a particular quality which causes him to have a very special place in comparison to the enormous majority of the dead, and this quality lies precisely in the fact that he is only the bearer *hic et nunc* of an ideal essence. It is this essence, and not his earthly personality, that is worshipped in reality.

So when Agamemnon in Sparta is worshipped as Zeus Agamemnon, it is not Agamemnon but Zeus, i.e. the permanent essence embodied in him, who is the object of worship. To put it more precisely, such names as Zeus–Agamemnon do not mean a deified Agamemnon, but rather an ideal Agamemnon, thereby indicating an aspect of Being that was always inherent in him.

This is a very abstract way of putting it. Did the ancient Greeks really think in this way? And did not the hero who performed the deeds of a god thereby share directly in his divinity?

But let us leave aside what can only be speculation after the event, and let us ask instead what was the nature of this divine cult. Greece provides us with ample material for this. Similar elements that we find later in Western Europe are only a faint reflection of what we see before us in Greek literature in full reality.

The cult of the hero is spread over the entire Greek world. But it is the typical worship of a dead man. Herodotus, speaking of the sacrifices to Heracles,[2] writes of a temple dedicated to this hero which he saw in Phoenicia. There he was worshipped as a god. Therefore the Greeks acted wisely in offering sacrifices to the one they called Olympus as they did to the immortal (*thuein*), and to the other animal-sacrifices as they did to a hero (*enagizein*). If the ritual was an animal-sacrifice, then the place of sacrifice (*eschara*) was a pit representing the grave. There the sacrificial animal was burnt in its en-

[1] Cf. 'Myth and Story', in *Numen* i (1954), p. 189.   [2] *Historiae* ii. 44.

tirety, whereas in the sacrifice to the god it was consumed by the participants.

The act of the cult therefore takes place on or beside the grave, which presupposes that it is performed—wherever it may take place —in a spot that is considered to be the grave of a hero. His grave is his sanctuary. The Christian saints too are heroes, *milites Christi*, and so the place where they are worshipped must also contain their bones (or at least some of them) as a relic.

In some cases an actual divine sacrifice is offered to the hero, such as to Hippolytus and Menelaus, to Alcmene and Helen. This is sometimes explained as a legend of apotheosis,[1] but often it is doubtful. It could be because such heroes were actual gods originally.

The tradition concerning Ajax is typical. His grave was shown on the Hellespont, and there a sanctuary was dedicated to him. But in his fatherland, Salamis, where he was not actually buried, he was worshipped as a god—with a statue in the inner sanctum of a temple.

Not only the sacrifice offered to him belonged to the cult of the hero but contests were held in his honour as in the case of Pelops in Olympia, Theseus in Athens, and Palaemon-Melicertes on the Isthmus. We are reminded of the contests held at the grave of Patroclus in the *Iliad*; in Etruria, too, gladiator fights belonged to the cult of the dead.

Hymns and other songs were also sung in the hero's honour. At the funeral pyre of Hector *aoidoi* sing dirges or *threnoi*, and the women burst into loud lamentations.[2] Later it became customary that every dead man—certainly one who had fallen in battle—received the homage due to a hero. In Thracia, monuments on which an heroic figure was depicted were placed on the grave; his cult was closely connected with the earth and its fertility; his sanctuaries stood in the neighbourhood of wells.[3] No wonder, for the dead living in the underworld can give the fruits of the earth to their descendants if they are powerful.

I will now give a few examples of hero-cult among the Greeks.

[1] Cf. F. Pfister, *Der Reliquienkult im Altertum* ii (1912), p. 481.

[2] Cf. *Iliad* xxiv. 720 ff.

[3] Cf. Wiesner, 'Fahrende und reitende Götter', in *Archiv für Religionswissenschaft* xxxvii (1941–2), p. 43.

We have already mentioned that Alexander, on his expedition to Asia, did not omit to offer a sacrifice to Achilles on the Hellespont. For a long time it was customary for a mission from Thessaly, where Achilles was born, to be sent there to worship him. But he also had a cult in many other places: in Epeirus, Boeotia, Laconia, Elis, and in numerous colonies both in the East and in the West.[1] He was, moreover, worshipped not only as a hero but also as a god; in Laconia, for example. The most important sanctuary lay on the road from Sparta to Arcadia. Every year the ephebes sacrificed to him before they began the battle in the forest of plane trees.

Jason too was worshipped everywhere, but here we can hardly speak of a hero-cult any more, for, like Asclepius, he was regarded as a healing god. For that reason the legend makes him spend his youth with the wise Chiron, and he marries Medea, skilled in magic art and herbs, the daughter of Aeetes, ruler of the sun-island.

Graves of Agamemnon were to be seen in Mycenae and Amycleia. The worship of Diomedes extended as far as Cyprus in the East and Italy in the West.

Menelaus was worshipped as a god, with sacrifices and contests in Lacedaemon. Temples were dedicated to him near Sparta, and at Therapne, where he is supposed to lie buried with Helen.

Hector's grave was in Thebes, and in spite of the many expressions of doubt about the correctness of this information, it has to be accepted as genuine and old.[2] The grave of Anchises was north of Mantinea at the foot of Mount Anchisia, and a sanctuary dedicated to Aphrodite stood nearby.

These examples may suffice to give an idea of the general spread of hero-worship. But, as in the case of real saints, their relics were also preserved and worshipped. The lance of Achilles was in the temple to Athene at Phaselis, and that of Meleager in the temple of Apollo of Sicyon. Memnon's sword was in Nicomedea in the sanctuary of Asclepius. The weapons of Heracles could be admired in the temple of Apollo in Croton. The shield of Aeneas was in Samothrace; that of Diomedes in Argos, where Menelaus is said to have hung up the shield of Euphorbus also. The sceptre of Agamemnon,

[1] Cf. W. Kroll, in *Neue Jahrbücher für das klassische Altertum* xv (1912), p. 174.
[2] Cf. Bethe, *Homer* iii. 82.

the history of which is told in the *Iliad*, could be seen in Chaeronea. The necklace of Helen was in Delphi, but her sandals were in Iapygia. The folding-chair made by Daedalus stood in the Athenian Acropolis in the temple of the Polias.

Even ships were preserved as relics in sanctuaries. The *Argo* was in Corinth, but its anchor in Cyzicus. Odysseus left much to later generations: ships and rostra were found as far away as Spain, his weapons were to be seen in Engyon in Sicily. The ship of Agamemnon was preserved in Geraestus, Euboea. And is it to be wondered at that Athens boasted the ship of Theseus and Rome that of Aeneas?

Evidence for the hero-cult is also provided by the numerous illustrations of heroic legends on temple walls. Pictures of the Trojan War could be seen in the sanctuary of Artemis in Ephesus as well as in the temple of Apollo at Delphi, which, as appears from archaeological investigations, was a Cretan foundation. On the Hera temple in the neighbourhood of Mycenae, according to Pausanias, sculpture could be admired representing the birth of Zeus, the war of the gods against the Gigantes, and the capture of Troy. The famous throne of Apollo in Amyclae was rich in illustrations of stories of gods and heroes, such as the picture of Theseus carrying off the Minotaur alive, and the dances of the Phaeacians to the singing of Demodocus. On the *metops* of the temple in Olympia the twelve labours of Heracles were depicted.[1]

If we realize the full purport of these examples—and they are only a selection from a large number—we must needs arrive at the conclusion formulated by Pfister: in the epic the essence of the heroes as men from a distant past is canonized as it were, and their claim to a cult is confirmed. The fact that the epic is rooted in a cult cannot be emphasized too much, and any investigation into its origin has to take it into serious consideration.[2]

But are they always heroes? In many cases one might be inclined to speak of heroicized gods; in these the hero of the epic was originally a god, and his deeds are in a certain sense godlike deeds. Let us take Agamemnon as an example, whom Gaster has used to demonstrate the essence of the hero. He was worshipped in divers

[1] See for this and other examples: Ch. Autran, *Homère et les origines sacerdotales de l'épopée grecque* ii, pp. 96–108.   [2] Cf. l.c., p. 546.

places—especially in the Peloponnese. He is said to have dug up springs in Aulis, Attica, and many other places, and 'Agamemnon's springs' is even a proverbial name for a large building. In the neighbourhood of Smyrna medicinal hot springs bear his name. He also planted sacred trees, such as the plane-trees in Delphi and the Arcadian Caphyae. The *Iliad* even says of him: 'In eyes and head resembling the lightning-hurling Zeus.'[1] No wonder that the Greeks speak of Zeus-Agamemnon, thus not of the hero Agamemnon as a 'particularizing symbol' of Zeus,[2] but Zeus himself. This hero is a more or less dethroned god. His name has possibly arisen from an older form *mgamed-môn*, which indicates the one who is the highest *basileus*,[3] a typical name for Zeus. The line from the *Iliad* quoted above suggests that even Homer still had a notion of the close relation between the hero and the god, if not of their identity.

The same may be assumed about Achilles. His worship is so widespread that one can hardly consider him as a hero only, however famous. In some places he was in fact worshipped as a real god, especially in Laconia. Here, however, the cult of Achilles must be of fairly late date: he belongs to Thessaly. His name, which is connected with those of the rivers Achelus in Aetolia and Acheron in Epirus, and, in addition, with the name of the town Aquilea, points to the meaning of 'water-god'—perhaps it is derived from a Pelasgian word *ach*, 'water'.[4] In the epic also he is the son of the sea-goddess Thetis. At that time he was regarded as the tribal hero of the Northern Achaeans, and was thus able to acquire a dominating position in Greek heroic legend. It remains uncertain how the Achilles of the *Iliad* should be explained. There are various possibilities. He may have been a mythical figure from Thessaly who was absorbed in heroic legend. People have also thought of the poetic creation of an heroic figure, but based on a mythical world-conception. It may finally be surmised that an actual historical personality lies behind him.[5] In the light of the other evidence I am myself inclined to prefer the first alternative.

---

[1] Cf. *Iliad* ii. 478.   [2] Cf. Gaster, l.c., p. 190.   [3] Cf. Autran, l.c., p. 163.
[4] Cf. A. J. van Windekens, in *Beiträge zur Namenforschung* ix (1958), p. 172.
[5] Cf. Drerup, *Das Homerproblem in der Gegenwart* (1921), p. 259.

Glaucus, the grandson of Bellerophon, is a Lycian figure. But he has namesakes, namely, a sea-god and a god of prophecy. He is said to have had a share in the building of the *Argo*. It may be a memory of his divine origin that, according to tradition, he had eaten of the plant of immortality and had thus become a god. But this also applies to his grandfather: his cult is found both in Argos and in Lycia.

The divine origin of Helen may be regarded as certain. Her cult was centred chiefly in Therapne, in the neighbourhood of Sparta, where there was a temple in which she was worshipped with Menelaus; here too was their joint grave. Excavations have shown that the temple goes back to the Mycenaean period. Helen can probably be regarded as the goddess of fertility, which would explain why she was so liberal with her love. Her relation to Menelaus and Paris recalls that of Medb to Conchobar and Ailill. The Dioscuri, who are also counted among her lovers in the legend, had a famous place of worship in that same Therapne. It is striking that all these places of worship have their centre in Argos.

I will not weary the reader with more examples. It must be clear by now that there are various points of similarity between Gods and heroes. But there always remains the difference that the hero is a dead man who has grown far beyond ordinary life. He is worshipped because of some quality or other, because of one or more exceptional facts, or a sorrow that is bravely borne. He may therefore—taking into consideration all differences in religious quality—be compared to the saint. And just as shortly after his death, or even during his lifetime, the saint reveals his holiness to believers by means of miracles, so the temporal hero too can arouse the admiring veneration of his *milieu* soon after his death, or he can be regarded as more than human even during his lifetime. Examples of such rapid heroization are Cyrus, Alexander, and Theoderic the Great.

When we turn to medieval Western Europe to see whether here, too, traces of a hero-cult can be found, our expectations naturally do not run very high. This literature was written down in the midst of a Christian society, and so only very faint traces of really heathen heroization can be discerned. If the hero was worshipped in a cult, this could only assume the form valid at the time, worshipping the saints. Although at first sight the lives of martial hero and Christian saint lie far enough apart to make a similarity in the worship of both somewhat unlikely, it appears that there are nevertheless some examples of a cult of figures from heroic legend.

It is, in the first place, the heroes of the *Song of Roland* who have become objects of worship, but in their role of *milites Christi*, defenders of the faith. In this respect they can be considered worthy of the glory of saints. Churches and monasteries already boasted of the possession of graves and relics of these martyrs at an early date, and legends were bound to be woven around them. Thus it is told that Charlemagne had his paladin Roland buried in the church of Saint-Romain at Blaye, with Roland's famous horn, the Olifant, laid at his feet. Later, however, the clergy of Saint-Seurin in Bordeaux were said to have appropriated it. The grave of Bishop Turpin was supposed to be at Saint-Jean de Sorde, while Belin, situated in the Landes of Bordeaux, was able to boast of holding the bodies of the holy martyrs Olivier, King Ogier of Denmark, Duke Garin of Lorraine, and many other warriors of Charlemagne. It was related in legend that Charlemagne had taken them there himself and had them interred in a collective grave. A sweet odour emanates from there and the sick who inhale it are cured by it.[1] In this connexion it is easy to understand that Charlemagne's own grave at Aachen was also the object of great worship. The opening of the tomb, first in the year 1000 by Emperor Otto III and again in 1165 by Frederic I, was not done merely out of curiosity. Towards the end of the eleventh century we hear that he was expected to return, and liberate the Holy Sepulchre. For this reason we can also understand why Charlemagne's enterprises against the heathen Moors in Spain remained alive in people's memory.[2]

If people did not have the precious body itself, they prided themselves on the possession of relics. The sword and shield of Ogier of Denmark were shown to the believers in Farmoutier, while the shield of Guillaume d'Orange could be worshipped in Brioude. History repeats itself. Just as the church of Saint-Romain at Blaye accused that of Saint-Seurin in Bordeaux of having appropriated the

---

[1] Cf. Bédier, *Les Légendes épiques* iii, pp. 334–60.
[2] Cf. K. Heisig, in *Zeitschrift für romanische Philologie* lv (1935), pp. 66–67.

horn of Roland, the inhabitants of Tegea accused those of Sparta of having robbed them of the bones of Orestes.

The demand for relics was great, both in pagan antiquity and in the Christian Middle Ages. In the latter case the remarkable thing is that people even wanted to worship as saints persons from secular heroic legend. It cannot of course be assumed that the cup of the Viking Gormont, which the abbey of Saint-Riquier in Normandy preserved among her treasures, was regarded as a relic, but nevertheless on certain occasions this apocryphal object was no doubt proudly exhibited; and it is a fact that something preserved in a church by this very means acquires an odour of sanctity. Thus all this indicates a close relation between Church and heroic legend, but the conclusion that the Church made the legend is not warranted. The Church only took it to its bosom. Before the Olifant could find a place in a church it must have been made worthy by a preceding tradition. That tradition could only be heroic legend.

While, therefore, in early medieval France, the old and much-sung heroes gained a place in Christian ethos without much diffi-culty, evidence for this is very sparse in the Germanic field. A remarkable piece of evidence to prove the significance of heroes in Church circles is provided not by legends of the saints but by a document of the tenth century, the *Miracula S. Bavonis*, which con-tains the information that a King Hermenrik was supposed to have founded his imperial castle in Ghent. This also explains how the Dutch poem *Reinaert* still knows about the treasures of this Gothic king, as we remarked above. The hero Heimo was said to be buried in a monastery near Innsbruck. He also belonged to the cycle of Ermanaric; the grave was thirteen feet long, of which two feet had been bricked up in the wall.[1] This description shows that, as so often, the hero of primeval times was thought of as a giant.

Siegfried's grave, too, could still be seen. For, in the year 1488, the Emperor Frederic III visited Worms and wished to see the grave in the churchyard of the church of Saint Cecilia, in which it was said that the bones of a famous giant were lying. That giant was Sifridus der Hörne. Moreover, the lance of this hero was preserved in the main church of the same town.

[1] Cf. Albertus Stadensis, *Chronicon* of about 1250.

Of some importance, too, are the cases in which peculiar mountain formations or old buildings are given the names of heroes. A small bed on the Feld Mountain near Frankfurt-am-Main is called Brunnihilde. We may compare the mountain tops in Ireland called the bed of Diarmuid and Grainne. In the neighbourhood of Kehl a Kriemhildenstein is to be seen. The Drachenfels on the Rhine was connected with Siegfried's dragon-fight already at an early age.

When we consider these examples of hero-worship it appears that they can sometimes persist in the most unfavourable circumstances. Even in Christian surroundings, the famous names of the *chansons de geste* manage to acquire a sacred place in church or monastery. Bédier attributed an important role to this hagiographical tradition in the origin of Old French heroic epic poetry; it is the sanctuaries—of course only pseudo-sanctuaries—which led to the rise of the poems about Roland, Guillaume d'Orange, or Renout of Montalban. According to Bédier, practical priests, who wished to secure greater fame and especially a more lucrative veneration to the relics entrusted to them, encouraged *jongleurs* to make poems on these canonized heroes and hawk these poems about. It is remarkable that these songs do not have the character of legends at all but are very worldly in content. We conclude therefore that it was not only the clergy who were interested in heroes and their deeds, but also a lay public consisting mainly of men of the sword. Neither of these groups can be neglected in considering the origin of the *chansons de geste*. The interest of the Church in these heroic figures is also indicated by the not infrequent cases in which the hero retires into a monastery at the end of his life, in order to atone there by pious service for a life of bloodshed and violence.

But what else would have been the reason for the clergy to have taken pleasure in exhibiting the tombs and relics of these remarkable martyrs and saints, unless it was precisely the fact that they were convinced of having a great treasure in their possession? These curious relics were not smuggled into the church by way of chronicles and written legends, but by way of popular tradition. In general the high dignitaries of the Church themselves came from the nobility and in their spiritual status did not belie the aristocratic traditions in which they had been brought up. The heroes of the past were the favourite examples of chivalrous behaviour, and they were no less so for those members of the nobility who had found a place in the Church. We remember the abbot of Lindisfarne who was reprimanded by Alcuin for allowing heroic songs to be read aloud in the refectory: how could he have come to such strange behaviour, if he had not been of the opinion that heroic legends were edifying reading-matter and also suitable for monks? The abbot of St. Gall was of similar opinion when he set his young monk the theme of Waltharius for poetic treatment. Is it not possible that there were also many such abbots in France? But I shall have to come back to this question in the next chapter.

In the Greek world the situation is entirely different. The heathen faith knew and sanctioned from the beginning the worship of heroes as a special form of worship of the dead. Like the dead they could exert great power, usually for the better, but sometimes also for the worse. They were honoured as much as they were feared. They could punish mercilessly if they were not given the honour due to them. The greater the living, the more powerful the dead. Hence these heroes could be *sotères*, a word that may be compared with our 'saviour'. They were also worshipped as *ktisteis*, i.e. founders of towns or colonies. They had their places in the lives of the Greeks. For them they were salutary forces that had themselves once been living men and had been raised above ordinary human level by courage, sacrifice, or other qualities.

The priests could not remain passive in the face of this urge for worship. They eagerly seized the opportunity to draw the cult of heroes within their sanctuaries. The *pia fraus* was very common. But that is what the people wanted. The evidence was there: they all flocked to the sanctuaries to visit the tombs and relics of the heroes, and to return fortified by them in body or spirit. The splendid feasts, processions, and contests linked with the names of these heroes gave this cult the consecration and sanctity which the medieval church mass also possessed.

The French scholar Charles Autran in particular, who has been the advocate of the 'Church' aspect of heroic legend, speaks of *origines sacerdotales* in the title of his book on the Greek epic. In his opinion, this epic would never have received its form, more especially its beautiful form, if it had not flourished under the protection of the priests. But we will not discuss this aspect of the problem here.

For there is yet another side to it. In the heroic epic the Greek priests gave expression to their ideals, and these were not the same as those of the aristocratic nobility. For the Middle Ages, the Christian tone of the *Chanson de Roland* can suggest some such thing, but it should also be remembered that Christian morals worked as a leaven among all ranks of society in a way entirely different from the way it could have happened in Greek polytheistical heathendom.

And yet, let us listen for a moment to the remarks made by Charles Autran on the *Odyssey*:[1] 'What gave lasting greatness to Odysseus' suffering is the tragic conflict revealed in each new adventure between the firm intention of the hero to do everything possible to return to his own home, and the obstacles that again and again were put in his way by the immortal powers to whom man, even if he is a hero, is never more than a mere toy. If one reads this poem seriously, as one should; if one considers the total exertion expected of the hero before he could eventually come back to his damaged and plundered home, and considers also the calm resolution, the persistence, the sacred ideal, expressed in so many dangers nobly sustained, and long ordeals by which he eventually achieved the cleansing of a home restored to new splendour; if the poet shows us every time how insignificant man is when he relies on strength alone, and shows on the other hand the limitless value of courage, intelligence, and energy; then one cannot but form the opinion that man's highest virtues are precisely these *moral* virtues that were valued so highly by Athene: the virtues that made the happy ending possible. A lesson with a moral. Does that not clearly testify to a sacerdotal origin?'

So Odysseus the sufferer is not merely the plaything of a cruel fate, nor is he the man of the many adventures that are often disposed of as fishermen's tales. He is the paragon of man as he should behave in a life of trials and dangers, in order to be able to exist in the eyes of Athene.

Priests, cult, and myth are inseparable. The heroic legend growing and living in such a *milieu* cannot but assume the character of a myth.

[1] Cf. l.c., p. 218.

A myth, not of a god, but of a man who raised himself to the level of the gods. It is the myth that we find wherever we look around in a world that originated from myth. The *Mahabharata* and the *Ramayana* of the Indians reveal this as much as the Greek *Iliad* and *Odyssey*, the journey of the Argonauts, and the legend of Theseus. And in the Germanic epic are not these same myths ready to hand in such poems as *Beowulf*, and those about the Norse hero Helgi, Wayland the Smith, or the race of the Volsungs from which Siegfried sprang?[1]

[1] See F. R. Schröder, in *Germanisch-Romanische Monatsschrift* xxvii, 1939, pp. 325–67.

13

BEGINNING AND END OF THE HEROIC EPIC

IF we try to sketch the development of heroic poetry, we should bear in mind from the outset that this development did not take place everywhere in the same way. First of all, we should make a distinction between epic poetry that is basically sacral and that which we should consider mainly as secular. In India and Greece, the situation was entirely different from that which existed among the Romance and Germanic nations. And there may well be some reason for not treating the latter two alike. For, while we may assume that the clergy had a share in the development of the *chansons de geste* in France, how large that share is still remains to be established. In Germany this seems at first sight not to have been the case, or, if it was, it was much less so. And yet *Waltharius* arose in a monastery, and the *Ruolandes liet* is the work of the priest Konrad.

A further distinction has to be made, in the nature of things, between such entirely literary heroic poems as the *Nibelungenlied* or the *Chanson de Roland* and that other poetry that still lives among the Russian, South-Slav, or Finnish peoples. Here the situation is entirely different. The question at once arises whether this kind of poetry is a reflection of popular epic poetry on which the German and French heroic epic was also based at one time, or whether we have to deal with some sort of symptom of decay here.

As it looks as if we can form a fairly clear idea of the development of Greek epic poetry, we shall begin with it. We have already seen more than once that the hero was worshipped in a cult, which therefore presupposes a priesthood concerned with the observance of the acts of the cult and also with having songs sung in honour of the hero at certain times. These will not have been in the form of heroic poems. One should think of them as lyric poetry. First of all there is the *dithyrambos*, a stanzaic song of praise originally developed in the cult of Dionysus, which later also derived its subject-matter from heroic legends such as that of Heracles or Theseus. But hymns, too, were sung, i.e. songs of praise of the deeds of a hero which could make him worthy of taking part in the higher life of the gods. The central point of the cult was the hero's grave. His death therefore had to be in the centre, and so we ought also to consider the singing of the dirge or *thrènos*.

We have already remarked that several terms of this cult-poetry —the word *dithyrambos* itself belongs to this—are of pre-Hellenic origin. The Hellenes therefore received strong impulses from the early Aegean civilization. It should not be forgotten that this civilization had its roots in a widespread layer of Oriental forms of civilization. If we look for possible examples, two of the most important civilizations of antiquity naturally come to mind, those of Mesopotamia and Egypt. Let us take a pyramid text as an example that belongs to the ceremonial for the dead Pharaoh. As a dead king he is compared to the god Osiris; for, like him, he will arise from death to a new and eternal life. One of the songs of this extensive ceremonial, in which the souls of the ancestors (that is, the gods of Pé) appear, is as follows:

> The gods of Pé have pity;
> They come to Osiris, hearing the
>   lamentations of Isis and Nephthys.
> The souls of Pé dance for thee,
> They beat their hands for thee;
> They shake their hair for thee;
> They say to Osiris:
>
> Thou hadst departed
> And thou hast returned.
> Thou wert awake
> And now thou restest.
> Mayest thou remain alive.
>
> Arise and see,
> Arise and hear,
> What thy son has done for thee.
> What Horus has done for thee.

> He slays him who has slain thee,
> He chains him who has chained thee,
> He subjects her to his eldest daughter,
> Who lives in Kédem,
> Thy eldest sister who joined thy limbs,
> Who took thy hands, who sought thee,
> Who found thee,
> Lying on thy side, on the shore of Nedyt.[1]

Both in form and content this song is significant. The content is partly of an epic nature, as it tells what happened to Osiris after he had been killed by Seth and torn to pieces: his mother Isis collected the limbs of his corpse and made him rise again out of death.

As to the form, one notices a pronounced tendency towards parallelism. The purpose of this stylistic feature is partly of liturgical significance and may be likened to a musical accompaniment which repeats the same melody. But at the same time, the psychological effect of the spoken word makes a considerably stronger impression. It is therefore—at least in form—the same parallelism as that found in the Finnish *runot*, and hence there does not seem to be much doubt that here too its origin is to be found in the form of magic formulae. May we now put beside this similar cases of doubling of lines, such as we found in the poetry of the Great-Russians and the Tartars? If so, then nothing is left of the liturgical character, for it is nothing but a stock feature of style.

In the Germanic world, too, we find the same form in religious poetry. In a charm relating to the god Heimdall we read that the god says:

> I am the son of nine maidens,
> I am the son of nine sisters.

In a magic song that will protect the warrior in battle Odin says:

> I sing under the shields and they stride with might
> > Sound to the battle,
> > Sound from the battle,
> > Sound they return home.

Naturally, the hymns to the gods also contain such a repetition of

[1] Cf. H. Frankfort, *La Royauté et les Dieux*, p. 169.

praise, but it would not have its full effect if the deeds of the gods were not glorified in them. This may be done succinctly, as in the following hymn to Thor:

> You have broken the thigh of Leikn,
> You have lamed Thrivaldi,
> You have felled Starkad,
> You stood over the dead Gjölp.

But soon the need is felt to give a more circumstantial account of these glorious deeds. This happens in the hymns of the *Veda*, in which the victory of Indra over the monster Vṛtra is sung repeatedly. Likewise, but even more elaborately and artistically, in the Homeric hymns. Even if they are largely of a later, post-Homeric date they are based on older models, and their form proves how much original nature has been preserved in them.

I will remember and not be unmindful of Apollo who shoots afar. As he goes through the house of Zeus, gods tremble before him and all spring up from their seats when he draws near, as he bends his bright bow.[1]

Here, or again, in the hymn to Hermes we have the typical repetition of the same thought in two corresponding lines.

Muse, sing of Hermes, the son of Zeus and Maia, lord of Cyllene and Arcadia rich in flocks, the luck-bringing messenger of the immortals whom Maia bare, the rich-tressed nymph, when she joined in love with Zeus——

And a little farther down:

For then she bare a son, of many shifts, blandly cunning, a robber, a cattle driver, a bringer of dreams, a watcher by night, a thief at the gates, one who was soon to show forth wonderful deeds among the deathless gods. Born with the dawning, at mid-day he played on the lyre, and in the evening he stole the cattle of far-shooting Apollo——

In this example we find all the features that have remained lasting characteristics of epic poetry; especially the epithets, without which it is impossible to mention a god or a hero. Their majesty alone demands these ornaments. Homer can never mention either gods or heroes without giving them a word of praise. This is not only a

[1] This quotation and the next two are in the prose-translation by H. G. Evelyn.

relic of an epic styl e that has become rigid, but it also springs directly from the reverence with which the poet thinks of these exalted be-ings. Typical of the epic, too, is what might be called the enumer-ative style that mentions morning, noon, and evening. In heroic epic poetry the growing-up of the hero is similarly described in this for-mal way. It may be said that the poet of the hymns imitates Homer, but then it can also be pointed out that Homer considered the epic style to be entirely in accordance with that of a hymn.

We have only to imagine the festive mood on a day when people flocked together to celebrate the hero in his sanctuary. There a sacri-fice was offered to him, and his bones or his relics were shown to the crowd. There miraculous cures were made. The priests chanted hymns and praised his deeds. The splendour with which all this was done can still be inferred from the testimony of Philostratus.[1] At the command of the Pelasgian oracle at Dodona—again that reference to a pre-Hellenic origin—the Thessalians sent a *theoria* to Sigaion to Achilles every year; they were accompanied by fourteen official delegates who brought everything that was needed for the sacrifice —including the fire—in a ship with black sails. They also brought along two bulls, one black, one white, the former destined for the *Manes* of the mortal Achilles, the latter for the god Achilles. During the night the funeral rites were celebrated, hymns were sung, Thetis, his mother, was solemnly invoked to appear at the cere-mony, and the mound was wreathed with immortelles brought from Greece.

A report such as this shows how much the hero-cult inspired a dis-play of all imaginable splendour at such sacrifices. The people gathered together attended the sacred deeds with reverence, but also looked on, admiringly, at the procession taking the animals to the altar. In the evening, when they returned to their tents or inns after a day full of so many different, strong emotions, and the festive mood was still with them, they continued the feast, consuming food and drink together. Would this not have given a singer his chance to add lustre to the meal? Would he not have sung the praises of the hero Achilles, but this time in a more worldly manner? For there was so much left to tell which the priests had only been able to hint at

[1] Cf. *Heroica*, p. 739 in the Loeb edition of Hesiod.

briefly, or had not even mentioned at all. On such occasions he might have sung a small *Iliad* in which there was perhaps no mention of Achilles' wrath at the seizing of Briseis, but which did contain his tremendous fight with Hector or Memnon and especially his treacherous death at the hands of Paris. But what meaning did Achilles' deeds have, unless they were given meaning by the context of the whole story of the struggle for Troy? How much could be told, from the carrying off of Helen to the often so tragic return of the heroes after the fall of Ilion?

In this connexion the reader will remember Bédier's words. He too shows us the *jongleurs* mingling with the hosts of pilgrims on the way to San Jago di Compostella and singing of the heroes that had fallen in the pass of Roncevaux. There is of course a considerable likeness between the two examples, but also a considerable difference. Bédier makes the birth of the great epic, such as the *Chanson de Roland*, take place in this way; in the midst of the hosts of pilgrims and by a *jongleur* who thus tried to earn some travelling-money. But I prefer to think of short epic songs in such surroundings, like those recited by the Greek rhapsodes. This *milieu* is not the place where the Homeric epic itself was born.

These epic songs were not only the pastime of the pilgrims at the grave of a hero. Anyone who had devoted his life to the acquisition of fame by an armed fight equally desired to hear songs about the glorious deeds once performed by the heroes of the past. Man needs an ideal in accordance with which he can shape his life. Daedalus and Wayland were able to arouse the desire of smiths and artisans to emulate them, Demodocus and Horant inspired poets and reciters, while Achilles and Heracles inspired the warlike nobility to perform manly deeds. No wonder that the rhapsode also went to the strongholds of Tiryns and Mycenae, where he would be joyfully received. There the songs of Heracles, Theseus, or the Argonauts were eagerly listened to. And this time his song may have struck an entirely different note, laying the emphasis on feats of arms, and on everything that was connected with fighting. It was a delight to hear with what weapons a hero girded himself and with what shield he went into battle (was not the shield of Achilles a work of art by a god himself?), and how the warriors with resounding armour marched over the plain towards their enemies. The words they exchanged before the fight began, the blows they struck each other, the wounds the opponent received, the thud of the falling body, the taking away of shield and weapons, the triumph of the return after the victory: what a response all this found with the lords of the stronghold who had also experienced it, yet not in such an intense and glorious manner as had the heroes of old! They wanted to hear of the hero during his life, not after his death. But the rhapsode had started in the temple and had learned his art there; that is proved by the poems which he recited. The hexameter, the hieratic formulae, had become second nature to him. For the making of a verse he could not do without them. They will always remain the same to the very end of epic poetry.

And when the noble lords, who would certainly not have been amused by long-winded poems, wanted to hear the praises of the heroes sung over and over again, one song followed another. They were connected, because they dealt with the same heroes; they could easily have been joined together to form a cycle. The cycle of lays about the struggle for Troy grew to comprise about a hundred in the end, almost half of which are taken up by the *Iliad* and the *Odyssey* alone. But this does not mean that, in content, we may equate the epic song of recitation, of which we spoke just now, with a book of the *Iliad*. This is an episode from a larger and coherent whole, very closely connected with the song at the beginning and at the end. In many cases it does not seem suited to independent recitation, for that is only possible when the listener knows the whole course of the story already. For the period between the fall of Ilion and the Homeric epic I should like to imagine the heroic songs being, on the one hand, the average size of a book of the *Iliad*, but on the other with much more self-contained contents. Thus the division of the larger epic poems into books, which applies not only to the *Iliad* and *Odyssey* but to all the parts of the cycle, could be a relic of the fact that in one evening the recitation would not have comprised more than about five hundred lines.

The reason why Homer has survived as the greatest epic poet is that he was an artist of genius. Unfortunately we cannot form any opinion of the *Aethiopis* of Arctinus or of the *Little Iliad* of Leschis, for they have not been preserved. The reason for this need not be that they were of less literary value. It may well be that their contents were not able to arouse such a lasting interest as the poems of Homer. And so we are faced with the question, why the *Odyssey* and not the *Argonautica*? For both had an equally richly coloured and fascinating scene to offer: that of the adventures which the seafarer may have on distant voyages. And was not an expedition to the Black Sea just as thrilling as the wanderings of Odysseus in a half-fabulous Mediterranean?

The answer must be: because Homer had more to offer than merely an interesting story of adventures at sea. His epic was not like the voyages of Sindbad the Sailor. He had managed to give it a deeper and more universal meaning. The words of Charles Autran quoted earlier have already pointed out the high ethical value of his epic. But the same applies to the *Iliad* in no less a degree. It may be the story of many brave fights around Ilion, from the desperate fight at the ships' camp to the heroic death of Hector. But that is not the entire content, nor even the real meaning of it. It is surely the wrath of Achilles. We see in him the very human hero who withdraws from the fight, because of his injured pride, and makes the Greeks suffer heavily for the injustice which Agamemnon had done to him personally. But how great is the penalty he has to pay for it! Through his fault his most loyal friend Patroclus falls, the greatest and most unexpected victim of Achilles' wrath. Now he repents. The unyielding heart softens with grief and the same hero, who, in unbridled anger, had dragged Hector's body round the walls of Ilion only a short while before, presently laments the fallen heroes with Priam, deeply grieved, and returns his son's body to him for an honourable funeral.

This too, as we have seen, is evidence of the influence of priestly circles, who could deepen a story of pure lion's courage and noise of battle into the inner struggle of a man caught in injustice. Did Homer come from the circles connected with those sanctuaries in which the cult of the heroes lived on? Who shall say? But it is certain that Homer was a man with a warm and gentle heart. That appears at once from the numerous similes which derive directly from life and which were certainly his own work. Here we find his real

I

interest in simple folk, in shepherds and peasants, swineherds and slaves. These were tones that were certainly not struck in the Mycenaean period. At the end of a long series of anonymous poets who for centuries had sung of the deeds of the heroes, a true artist appears, and with him this whole epic tradition comes to a close. In future only Homer will be recited. That was what the epic had to be like, in order to appeal to Pericles' contemporaries. And that is why it still finds an irresistible response in the hearts of modern men, too.

Concerning the epic poetry of Western Europe, we are much better informed. We find evidence of epic song stretching over many centuries. Of course these testimonies were accidental and depended on the passion for writing on the part of some scribe or other who found time to write them down and took pleasure in doing so. We should therefore be grateful for the meagre remains that have come down to us. They begin as early as the seventh and eighth centuries and continue up to the time when, at the end, the great epic poems appear: in France from the end of the eleventh century, in Germany about a century later. Here again the great epic poems appear to be the end of an epic tradition.

We shall begin with the latter group. Our main purpose will be to establish whether epic songs existed in the centuries preceding the written tradition, and if so, what they may have been like. The Germanic tradition gives us the firmest ground to build on. Earlier on we mentioned such poems as the *Lay of Hildebrand,* the *Waltharius,* and *Beowulf,* which belong to the eighth or ninth centuries.

Let us, then examine first what pre-epic poetry there was—i.e. the whole literature of songs of praise and of satire, laments for the dead and war-songs, of which similar indications were also found in Greek literature.

After a victory or a defeat the poet does not remain silent. We have seen that among the Slav nations and the African Fulbe such songs arise spontaneously. Obviously this must also have happened in Western Europe. An example of this has been preserved: the so-called *Ludwigslied,* made on the occasion of Louis III's victory over the Vikings at Saucourt in 881. As this ruler died suddenly in the following year, and as there is only joy at his victory in the poem, it

must have been composed immediately after the battle. It is a genuine song of praise—an encomium—in which, however, the facts
are also briefly mentioned. It has only 59 lines and is written in the
Rhenish–Franconian dialect. It is noteworthy that, just as is said of
Charlemagne in the later epic, Louis only proceeds to the battle after
he has been urged on by God himself. Thus he fights like a real
miles Christi against the heathen.

As soon as he encounters the Norsemen on the battlefield, the
army sings Kyrie eleison and then:

> The song was sung, the battle begun;
> Blood shone in the cheeks, the Franks played the war-game;
> There no hero fought like Louis:
> Mighty and brave, that was innate in him,
> Some he struck in two, some he pierced.[1]

It strikes us at once that this song of praise also shows the universally
popular technique of variation of thought expressed in parallel lines.
The form of this song would lend itself eminently well to the treatment of epic subject-matter.

And is it not remarkable, therefore, that in the other, western part
of Franconia this glorious battle did in fact provide the impulse for a
purely epic treatment: the *Chanson de Gormont et Isembart*? It seems
to have linked the French and the German reaction to these events,
and makes it plausible that not only in East Franconia, but also in
Neustria, the battle of Saucourt was sung. It seems that in the
western part an epic poem arose out of this, the last reflection of
which we find in the *chanson de geste*.

But we can go still further. Tacitus gives us a valuable indication.
In his *Germania*[2] he says: 'Hercules, among others, is said to have
visited them, and they chant his praises before those of other heroes
on their way into battle.' Leaving aside what he means by this 'Hercules'—certainly not the Greek hero, but some Germanic god or
hero—what is important for us is that we learn from Tacitus that
people clearly prepared for battle by singing songs praising the deeds
of former heroes.

[1] For the text see W. Braune, *Althochdeutsches Lesebuch* No. xxxvi.
[2] Cf. ch. 3.

The custom survived for a long time, although naturally later sources only give us very exceptional examples of it. I have mentioned before the heroic song sung at the request of King Olaf the Saint before the battle of Stiklestad in 1033. The Icelandic historian Snorri Sturluson has this to say about it: 'The poet Thormod recited the old *Bjarkamál* and this is how it begins', and he quotes two stanzas of it. In the reconstruction of it by the Danish scholar Axel Olrik —for we only know the poem from a Latin paraphrase by Saxo Grammaticus—it contains 35 eight-line stanzas,[1] or about 140 epic lines. It seems to me that this is not too long for a poem whose purpose is to encourage an army before the battle.

The case of Taillefer is different. He is supposed to have recited the *Song of Roland* in 1066 at the beginning of the Battle of Hastings. Surely not the poem that we know now; the enemy would not have allowed the singer enough time to complete the recitation of four thousand lines, nor would William the Conqueror's men have had the patience to listen to so much. So what did Taillefer sing? Only the beginning? But the opening of the *Song of Roland* has not nearly the inspirational power that the first stanzas of the *Bjarkamál* possess. Did he make a choice and recite one of the most stirring parts of the extensive poem? This would presuppose that each of the warriors present knew the story in broad outline. Or was it an entirely different song which, in a much more compressed form, dealt with the defeat at Roncevaux? Or did Taillefer improvise a poem of encouragement by picturing to the soldiers the fight at Roncevaux?

We have to resign ourselves to the fact that we do not know. Yet one thing is significant: both the *Song of Roland* and the *Bjarkamál* deal with defeat. A strange choice, one would think, to urge an army on to victory. Yet on closer inspection the choice is understandable. The pathos of courage, contempt of death, and self-sacrifice is nowhere praised more gloriously than precisely in these two poems about defeat. And that was the point in both cases: the impending battle was a precarious undertaking. Victory was by no means certain. But even if the fortunes of battle should turn against them they would fight with the same fiery zeal of which both poems give such fine evidence.

[1] Cf. *Danmarks Heltedigtning* i (1903), pp. 46–59.

The lamentation for the dead should also be briefly mentioned here. The Greek historian Priscus tells us, in connexion with the death of Attila, that the ruler lay in state in a tent and that a selected band of Hunnish raiders played a game of war around it and sang a dirge. The Gothic author Jordanes gives us some information about the contents: 'Eminent King of the Huns, Attila, born in Mundzuk, ruler of the mightiest nations, who alone conquered the formerly mighty kingdoms of the Scythians and the Germanic nation, terrified the two parts of the Roman Empire by capturing towns, and contented himself with an annual tribute so that they should not be left a prey to plunder. When he had successfully achieved all this, he died not by a wound which enemies inflicted on him, but in the midst of joy, without any feeling of pain.' [1] This is undoubtedly a very much shortened version of a song about the tremendous deeds done by the ruler in his lifetime and the way in which he met his death.[2]

It is generally assumed that Attila's dirge was really sung by his Germanic bodyguard, especially as a similar custom is found later among the Germanic tribes. This is of course merely a surmise; why should it be doubted that among the Huns also, as with so many other nations, the dead were honoured in songs about their great merits during their lifetime?

At any rate the dirge at the mound of Beowulf is a Germanic counterpart. Twelve noble youths ride round the mound and sing a song in which they praise their king. They extol him because he has become famous all over the world, has been mild and merciful to his men and generous to all his people, and had always striven for fame.

The conclusion must be drawn that such a dirge was made immediately after a person's death. It will have been adorned with all the ornaments of the art, for the dirge requires hyperbolic forms. The poet was probably the *scop* who during the ruler's lifetime was a member of his retinue and whose task it was to compose songs of praise about his lord and his famous deeds.

It is the Scandinavian North especially that gives us a clear picture

[1] Cf. ch. 49.

[2] Attila, for example, died from a sudden haemorrhage in the night after his marriage to the Germanic princess Hilda. Soon the rumour arose that the princess had killed him in his sleep: a starting point for the legend of Kriemhild–Gudrun and Etzel–Atli.

of the activity of such poets. A great number of similar songs about rulers have come down to us in whole or in part. The court-poet was here called the *skald*. His task was to glorify the ruler after gaining a victory and to lament him after his death. Naturally we should not expect songs recited at the courts of Scandinavian kings and jarls from the ninth to the twelfth century to have been of the same kind as the Anglo-Saxon and Franconian ones of even earlier date. But they are sufficiently important to dwell on for a while.

This is court poetry in all respects. It is highly artificial, with an almost exaggerated splendour of style and language. But the metrical form is also a showpiece, hardly equalled anywhere in other literatures. Though based on the ordinary Germanic epic measure, it is characterized by an ingenious but strictly regulated use of internal rhyme and assonance in a stanza of eight lines. But even more strange is the use of a picturesque figure of speech, the *kenning*, which describes in a very original way almost every nominal idea suitable for description which at once veils and glorifies. But what is striking is that in these descriptions the names of gods or mythical beings, especially allusions to mythical stories, play a very special part. Thus the description of gold as 'tears of Freyja' or 'language of the giants' or 'flour of Fródhi' is derived from mythology, or (with a clear allusion to the Nibelung legend) as 'ore of the Rhine' and 'burden of Grani'. This is not the place to quote from other examples what curiously complicated descriptions were made, which have to be solved like crossword puzzles. In any case, we have to assume that the listeners for whom such enigmatic figures of speech were meant at once remembered the appropriate motif from the legends of the gods and heroes, and were able fully to enjoy such artificial language.

But two points may be made here. First, similar descriptions, although in a much similar form, were also often used in Old English poetry, from which we may conclude that it was a general Germanic custom. Further, there are indications that this peculiar scaldic language originated in a sacral atmosphere, particularly since names of gods are used with such obvious preference as the basic words of the *kennings*, or allusions are made to myths. We might perhaps be justified in deducing from this that their origin is to be found in the hymns recited in the cult, and that in these a very luxurious language was developed. On the rune-stone of Eggjum, dated about 700, there is a magic inscription with similar poetic descriptions. Hence, just as is probable in the case of Greece, there may have been a connexion between cult songs and songs of praise.

Among the oldest examples of existing scaldic poetry are some so-called 'shield-songs'. These are poems in which a scald expresses his gratitude for a beautifully ornamented shield. Evidently such shields had pictures from myths and heroic legends on them; perhaps they were not even so mythical—as the famous shield given to Achilles by Hephaestus! The oldest poem of this kind was by Bragi, who lived in the ninth century. It is remarkable for a series of very bold *kennings*. Thus he names the object of his song of thanksgiving, that is the shield, with the following allusion to a well-known myth: the leaf of the soles of the thief Thrud; a giant, namely, is said to have put his shield underneath his feet in a fight with Thor. The pictures on the shield were: the fight of Hamdir and Sörli in Ermanaric's hall, the legend of Hild and the fight of the Hjadnings, and two myths: that of Gefjon who ploughed the Danish Sjelland loose from Sweden and that of Thor's fight with the world serpent.

Consider what it means to find a legend of Ermanaric in ninth-century Norway. Here this legend must have been so well known that a shield could be decorated with it. Familiarity with this legend can only have been possible if a song had been made about it. But Ermanaric was a King of the Goths, who lived in the fifth century and suffered the disaster of being invaded by the Huns. We must therefore assume that this tragic fall was treated in an epic song, and that this must have happened in that part of Hungary to which the Goths had been carried along by the Huns. By what intermediate stages did this song come to Norway? Already at such an early date there must have been an exchange of the subject-matter of legends between the various tribes. And that can only have taken place through poets and singers of such epic songs, who evidently went from tribe to tribe and thus spread the famous heroic legends to the farthest corners of the Germanic area. What a perspective this opens up of the intense life of the heroic legend, and no less of the heroic song, in these early centuries!

Is it possible to form an idea of the shape of the heroic song at that time? The only support here is the *Lay of Hildebrand*. This was a poem of about a hundred to a hundred and fifty lines which dealt with a single tragic event, mainly by means of lively dialogue. The heroic songs of the *Edda*, which may belong to the same period, are of a similar size, but they differ in their being not stichic, but stanzaic. There is therefore reason to suppose that the stories of Sigurd and the fall of the Nibelungs, of Theoderic the Great, of Wayland the Smith, of Walter, and of many other heroes were sung in such songs. We may take this as a firm starting-point for our further observations.

I should like to add the following point. Who would still believe nowadays that the Franks on one side of the Rhine knew such songs, but that the Franks on the other did not? At the courts of the feudal lords (who up to Charlemagne's time and even later spoke their old Franconian language) heroic song flourished, and, as we know, they so fascinated Charlemagne that he ordered them to be written down. Gradually this nobility became gallicized. Must we, then, also assume that with the change of language there came a change in manners and customs as well, and that the poets disappeared and the banquets were held without music and singing?

But, it will be objected, surely the interest in old Germanic legends must have flagged considerably? This is indeed true. Those noblemen, spread throughout France in their castles and now speaking the language of the native population, did not feel very much attracted towards the legends of Ermanaric, Siegfried, or Gunther. It seems that only Wayland the Smith was not entirely forgotten, but for the rest they lived on the traditions of the Merovingians and Carolingians who had made the history of their France. Therefore one may well ask oneself the question whether figures like Roland or Guillaume d'Orange are not equally suitable for the provision of material for heroic songs as those other heroes, once celebrated in the Germanic heroic songs. The shock caused by the defeat at Roncevaux must have been great in the Margraviate of Brittany, and one cannot but believe that a singer returning from the disaster must have sung about it, at first perhaps in the form of a dirge, but later also in that of a narrative song. The French heroic song took the place of the Franconian one, but it was not at all a direct continuation of it. It was a new age and a new nation, which worshipped new heroes and celebrated them in new songs. There was undoubtedly a breach in the tradition. But the demand for heroic song remained undiminished.

This must be assumed, if only for the reason that the conditions for this art were present in the same degree. Here too lived a powerful, stubborn, and turbulent class of nobility, proud of its descent, which, equally unconcerned with regard to ruler and members of its own class, called upon fancied rights and claims and gave free rein to its lust for power and thirst for fame. The attitude of these noble lords is clearly drawn in the later *chansons de geste* such as the *Couronnement de Louis* or the *Geste des Loherains*. Neither must we forget the church prelates. Nearly all of them came from the nobility. They lived like knights, hunted, and went to war. They did not ride Jesus's mule, but the proudly harnessed horse. Usually they combined church office and worldly possessions, and in times of war placed themselves at the head of their men, in shining armour and with glittering sword, just as Bishop Turpin took part in the battle at Roncevaux. If they beguiled the time in their monasteries and abbeys by listening to stories, these were not always of an edifying nature, but stories full of the noise of war and the clang of arms. The abbot of Lindisfarne had his counterparts in France and in Germany. It is in such circles that the *Waltharius* arose. It was in the abbey of Saint-Requier that the song of *Gormont and Isembart* was so well known.

But the chronicler of Saint-Requier reveals at the same time that there were other circles interested in such stories. He does not render the whole of the *Chanson de Gormont* in his chronicle, because it is still alive in everyone's memory, and therefore also among the country-people of Normandy. This is confirmed by what other chronicles say in some places. Bédier will not accept this as evidence, but these places are too numerous to be ignored. How often do we read in these chronicles of persons or events *quae de illo concinnantur vulgo et canuntur*, or similar utterances? This applies to people who lived as early as the tenth century.[1] But by these *vulgares cantilenae*

---

[1] See examples in Ehrismann, *Geschichte der deutschen Literatur bis zum Ausgang des Mittelalters* i (1954), pp. 95–97.

must songs other than those which were recited at the courts of nobility have been meant.

There is sometimes a tendency to represent the gap between the nobility and the people in the early Middle Ages as almost unbridgeable. Perhaps it was considerably wider at the time of the court nobility of Louis XIV. For in the Middle Ages a vassal who went to war stood at the head of an army that consisted not only of young knights but also of armed farmers' sons. When he had to defend the country, the people did not leave him in the lurch. And when he returned laden with glory, his people also basked in his glory and admired him for his brave deeds. His victory was theirs also. Why should they not also have had pleasure in listening to stories and songs of things they had themselves experienced?

But it was not the court poet, not the *scop*, who addressed himself to these people. A different kind of reciter was required for them. In Germany he is called the minstrel (*Spielmann*), in France the *jongleur*. We have already made their acquaintance earlier on as a questionable scum of jugglers and rope-dancers, very like the Russian *skomorokhi*. If they made heroic songs, these must have had an entirely different character from the chivalric romances. The people to whom they addressed themselves wanted simpler fare. Little can have been left of the pathos of the old epic poetry. We ought to imagine instead a more or less burlesque type of poetry, in which figures like Rainoart were in great demand. But it is impossible to form a clear idea of this kind of song. The expression *cantare* need not necessarily point to a sung type of song, as has already been said above, but it may very well be applied to such a type. Should we imagine a stanzaic form such as can still be discerned in the *Chanson de Gormont*, or a strongly modulated recitation that could be taken as a kind of singing? This much is certain, however: the chivalric romance did not stand alone. Other forms of narrative poetry existed by the side of it, just as in Germany there were the minstrel's songs and even recited songs with epic contents side by side with the knightly epic. We shall come back to this presently.

How did the transformation into the large epic take place? How did great poems like the *Chanson de Roland* or the *Nibelungenlied* arise? In the history of the development of the epic, poems such as the *Waltharius* and *Beowulf* should, to my mind, be eliminated. They stand alone and are, as it were, heroic epics prematurely born. The *Waltharius* is the task given to a young monk who had to prove his familiarity with the Latin language and versification; and he proved himself beyond expectation. But what happened to this poem then? Perhaps it was praised so much that copies were sent to friendly abbots. They probably also admired the poem, and in the end these copies must have found their way into the libraries of the monasteries. What outside influence can it have had? Was it really a much used reader in monastic schools? I cannot support the view, occasionally expressed, that the *Waltharius* contributed towards the making of the *Chanson de Roland*, of course via the Latin *geste Francor*. This is not where we have to look for the origin of the epic in the vernacular.

And what about *Beowulf*? This poem, too, remained unique. We have no other English heroic epics that followed the example of *Beowulf*. If there was any imitation, it lay in an entirely different field. English literature has a fairly large number of poems of religious content, such as paraphrases of books of the Bible, written, strangely enough, entirely in the traditional epic style. But these were all meant to be read in monasteries. A remarkable offshoot of this branch is the Old Saxon song *Heliand* or the Saviour, a biography of Jesus in heroic verse, likewise a poem of and for the monasteries. Its place of origin is generally assumed to have been Fulda. This poem, preserved in a manuscript of the ninth century, originated under direct Anglo-Saxon influence, and therefore proves nothing at all about the existence of an Old Saxon secular epic at that time.

We ought rather to think along different lines. The *Heliand* could never have been written in this form if the poet had not been able to base his ideas on a long epic tradition that preceded him. Style and language show this clearly. Its spirit is not that of the pious monk, but the warrior. Jesus and His disciples are represented as a proper *dux* with his *comitatus*; the loyalty of the disciples is expressed in the same words as in the *Bjarkamál* or in *Maldon*. This is more evidence for the early appearance of heroic epic poetry; and also its great popularity in monastic circles.

The transition of the short heroic lay to the full epic is very smooth. We cannot even say when it took place. When the *Chanson de Roland* and the *Nibelungenlied* appear, they are like new stars in the literary firmament. But is that what they really were? Or do we have an example here of what so often happens: the successful work of art overshadowing all its predecessors to such an extent that they sink into oblivion? The Moor has done his duty and nobody thanks him for it. Homer did the same to all his anonymous predecessors.

All one can do, therefore, is to ask what the changes were which took place in the transition of the short heroic lay to the large epic. And one cannot do much more than hazard a guess. Andreas Heusler has dealt with this problem in a clear and sober manner.[1] In the case of the *Nibelungenlied*, when we compare the epic with its earlier forms, we notice that there has been considerable broadening. The number of characters has been increased with the appearance of new figures. Episodes, such as the fight with the Saxons, described elaborately and with such pleasure have been inserted. In particular the poet applied himself to the detailed description of incidental scenes: a wedding, a messenger's journey, a tournament. It is especially in the last instance that detailed description of insignificant details suggests an audience making different demands. This theory is called the theory of 'swelling': a certain given subject-matter swells as it were from inside by the addition of ever increasing detail.[2]

There are of course many other means at a poet's disposal for treating material handed down to him in greater detail. He can combine diverse material, as was done by the poet of the *Nibelungenlied*. For he probably built on a poem roughly thirty years older, *Der Nibelunge not*, which dealt with the fall of the Burgundians only. By way of introduction to this he added the legend of Siegfried.

Another way in which poems can be expanded is by duplication of the material, as it were. Perhaps this really testifies to poverty of mind, but it is effective. The poets of the minstrel epic liked making use of it. In a certain sense the famous Baligant episode in the *Song of*

---

[1] *Lied und Epos in germanischer Sagendichtung* (1905).

[2] Cf. Brinkmann, 'Erbe und Abendland', in *Dichtung und Volkstum* xliv (1943), pp. 154 ff., and S. Beyschlag, 'Zur Entstehung der epischen Großform in früher deutscher Dichtung', in *Wirkendes Wort* v (1954), pp. 6–13.

Roland may be taken as exemplifying this technique. Hardly have the Saracens taken to flight, when a new Moorish force appears forcing Charlemagne to a new battle. But there the poet reveals himself, for he does not merely give us a purposeless repetition, but a climax which in fact makes Charlemagne the victorious champion of Christianity.

It seems to me, however, that the impulse towards this gradual swelling also lies in epic recitation itself. We who live in an age that hungers for novelties and is always hankering for a new 'pop' song, can hardly imagine the people of the Middle Ages listening indefatigably to the same stories, century after century. How often did the lord of the castle listen to the recitation of the *Chanson de Roland*, and then another singer appeared to offer the same well-known poem! Why let him start at all? Perhaps people were never tired of hearing songs about the old heroes—that is, until the appearance of Arthurian Romance with new inventions and materials. Then the popularity of the Carolingian stories was finished.

This may be so, but the lords of the castles were not like children who always want to hear the same fairy-tale. They were adult men of judgement and taste. Not every *jongleur*, even if he recited the *Song of Roland*, was sure of success. In those days more attention was paid to form than to content. The fascinating thing was to see how a singer would recite old material or, from the point of view of the *jongleur*, how intent he was on creating a new and fresh impression—not in the story itself, for that was inviolable, hallowed by tradition as it were—but in the form in which he offered it. A racy description of some new detail could work miracles. In the beginning Ganelon's journey to Saragossa would have been described briefly, but how much could be made of it! The conversation with the Moorish envoys on the way, the reception in Saragossa, the conversation with the Emir Marsilies who grows angry about the shameless demands of Charlemagne, the figure of Queen Bramimunde, and the presents promised to the traitor.

The poem was so well known that every new detail was noticed, and greeted with approval if it was successful. The poem was continually on the move, not because of a fluctuating oral recitation, but rather because of the conscious work of many generations of rhapsodes who were also more or less *aoidoi*. And then suddenly a really talented poet arose and gave new lustre to the old epic.

The important point is the transition from oral recitation to written document. As soon as the reciter is able to make a rough draft and work it out in writing, he can spread his wings more widely. It is not till that stage is reached that a large epic can arise, as we have seen in the case of Homer.

This must have taken place long before the epics known to us came into being. In Germany, prior to the *Nibelungenlied*, there are some poems usually called 'minstrel's epics'. Poems like *Rother*, *Orendel*, and *Oswald* breathe an entirely different spirit from that of the heroic epic. They are poems of adventure and they even have rather a vulgar nature. They seem to have been intended for an audience that made no great demands, that liked coarse jokes, and shrill colours. The age of the Crusades had revealed the East to the world. People never grew tired of hearing about the wonders there. But it had to be laid on thick: kingdoms of tremendous size and princes of incredible ostentatiousness, that is what the little man in his everyday world wished to hear about.

The minstrel was able to offer this to him in abundance, and he did not forget to give himself the leading part: a journey to the East for the sake of a beautiful princess, but with the greatest dangers attached to it. Hence the hero is preferably disguised as merchant or minstrel in order to lure the princess craftily to the ship. And, of course, the princess falls into the hero's arms. If the story was liked a new one could be started at once: the princess is forcibly taken back by her father and the wooer must again go out to win her. The minstrel knew how to manage with a minimum of material. Its duplication came to him easily. And he always knew how to season the song with piquant new details and embellish it with marvels.

The French *jongleur* knew this kind of song equally well. An excellent example of it is the humorous description of Charlemagne's *Journey to Constantinople*. The paladins boast rather vulgarly about what they will do at the Byzantine court; the emperor hears about it and forces his guests to translate their boasting into fact. But however funny it is, the poem is unworthy of a figure like Charlemagne.

Sometimes the minstrels do not hesitate to make use of the old heroic legends. The *Lied vom Hürnen Seyfrid* is a sad example. Written in eight-line stanzas, it tells a strange story, in which here and there old features known from elsewhere can be discerned with difficulty, but which for the rest tells the old legend in a very confused manner. (The dwarf Eugel and the giant Kuperan are at any rate new figures in this old material.) The distance between this song, intended for the people, and the epic of the Nibelungs is very great indeed.

And yet here, too, there are mutual influences. The Staufen poem received its present form through influences from various directions. We have pointed out the great influence of the Arthurian Romance from France, which gave the old heroic legend a slight veneer of modern chivalry—a revelling in the description of pomp and splendour—and also a little sentimentality to the relationship between Siegfried and Kriemhild. If the heroic core had not been so solid, the song would have been in danger of degenerating into a poem of adventures like one about Arthur.

But the minstrel epic, too, should be taken into consideration. Its influence on the *Nibelungenlied* was slight—the scene in which Hagen throws the chaplain into the Danube is an example—but in course of time it became much greater. The later poems of Wolfdietrich and of the wanderings of Dietrich of Bern, written in the second half of the thirteenth century, were obviously made for a much less exacting audience.

About this time, too, vast compilations arose, and curiously enough it is Norway which gave them their final saga-form: the *Karlamanna Saga* and the *Thidriks Saga of Bern*. The former is based on the French *chansons de geste* which were translated and then combined into a continuous story; the latter is based on poems that were current in North Germany, which offer a surprisingly rich and varied content, out of which the figure of Dietrich emerges as the binding element.

Meanwhile in Norway, and partly in Iceland also, a new trend had been given to the old Eddic poetry. Here too the new age had exerted its influence: a stream of French literature was gradually becoming known. An entirely new kind of poem appeared which was similar in form to the old poetry but differed greatly in content. A younger generation saw Kriemhild and Brünhild, or, as they are called here, Gudrun and Brynhild, as women, but women of a baffling nature. Brynhild especially seemed a problem: she loves the hero Sigurd and yet she is the cause of his death. What can have moved her to come to such a decision? The poet of the *Nibelungenlied* allows her to disappear unnoticed from the scene; the *Edda* poet tries to go into the problem which she presents. And so we have a lay of Brynhild in which this passionate woman takes the decision to follow Sigurd in death by burning with him on the funeral pyre. But before this supreme deed she first has to pour out her heart, and in a long monologue she surveys her whole life and tries to explain how her destiny came to take this course.

It has been justly remarked that in language and style these Eddic poems betray their late origin, because they are influenced by an entirely different kind of poetry: in these centuries in ferment, the ballad had come into being[1]—a dancing song, as its name tells us—and in some parts of the North Germanic area it remains so up to the present day. It can be traced back to eleventh- and twelfth-century France. Knights and maidens held hands while a singer in the middle started up a song and the circle moved slowly round in measured tread; only with the refrain, which was sung and had a more lively measure, some quicker dance-steps were made. The contents of these songs were derived from the everyday life of the nobility: the love of a knight for a maiden; a girl who lived under the discipline of a stern mother or who sewed and embroidered all day. Gradually —we cannot say how or when—stories and legends came to be chosen for these songs; thus the ballad proper arose: a stanzaic song with epic contents. It spread rapidly, undoubtedly with the expansion of French chivalric civilization; it is found from Italy and Spain to far-away Norway and Iceland. Songs like *Heer Halewijn* and *De Twee Koningskinderen* in Dutch literature belong to this type of poetry.

In Scandinavia too, ballads were originally limited to the circle of the nobility; but, when the nobility lost the taste for them, they were taken over by the people. Even today they are still alive as

[1] Cf. H. Mohr, in *Zeitschrift für deutsches Altertum* lxxv (1938), pp. 217–80.

popular songs, and on the Faeroes, love of dancing has remained so great that poems of a hundred or more stanzas are sung in the old way to the 'measured dance'.

Some examples have been preserved which show that the old heroic legend was also used as material for such ballads. Thus the Danish song of *Sivord and Brynild* begins in this way:

> Sivord rides away on his foal;
> He took Brynild away from the mountain.

(*Refrain*: The King's sons of Denmark)

> He took Brynild, who sat on the mountain,
> And gave her to Hagen as a pledge of friendship.

> Brynild and Signild, the maidens proud,
> Went and washed the linen in the river.

We notice how far the legend has wandered from its original. Neither the names nor the facts themselves have been correctly preserved. It is also striking that the story advances in such tremendous bounds. We cannot but assume that the singers had some notion of the contents of the legend, but this is indeed the end of a glorious tradition of heroic legend.

Another way in which the tradition comes to an end is the dissolving of the legend into a prose story. We mentioned the Norse Saga of Dietrich of Bern which was made in the thirteenth century. In Western Europe cheap popular books were later printed which repeated the old heroic legends in simple prose. They remained popular for a long time; the story of the *Vier Heemskinderen* in Dutch well into the nineteenth century.

Now that we have come to the end of this outline of the Germanic heroic legend, the question still remains: did it live exclusively in the form of songs? This is how Heusler imagined it. For him the heroic song was literature. The chain of the tradition was a long series of poetic versions, the greater part of which had sunk into oblivion, but some of which were saved purely by chance. The Eddic poems of Sigurd and the Nibelungs, which almost certainly belong to the ninth century and may perhaps be considerably older, go back to Frankish models which may be reckoned to belong to the sixth century. To build a bridge from there to the *Nibelungenlied* of about 1200 is impossible without piers. But Heusler had to construct these piers. He lists a number of intermediate stages, the contents of which he tried to determine. But they themselves lie centuries apart.

Is it necessary that a poet who wanted to deal with this legend need always have taken an older song as a model? Could he not also have drawn from an oral tradition which may be imagined as a story, as a popular legend? Heusler has contested this fervently. Legend was to him far too vague a notion. In the age of romanticism and later people had wanted to prove so much with it. But that is no reason for ignoring it altogether. We have pointed out that often these songs could only be understood if the listener was already familiar with the story. Is there any reason why people should not have told stories of the deeds of heroes when it so happened that no singers were available? The people will only have been fortunate enough on rare occasions to have a *jongleur* in their midst who could recite a song. Surely they must have felt the need for reviving these old legends in the long interim periods?

The heroic legend formed such an integral part of the spiritual life of those early days that it was always and everywhere present. It lived in song in the first place, but also found its way into monastic chronicles (like those of Novalese and Saint-Requier), came to be written down in a manuscript, and also spread to all strata of the population. Hence it is almost unimaginable that a poet who wanted to compose such a song should never before have heard it recited as a story.

The heroic song in the oral tradition of the people is rare in the West. Two examples have been preserved in Germany: the late *Lay of Hildebrand* and the song of *Koninc Ermenrikes Dot*. They are stanzaic in form and clearly show how much the contents of a legend can change in the course of a long and unhampered tradition. A later generation could no longer bear the old tragic ending of the Old High German poem of Hildebrand. They replaced it by a reconciliation of the two relatives, and a cheerful ride to the mother who had been lonely for so long.

In the Slav countries, in Finland and Estonia, the tradition was naturally more persistent, because here the old civilization had the chance of preserving itself intact for a longer period of time. Wherever there is a continually developing civilization that takes on new forms, the old is rejected. But where no new impulses, or very few, are at work, the old traditions must be adhered to. Yet they gradually lose something of their tension and freshness. The tradition becomes rigid, something new can arise only from within, and so it is tied up with the old fixed forms from the outset. The village poets may sometimes have considerable talent, but they do not possess real originality.

The tendency to vary a thought in a second line is remarkable. This produces a certain amount of diffuseness. The story never really makes headway. An empty repetition of each line springs from the parallelism of the old poetry, which possessed the means to underline the important moments in this parallelism. Thus one gets the impression of a mechanical recapitulation, and involuntarily one thinks of the advantage to the reciter of being able to think of the next line. But this is not the real reason. In general the memory of the singers is so well trained, and they are so skilled in versification, that they do not need such props. It does seem to me, therefore, that an old style has become a mannerism.

But there is another, more important point. At one time the question was fiercely disputed whether heroic poetry was a collective product or an individual one. It seems a strange question, put like this. A remark by Jakob Grimm about 'the verse-making people' gave rise to this controversy. In a more realistic time than the somewhat over-enthusiastic romantic period, people raised the objection that no single piece of literary creation can ever have risen collectively: there is always one person who makes a poem. Now Grimm, of course, never intended his remark to be taken so naïvely. He wanted to say that the poet of such a song could only be imagined as a member of a community receptive to it. The idea of the modern poet behind his typewriter should never arise in this connexion. The epic poet had an audience in mind and worked for it: he had to calculate the effect of his recitation; he had to gauge the taste of his audience. In a certain sense, therefore, he was the mouthpiece of this audience.

But the audience eagerly absorbed his poem and preserved it, and so it remained very much alive. It is unthinkable that a *jongleur* should change a universally known legend out of all recognition. The audience would have been anything but grateful to him. The legend had a fixed form, and so was hallowed, in a kind of way. To the audience it was a true story of a venerable past, not at all a poetic invention. People are not apt to deal lightly with their own past. If the word *geste* also had a genealogical meaning it is only natural that such a song would have to be truthful. So the audience played the active part that any audience always plays—by its approval or rejection. The poet was the means of expressing the inner life of the community. This is the sense in which one can say that the people make poetry. They determine what and how the poet shall create.

The Spanish author Menendez Pidal expressed this with great clarity:[1] 'The popular song is an individual creation. But it can only become popular if it is assimilated by the people, when they repeat it again and again and do not remain passive in this repetition, but adapt the poet's creation to the general feeling, recreate it, and give it new life through new impulses which in their turn are creative, however scattered and imperceptible each of them may be.'

For this reason a distinction should be made between traditional and popular poetry. The latter always reduces the value of a song; the former derives its significance from the fact that it arises and assumes its form not at a certain moment but in a series of creative moments, and that it owes its foundation and style to the very fact of communication.

The term 'national epic' has sometimes been used. It is a dangerous term, for when one considers the *Nibelungenlied* one cannot say that any national feeling is expressed in it. The Huns may be a different nation from the Burgundians, they are not inferior—nor are they the arch-enemy. Etzel is drawn sympathetically: no shadow of national prejudice falls on him. Moreover, these legends travelled from nation to nation. What had happened among Goths and Franks and Burgundians was sung with equal enthusiasm in the far North. The subject-matter would appear to be almost more international than national.

[1] Cf. *Revista de Filología Española* iii (1916), p. 272.

Occasionally, however, a flicker of national pride seems noticeable—most clearly in France, which was the first country to acquire national self-consciousness. The tenderness with which the poet of the *Chanson de Roland* speaks of 'la douce France' can only spring from a heart that beats warmly for its own country and people. In the course of time, people did indeed take the heroic song as the glorification of their own national past.

But if the epic is not really national in its essence, it has clearly been of enormous importance in the development of national feeling. Charles Autran is certainly right when he points to the role played in this by the epic. In connexion with the Indian epic he speaks of an 'heroic tradition' and says: 'A tradition which to a large number of people was for some time a means of forming a concrete picture of the warrior virtues, the courage and behaviour of brave men, this was a type which made it possible to create a clearer sense of national solidarity.'[1]

The significance of the Homeric epic for the realization that all those Greek townships did indeed form a unity through a common civilization must have been very great. It is easy to understand that the *Nibelungenlied*, common hereditary property of all German nations, became the touchstone of German unity in the nineteenth century. What a heroic epic means to nations struggling for political and cultural independence we noted in the case of the Finnish *Kalevala*, and the Estonian *Kalewipoëg*.

A modern observer could easily disparage an heroic epic as an antiquated monument of a perished civilization. He might perhaps judge it as the typical expression of a class of nobility and talk of a class culture. But if this class, at a certain time in history, set the standards of noble behaviour and maintained them, it played the role allotted to it by history. The life of every nation springs from its past, and the heroic epic is a precious monument of that past. Modern man must have wandered far from the foundations of his own civilization if he sees in the heroic song merely a memory. Does it not still meet with response as the radiant image of ideals that, even in our own day, have not become entirely extinct?

[1] Cf. *L'Épopée indoue* (1946), p. 285.

INDEX